Rising Sun, Divided Land

.

Rising Sun, Divided Land

JAPANESE AND SOUTH KOREAN FILMMAKERS

KATE E. TAYLOR-JONES

WALLFLOWER PRESS
LONDON & NEW YORK

A Wallflower Press Book
Published by
Columbia University Press
Publishers Since 1893
New York • Chichester, West Sussex
cup.columbia.edu

Copyright © Kate E. Taylor-Jones, 2013
All rights reserved.
Wallflower Press® is a registered trademark of Columbia University Press

A complete CIP record is available from the Library of Congress

ISBN 978-0-231-16586-0 (cloth : alk. paper)
ISBN 978-0-231-16585-3 (pbk. : alk. paper)
ISBN 978-0-231-85044-5 (e-book)

Design by Elsa Mathern

∞

Columbia University Press books are printed on permanent
and durable acid-free paper.
This book is printed on paper with recycled content.
Printed in the United States of America

c 10 9 8 7 6 5 4 3 2 1
p 10 9 8 7 6 5 4 3 2 1

Contents

Acknowledgments

Thanks must be extended to the British Academy and the Great British Sasakawa Foundation for their support with various aspects of this project.

Warmest appreciation is extended to my friends and colleagues from around the world who have helped me throughout this process. Key people who have played invaluable roles at various stages need a mention here: Di and Howard Gorindge, Hiro and Yuri Kiyama, Dee-arne Caire, Jun-rock Seo, Miki-chan, Alison Armstrong – thank you all for your friendship, hospitality and advice over the years. A big thank you to all my current and former colleagues at Bangor University including Stephanie Marriott, Gwen Ellis, Eben Muse, Amy Chambers and Lyle Skains. As usual, my deepest thanks are given to all my family for all the care and support they have extended to me over many years. This has been a long process for a variety of reasons and I now have two key additions in my life who were not with me at the beginning! My loving and supportive husband Nick Taylor-Jones and our beloved daughter Amelia who joined us in late 2012 – to both of you I send all my love.

Introduction:
Rising Sun and Divided Land

Cultural traditions [...] are preserved and continue to live not only in the individual subjective memory of a single individual and not in some kind of
collective 'psyche' but rather in the objective forms that culture itself assumes.
(Bakhtin 1982: 249)

Towards the end of the twentieth century East Asian cinema began to take the
world by storm. Directors from Hong Kong, Taiwan, China, Japan and South
Korea all had films succeed on the popular international stage. Whilst Japanese
directors such as Kurosawa Akira, Ozu Yasujirō and Mizoguchi Kinji had historically achieved acclaim and recognition among aficionados of world cinema
this new wave of East Asian film appealed to a wide range of film-goers from
young to old. Whilst Studio Ghibli products such as *Howl's Moving Castle* (*Hauru
no ugoku shiro*, 2004) and *Spirited Away* (*Sen to Chihiro no kamikakushi*, 2001)
thrilled a younger audience, teenagers became avid consumers of Asian horror
franchises and older audiences were engaged by the visual splendour of films
such as Zhang Yimou's *Hero* (*Ying xiong*, 2002). Whilst the influence of the West
has always been strong in East Asian cinema (as seen in the raft of films that seek
to offer Hollywood models of narrative and genre), the impact was beginning to
work both ways. East Asia's approach to action, horror, melodrama and animation began to infiltrate the cinema industry on a global scale. As Leon Hunt and

Wing-Fai Leung state, 'East Asian cinema has arguably never had a more visible presence in the West than in does at present (2008: 2).[1]

Rather than engaging with the myriad of reasons for this media interplay, a topic which several recent studies have begun to deal with (Lau 2003, Katzenstein and Shiraishi 2006, Davis and Yeh 2008, Hunt and Wing-Fai 2008), this book will concentrate on directors from two of the countries that have been key in this development: Japan and South Korea. This study will examine eight directors in total: Fukasaku Kinji, Im Kwon-taek, Kawase Naomi, Miike Takashi, Lee Chang-dong, Kitano Takeshi, Park Chan-wook and Kim Ki-duk. The aims are to present the works of these directors on multiple levels: as reflections of personal visions but also as works that are part of the ongoing debates concerning, respectively:

> Colonialism, post-colonialism, multinational capitalism, globalisation, the complex and multifaceted interplay between the Asia Pacific and the Euro-American Pacific, and their diverse and intersecting productions. (Geok-lin Lim *et al.* 1999: 3)

The debates involved in the relationship between cinema and nation are complicated (see Hjort and Mackenzie 2000). Does cinema reflect the nation from which it emerges? Is French, Russian, Japanese cinema and so forth the way it is because of the countries that it emerges from? This premise would indicate that there is a defined, unique concept of nation and nationhood that continues to function as a marker in cultural production for the respective nations that it comes from. As David Morley and Kevin Robins state, 'the idea of the 'nation' …involve(s) people in a common sense of identity and … work(s) as an inclusive symbol which provides integration and meaning' (1995: 91). The cinema therefore provides the audiences of a specific nation their symbols of identity that 'accurately expresses, describes and itemises the salient concerns and features of a given national culture' (Hjort and Mackenzie 2000: 4). National identity is consequently based on a common sense of unity with one particular social grouping. Nationhood therefore will function as the answer to a 'felt need for a rooted, bounded, whole and authentic identity' (Morley and Robins 1995: 103).

There are several issues with this approach; least of all that of cultural determinism. Must the nation be defined by opposition to an 'other'? Although questions of the national continue to play an important factor in film studies, cross-cultural, interdisciplinary practices that can be seen to work against the binary concept of them/us have been a growing field of study. These approaches have had particular effect on the discussion of cinema and media (Darrell William Davis refers to the process as 'film as syncretism' [2001: 66]). Several recent studies have focused on East Asian cinema at the centre of the transnational and the global as a method to overcome the sometimes-limiting approach to seeing film as a method of legitimising an essentialist discourse of the national. These studies can be seen in engaging in the global consumption of Japanese Horror and Hong Kong action films (see McRoy 2005, Morris *et al.* 2006), the continuing Hollywood remaking of successful Asian films (Marchetti and Kam 2007), and the role that international film festivals are playing (Iordanova and Cheung 2011). Globalisation in all its forms, both negative and positive, has had an undoubted effect on film. With reference to Chinese cinema (but in an argument that can easily be transferred to other regions of East Asia), Sheldon Hsiao-Peng Lu identified 'an era of transnational post-modern cultural production' (Lu 1997: 10). Hunt and Wing-Fai's (2008) work on transitional East Asia cinema, Iwabuchi's debates around the global consumption of Japanese television and popular culture (2003, 2004), the work of Chua *et al.* (2008) work on Korean Television, and Davis and Yeh's (2008) examination of the East Asian media industries all highlight the fact that 'national cinemas', as traditionally defined, can no longer exist in isolation. Davis and Yeh note that 'the East Asian screen industry has characteristically negotiated the passing of studio modes to re-emerge as a flexible industrial-cultural force responding to challenges of global capitalism' (2008: 3). This is not to deny the impact that an individual national history, culture, economy and traditions have on the cinema from this region. Cinema is in many ways an ideal tool to chart and evaluate a national culture but the point that needs to be made is that cinema does not act, and has never acted, in isolation from the world that surrounds it. There is always constant interplay between the nation and culture as concept and the realities that traverse it as part of wider dialogue of internationality and globalisation. As Davis and Yeh state:

> A national cinema, then, is not a one-way reflection of culture, but neither is there only a dialectical, intertextual relation between cinemas and cultures. Instead national cinema is both of these, a reflection and a dialogue, plus the next stage of its evolution. (2001: 95)

In a similar fashion, the individual director is imbued with a notion of cultural and national identity but concurrently, the individual works with and against these discourses. In short, the director can be seen to simultaneously inform and *be informed by* their individual notions of identity as well as the cultural and national discourse that they work inside. Susan Hayward writing on auteur theory concluded that,

> To speak of a text means too that the context must also come into play in terms of meaning of production: modes of production, the social, political and historical contexts ... One cannot speak of a text as transparent, natural or innocent: therefore it is to be unpicked, deconstructed so that its modes of representation are fully understood. (2006: 38)

In short, any evaluation of an individual director's *oeuvre* must also look to the much wider cinematic and cultural field to be able to fully assess their filmic works. To this end, film scholarship has engaged with the directors and cinema of Japan and South Korea in a variety of different ways.

Arguably people in the West have historically been more aware of the cinema of Japan than that of South Korea. This is primarily due to international presence; whilst Japan has been a key player in world affairs for over a hundred years, Korea suffered from a variety of events from colonisation to partitioning, and has trod a long path to its current global status. In the last few decades South Korea's high economic growth rates and commercial expansion have seen this small nation become one of the so-called 'Asian Tigers'. At the other extreme, North Korea is best known for its isolation and as a potential nuclear threat. The culture of this region however, including its cinema, is often ignored when compared to the amount of scholarship regarding its neighbours Japan and China. Although there has been a marked increase in the number of English-language publications dedicated to Korean film in the last few years, Korean cinema as a whole still remains relatively unexamined. In general terms the two main dialogues that have taken place are related either to the recent success of what has been labelled the Korean New Wave (see Leong 2003, Shin and Stringer 2005, Paquet 2009) or a more socio-historical approach that relates to the socio-economic history and status of film as a reflection of social experiences and narratives (see Lee 2000, Kim 2004). Excellent recent scholarship devoted to studies of individual films (such as Gatewood 2007), directors (James and Kim 2001) and periods (Abelmann and McHugh 2005) has emerged over the last few years and these approaches have been enhanced by works that seek to debate the conception and production of cinema and culture on a transnational scale (see Lau 2003, Hunt and Wing-Fai 2008, Chua *et al.* 2008, Choi 2010, Kim 2011).

In contrast, Japanese cinema has maintained a unique place in the world cinema canon for many decades. English-language scholarship has historically tended to engage with Japan far more readily than with other Asian cinema industries and it offers a wide range of approaches. Yoshimoto Mitsuhiro sums up the history of English-language engagement with Japanese cinemas as falling into three distinctive strands:

> (i) Humanist celebration of great auteurs and Japanese culture in the 1960s (ii) Formalist and Marxist celebration of Japanese cinema as an alternative to the classical Hollywood cinema in the 1970s (iii) Critical re-examination of the preceding approaches through the introduction of discourse of otherness and cross cultural analysis in the 1980s. (2000: 8)

Early cinematic scholarship on Japan was often insistent on seeing the visual arts as a sign of the country's position as a unique and consolidated 'other' that engaged with film in a unique and culturally specific way (see Kirihara 1996: 504–6). As a key example, Joseph Anderson and Donald Ritchie's *The Japanese Film: Art and Industry* (originally published in 1960, republished in an expanded edition in 1983), offered an examination of the 'Japanese character' and its reflection in film. They literally see Japanese cinema as a 'mirror' perfectly reflecting Japanese culture and national identity. The most famous study of national character is Ruth Benedict's *The Chrysanthemum and the Sword* (1946) that presented an eternal unchanging and alien Japanese culture. This presentation of Japan saw the nation established as the perfect 'other' to America and the West. These concepts developed into a binary situation where the cinema of Japan was positioned as a unique alternative to dominant Western modes of filmmaking. This approach is personified by the writings of Noël Burch (1979) and in David Bordwell's examination of the 'unique' filmic work of Ozu Ysujirō (1988). This vision was, in essence, based on the flawed notion that 'Japan' was eternal and unchanging and therefore this approach was combined with comparatively little evaluation of Japanese society a mutable and changing force.

Over the last few decades, however, a variety of other approaches have engaged with Japanese cinema from a multitude of angles. Writers such as Audie Bock (1985), Catherine Russell (1995, 2003, 2008) and Mitsuyo Wada-Marciano

(1998, 2005) have opened up the debate in relation to gender representation and cultural dynamics. Yoshimoto (2000) and Aaron Gerow (2007) are just two of the writers that have chosen to focus on the work of specific directors in an approach that seeks to place them not only in terms of their individual filmic 'style' but also in terms of the surrounding cultural and social questions. Isolde Standish (2000, 2005) has been an important figure in focusing critical attention towards 'popular' cinema genres such as musical and *yakuza* films that for many years were ignored by critics who chose instead to concentrate on more 'worthy' and artistic films. In his work Eric Cazdyn (2002) has sought to reposition Japanese cinema in direct relation to the competing models of Marxism and imperialism. With her studies of individual films Keiko McDonald (2006) offers a socio-cultural reading of Japanese films as they relate to specifics of Japanese history and society, with a desire to provide non-Japanese readers with a methodology with which to engage with Japanese cinema on its own terms. At the other extreme Scott Nygren (2007) offers a cross-cultural analysis that seeks to evaluate the previous theoretical positions that have been taken and to examine films from a multitude of theoretical angles, both Japanese and Western.

In many ways this book lies at the intersection of many of these approaches. This project is in no way aiming to place the directors and their work as part of a narrative that would see Western film theory and beliefs as the only active critical tool. Rather the aim is to open up to the maximum number of people (including those without a developed knowledge of East Asian cinema) the relevant debates around and analyses of these directors and their work. Many more directors could have been included and this work will refer to other key directors and provide a viewing list for further interest at the end. These eight directors and their works, however, were felt to provide rich grounds for analysis. The aim is not simply to offer a series of critiques based on the ideas offered by auteur theory. Undoubtedly the personal experiences and beliefs of the respective directors play a key role in their choice of narratives and styles but the aim is also to take into account the mixture of what Alastair Phillips and Julian Stringer call 'text and context' (2007: 1). Thus the wider questions of gender, history, nationalism, economics, artistic movements and war are discussed together with evaluation of the interplay between the global and the local, national and international. The aim is not an analysis based on socio-history but an inter-disciplinary one that will see the directors and their works as integrally involved in the wider cultural debates that are taking place on a regional, national and international scale. Chris Berry writes in his discussion of the methodology of examining 'one film at a time', arguing that 'cinema studies requires a range of approaches … that understand the singularity of the film and the importance of the cinema as an institution without trying to divide them or set them in opposition to each other' (2003: 3). Therefore at the conclusion of each chapter in this volume there is a close analysis of a selected film text. All of these films are available on the international market and have been chosen since they are key examples of that particular director's work and the readings that are inherent in the film texts.

Selecting directors for this type of project is always controversial but at the centre is the belief that all eight offer an excellent overview of contemporary Japanese and Korean film. Many of their works are available with English or French subtitles that opens their films up to a much wider audience. This is vital in allowing their works to be seen by a larger non-specialist audience and all the films used in the close textual analysis sections are relatively easy to source or acquire.

The older directors also serve to illustrate the main trends that have taken place in the South Korean and Japanese film industries. Im Kwon-taek and Fukasaku Kinji both commenced working in the film industry in the 1950s and examining their respective careers highlight many of the changes and narratives that took during the several decades of both Japanese and South Korean history until the present day (Fukasaku died in 2003 but Im is still working).

The other directors have all been chosen since their respective careers illustrate important aspects of the industries they work in. As S. Louisa Wei (2012) notes, women have been very underrepresented in studies on Asian cinema and therefore the inclusion of Kawase does not just address only her work but the wider status of women directors in Japan. V-Cinema has been highly influential on the Japanese cinema scene and Miike Takashi is a director who has worked in both the V-Cinema format as well as directing feature films that have performed well on the local and global stage. Lee Chang-dong's films engage with the various tensions that have imbued South Korean society since the 1980s and Kim Ki-duk takes this social critique one step further in his controversial, often violent and highly criticised reflections on the state of modern Korean society and art. Kitano Takeshi has become one of the most powerful media players in Japan and his domestic and global influence as a media figure *extraordinaire* is a vital aspect of the contemporary Japanese cinemascape. The directors are also all interesting for the respective positions that they hold on both the domestic and international film circuits. Kawase, for example, may not be the most commercially successful of Japanese directors but she has consistently represented her county in film festivals to great acclaim and thus is worthy of examination. The work of Fukasaku Kinji is often critically dismissed as nothing more than basic action films yet over the last few decades his films have proven to be incredibly popular at the Japanese box office and his last film, *Battle Royale* (2000), was an international success. Lee Chang-dong is a highly successful Korean director and his films have demonstrated popular appeal whilst Kim Ki-duk is a well-known international name and yet many in his home nation dismiss and ignore his work. In this way the tensions between art and commerce are represented and illustrated via the directors chosen.

In his preface to the book devoted to Im Kwon-taek, David James states that the contributors' aims were to 'forestall the construction of an idea of Korean cinema as either a reflection of the Western one or an exotic, orientalised other; but also, and more fundamentally, we hoped to forestall the construction of any binary that would have Western film theory at its centre and Korean cinema as its passive object' (2002: 3). In a similar fashion this book will aim to avoid these pitfalls but also, more importantly, aim to not conflate in any way the two nations that the directors hail from. Korea and Japan are undoubtedly separate nations with strong national traditions and histories of their own; however, as Justin Bowyer writes, 'the complex relationship between Korea and Japan provides a fascinating and inextricably linked "pair" of national cinematic identities, which are at once complementary and, paradoxically, conflicting' (2004: 7). As the debates on transnational cinemas continue what is clear is that seeing nations in total isolation is not the most effective, or indeed accurate, way to evaluate their cinematic output. Japanese and Korean histories, cultures and futures are inevitably entwined, although this in no way conflates or reduces their individual impacts. The in-depth examination of the work of directors from both regions can reveal a concurrent matrix of differences as well as similarities and it is in this dialogue that new connections can be made.

Note: This book is organised into nine main sections. The first chapter offers an overview of Japanese and Korean cinematic history, which is aided by a further reading list at the back of the book together with a list of some key directors and films from the region. The chapters on the individual directors are each followed by a short analysis of a selected film.

All names in the book are presented surname first according to Japanese and Korean style. For readers' convenience the films will be referred to by their English titles although the original titles will be offered in the first instance.

NOTES

1   This presence is perhaps not always to the benefit of the East Asian products as arguably a degree of cultural appropriation and eradication is clearly taking place. This can be demonstrated in remakes of films such as *Infernal Affairs/Wu Jian Dao* (*The Departed*), *Ringu* (*The Ring*), *Ju-on* (*The Grudge*) and the forthcoming Spike Lee-helmed *Oldboy* adaptation. For a more in-depth analysis of this phenomenon see Lau 2003, Katzenstein and Shiraishi 2006, and Hunt and Wing-Fai 2008.

Cinematic Japan and Korea:
A Long and Turbulent History

They said, you're Japanese.
They said, stop being Korean.
I came by boat.
When raising my children
I wore a Kimono.
To rent a house
I wore a kimono.
I put my chŏgori.
Away in the dresser.
I will give my fingerprints
For alien registration.
I'll make my children give theirs.
But,
I don't want to make my grandchildren give theirs'
– 'On Fingerprinting' by Mun Kon-bun (quoted in Ryang 2002)

This opening poem was written by *zainichi* (Japanese-Korean) female poet Mun Kon-bun. In this simple but effective musing she vocalises many of the issues facing people of *zainichi* descent living in contemporary Japan. Ethnic Koreans make up the biggest immigrant community in Japan and these communities, particularly those located around Osaka, have been in Japan for many decades.

They continue, however, to frequently suffer economic, social and educational exclusion in the country that has been their home for several generations. The presence of the current *zainichi* community in Japan is a legacy of the tumultuous events that took place at the beginning of the twentieth century. At the same time as Europe fought on the fields of France and Belgium in the first 'modern' war, Japan was consolidating its hold on Korea, a nation it had invaded in 1910. The modern era had been proclaimed around the world: transport, economics, culture and ideology could now reach a global audience. Just before the beginning of this new modern century the Lumière brothers first film, *Employees leaving the Lumière factory/La Sortie des usines Lumière* (1895) had heralded the beginning of what has become a fantastically popular, often highly politicised, global phenomenon, namely cinema.

Cinema quickly travelled around the world and has become one of the most popular and enduring modern art and entertainment forms. In Japan, Shiro Asano imported the first motion picture camera in 1897 and the medium was quickly embraced by the whole population and over the next decade became a popular method of entertainment. 1903 saw the opening of the first cinema and 1908 witnessed the creation of the first Japanese production company. Like many national cinemas Japanese film was deeply indebted to the legacy of the theatrical arts and, as Donald Ritchie states, initially the Japanese audiences indeed saw cinema as 'a new form of theatre' (2005: 22). *Kabuki* and *shimpa* (new style) theatre traditions greatly influenced early Japanese cinema in terms of form, narrative and acting styles. Realism was secondary to style and the theatre traditions maintained a strong hold on cinema for a couple of decades in the fixed position of the camera, the use of male performers in female roles and the traditional narratives. As Keiko McDonald states during this period, 'the three definitive characteristics of Japanese cinema are its use of *onnagata* (female impersonators), *benshi* (commentators) and centre-front long shots following strict continuity' (2006: 2). Cinema quickly divided into two distinct genres: *jidai-geki* (period drama) and gendai-geki (new or contemporary drama)[1] and the 1910s saw a huge expansion of the Japanese film industry. Two large production giants, Nikkatsu and Tenkatsu, had began to imitate the vertically integrated production model of their American rivals and a vibrant star system developed with fans able to follow the exploits of their favourite stars such as Matsunosuke Onoe in the new raft of film magazines that appeared at this time. By the 1920s the call for more realistic acting styles, modern narratives and an increasing focus

11

on cinema as an art form in its own right, separate from theatre, saw the industry transform even further. The 'pure film movement' (*jun'eigageki undō*) originated around 1910 (see Bernardi 2001) and would be enhanced and developed further into the 1920s with the founding of two studios, Shōchiku and Taikatsu. Those who believed in the focus on 'pure film' were determined that cinema should move away from the theatrical traditions that had dominated since its conception and offer a new, formalised approach to cinematic storytelling. Heading this transformation was the newly established Shōchiku Company that, like its rivals, had copied the integrated American model. Editing techniques such as cross-cutting and parallel montage, taken from foreign directors such as D. W. Griffith (*Birth of a Nation*, 1915) and Sergei Eistenstein (*Battleship Potemkin/Bronyenosyets Potyomkin*, 1925) were embraced, and films such as *The Enchanted Snake* (*Maji-nai no hebi*, 1917) and *Island Woman* (*Shima no Onna*, 1920) broke with the tradition of female impersonation and actually starred a woman playing the female role (see Bernardi 2001, Macdonald 2006). Benefiting from the new wave of technicians trained overseas, films such as Kinugasa Teinosuke's surrealist *Page of Madness* (*Kurrutta ippeiji*, 1926) opened up further debate about the potential of the cinematic image. At the end of the 1920s they had 'created a style of filmmaking that gave the public a glimpse at a visually defined concept of modernism, later to be equated with "Americanism", that had been adapted to meet the demands of the rapidly changing society' (Standish 2005: 37).

Jidai-geki, or period film, of this silent era rapidly developed and the inclusion of more and more exciting action sequences saw the hero break free of the formalisation of *Kabuki* to reach new heights of popularity with cinema audiences. A subsection known as *chambara*, after the dramatic sword play sequences, with films such as *Chūji's Travel Diary* (*Chūji Jynuisada*, 1925, Daisuke Itō), *Streets of Masterless Samouri* (*Rōningai*, 1928, Masahiro Makino) and *The Serpent* (*Ocohi*, 1925, Buntarō Futagawa) proved to be especially successful. By 1928 Japan produced more films annually than any other country and would continue to be one of the most prolific cinematic producers of the decade (see Ritchie and Schrader 2005: 44).

As the decade rolled on, *Onnagata* and then *benshi* saw their influence and use diminish. During the early days of cinema *benshi*, who provided the audience with narrative, meaning and 'emotional overlay' (Kirihara 1992: 61), had been popular stars in their own right. The new editing and narrative styles meant that they were no longer needed as an integral part of the film viewing as narrative could be conveyed to the audience via other means. The legacy of their labour and pay disputes with the studios together with the coming of sound in the 1930s would see the once powerful *benshi* consigned to cinematic history.

The arrival of sound in the 1930s was ushered in with Gosho Heinosuke's *The Neighbours Wife and Mine* (*Madamu no nyōbō*, 1931). Starring lead actress Tanaka Kinuyo, the film achieved huge acclaim and soon all the studios had embraced the new sound technology. Famous and iconic Japanese directors such as Ozu Yasujirō, Yamanaka Sadeo and Mizoguchi Kenji began to produce some of their most famous and remarkable works. Films from this period such as *I was born but…* (*Umarete we mita keredo*, 1932, Ozu), *Humanity and Paper Balloons* (*Ninjō Kamifūsen*, 1936, Yamanaka Sadao), *Osaka Elegy* (*Naniwa Eriji*, 1936, Mizoguchi) and *Sisters of Gion* (*Gion no Kyōdi*, 1936, Mizoguchi) remain cinematic classics to this day. A new player joined the cinema game and began to compete with Nikkatsu and Shōchiku in all film genres. Tōhō studios spurred the competition to provide films that appealed to all areas of the cinema market: slice-of-life realism, melodrama, *shomin-geki* (lower-middle-class dramas), literary adaptations, comedies, musicals and romantic tragedies were all seen by Japanese audiences and a few films even made it to the international market (see Okubō 2007).

The cinema of the 1930s also became increasingly marked by the dual narratives of nationalism and militarism that were sweeping the county. From the isolated state that American Commodore Perry had forced into international trade by threat of violence in 1854, a few decades of development had resulted in a Japan that was now a centralised state under the name and rule of the Emperor with a powerful navy, a modernised army and the beginnings of an industrialised economy. In tune with the empire building that marked that age, Japan quickly embarked on a series of military excursions and conflicts to expand the nation's sphere of influence. The aims and reasons for this development have come under much scrutiny: most history books inside Japan support this expansion as the pre-emptive need to defend themselves against the ever-present threat of China and Western powers such as France, America and Britain that were seeking to expand their already considerable overseas territory. For those from outside the nation, particularly from countries that suffered under Japanese invasion and colonisation, it was not considered self-defence but rather the aggressive desire to establish Japan as the dominant cultural, economic and military force in the region.[2]

As with all modern periods of political upheaval, cinema was seen as an important tool. In 1939 the Film Law was passed resulting in the film industry coming under the control of the Cabinet Propaganda Office. The 1940s would usher in a period of cinematic censorship and control, and films were rigidly assessed at all stages of development. Any sign of dissent from the official discourses of military glory, self-sacrificing nationalism, traditional family values and the exultation of the Emperor would result in the termination of production and, as the sad case of director Yamanaka Sadeo illustrated, a possible posting to a dangerous warzone.[3] All production companies, including Nikkatsu, were split into two huge structures: Tōhō and Shōchiku respectively. National Policy films (*Kokusaku Eiga*) were designed specifically to offer the audience the 'correct' vision of Japan and the Japanese people. Naruse's *The Whole Family Works* (*Kararaku ikka*, 1939) showed an entire family contributing to the work which is required on the 'home front'. (Japan had been at war with China since 1937 and after Pearl Harbor Japan entered World War II.)

Films such as *The Sea War from Hawaii to Malaya* (*Hawai-Marei Oki Kaisen*, 1942, Yamanoto Kajirō) and *Our Planes Fly South* (*Aiki Minami Tobu*, 1943, Sasaki Yasushi) show both the spirit of nationalism and self-sacrifice that all people were been called upon to offer. They both feature mothers actively encouraging their sons to participate in and die for the Japanese war effort. Young men were encouraged to engage with the war by their mothers and there were a series of feature films dedicated to the heroics of the Japanese soldiers on the front line. *Mud and Soldiers* (*Tsuchi to heirai*, 1938, Tomotaka Taska), *Chocolate and Soldiers* (*Chocolate to heitai*, 1938, Sato Takeshi), *The Story of Tank Commander Nisihizumi* (*Nishizumi senshachō-den* 1940, Yoshimura Kōzaburō) and *Navy* (*Kaigum*, 1943, Tomotaka Taska) all offer a vision of the noble, obedient and honourable Japanese army fighting to defend the Emperor and Japan. This period, however, would soon draw to a close. In 1945, after extensive military losses, the fire bombings of Japanese cities and then the atomic devastation of Hiroshima and Nagasaki, Japan surrendered to the Allies. The subsequent American occupation and the several previous years of warfare had resulted in the destruction of a huge amount of early Japanese cinema. Yet the 1950s and the subsequent decades would see the recreation and revival of Japanese cinema and the radical development of the nation, on all fronts.

Across the Sea of Japan, the 1945 defeat heralded a new beginning for another cinema, that of Korea. Korea had suffered the dubious honour of being one of the first territories that had caught the attention of Japan in its colonial march. Korea had always been a country that had suffered as a result of powerful neighbours. Since the beginning of East Asian civilisation, the mixing of cultures from China through Korea to Japan was well established. Trade, arts, culture, food and people moved throughout the regions and the individual nations were often engaged in trade and territory disputes. Gradually, over several centuries, distinct countries were born and Korea as a unified entity came into being in the year 918 with the Goryeo dynasty (the English name of Korea derives from this). Despite invasion attempts by the Mongolian empire in the thirteenth century and Japanese invasion in the sixteenth century, Korea managed to maintain its independence and unique culture, language and writing system, although it kept a close link with Qing China as a tributary state. All this changed in the late nineteenth century when the struggles for influence in the region saw many international eyes turn to Korea as a strategic point for East Asia. Its central location and numerous seaports made it a vital part of any campaign to control the wider region. Japan initially sought to transform Korea into a satellite state, in part to act as a buffer against China. This process saw the signing of the unequal treaty of Ganghwa which came into being on 27 February 1876 and was highly reminiscent of the treaty forced on Japan by Commodore Perry a few decades earlier. Korea was forcibly opened up to Japanese and international trade and was made to declare its independence from China in foreign relations. The treaty marked the beginning of a power struggle for Korean domination. Although China by this point was weakening as a power, it made consistent attempts to maintain influence over Korea that through a complex and involved process of uprisings, rebellions and protests, resulted in the first Sino-Japanese war. This ended on 28 July 1894 with Japanese troops entering Seoul and from 1910 onwards Korea was an official Japanese colony.

Although there had been a private screening of the new cinematic equipment for the court in 1897, cinema was introduced to the general Korean public in 1903. The Korean film industry, however, had a difficult start and it struggled to emerge from under the control of the Japanese. As a result the first Korean film was not actually produced until 1919. *A Righteous Revenge* (*Uirikŏk Kut'u*, 1919, Kim Tosan) is generally accepted to be the first film although there have been some spirited debates on the validity of this fact (see Lee 2000: 19). In the early part of the century (roughly 1910 to 1920) the Korean film market was dominated by Western and Japanese imports. Commercial theatres flourished, although they were often divided into cinemas for the Japanese and cinemas for the Koreans (see Lee 2000: 21). Despite the difficult circumstances the 1920s saw the production of some Korean films with a decidedly nationalist flavour. The most notable is *Arirang* (1926, Na Un'gyu). This film, whose title comes from a Korean folk song, offered clear anti-Japanese sentiments and helped to provoke a national interest in Korean independence and a national cinema. The Korea Art Proletarian Federation (KAPF) was a group of young filmmakers who were at the forefront of the 'tendency film' genre that was generally anti-government and pro-labourer (Lee 2000: 28). Any film that went against the Japanese discourse of obedience and unity went directly against the colonial rule and as a result by 1931 most members of KAPF were in jail and the burgeoning Korean film industry was being crushed to death by the might of the colonial machine.

The fragile industry was fighting a losing battle from before the first Korean film was ever made. The Japanese were well aware of the power of film and in 1920 the colonial government established a motion picture section that would produce propaganda films for general consumption. In 1922 the Entertainment and Theatres Regulations Act started the process of strictly censoring any film shown in Korea. Western cinematic imports and Korean films were all closely monitored for any dissent or criticism of Japan and the Japanese policies in Korea. The censorship regulations were strengthened and tightened over the next couple of decades and by 1940 the Chosŏn Film Regulations came into force. Korean companies were forced to create pro-Japanese products and fines and possible imprisonment would follow if this was disobeyed. The government controlled all aspects of the cinema from the production and financing to distribution and exhibition. In 1942 the Chosŏn Film Production Company was founded and revoked the licences of all Korean production companies. Films would now only be made in Korea by the Japanese and they were very clear about the messages that they wanted to be given to the Korean population. The Korean Language Prohibition Law came into force in 1938 and forbade the screening of any Korean-language film, and enforced the compulsory usage of Japanese in schools and official situations. Sound had arrived in Korean cinema in 1935 but it would be rare (and technically illegal) to hear Korean on the cinema screen. There was a concerted effort to 'eradicate "indigenous lifestyles" and make people more "useful and efficient", including campaigns for short hair on men, wearing coloured clothes (as opposed to traditional white Korean dress), and saving money' (Moon 2005: 22). The colonial film board would make sure that all of these aims would be reflected in cinema and pro-Japanese films such as *The Volunteer* (*Chiwŏnbyŏng*, 1941, Pak Yŏnghŭi) rendered the colonial government's desire to 'remould Koreans into colonial subjects of Japan' cinematically (ibid.). *The Volunteer* is the tale of a young Korean man who is desperate to join the Japanese army and fight for the Japanese Empire overseas. He studies Japanese with due care and attention and speaks passionately about how he sees Japanese colonial rule as a positive and important step in Korean development. With the support of his mother and fiancée, eventually his dreams come true and he departs for military training as his family and friends wave Japanese and Korean flags in celebration. *Mr. Soldier* (*Byeongjeongnim*, 1944, Baek Un-haeng) focused on drafted Korean military recruits as they learn how to conform to Japanese army standards. The army is seen to offer the young Korean men purpose, discipline and development and they happily go off to the front to fight for the glory of the Japanese nation. Made at the height of the Korean-language prohibition laws there is no Korean spoken throughout the film and the clear theme of the film is the 'benefits' that the Korean populace are receiving by being part of Japan. There is little information about how such propagandistic films such as these were received by Korean audiences but one thing was certain: the Korean national film industry would never succeed under Japanese rule.

1945 saw Japan defeated and enter into a period of US occupation which lasted until 1952. Cinema under the Americans was closely controlled. They established the Civil Information and Educational Section (CIE) on 22 September 1945 only a month after entering Japan, emphasising just how powerful a tool cinema was seen to be in the occupation ethos. CIE films, in a similar fashion to their earlier *Kokusaku Eiga* counterparts, exalted the beliefs and opinions that the occupiers believed the new and peaceful Japan needed to embrace. For Japan to participate in international society the Japanese people must be made to understand 'the basic political ideals of law and democratic representative government, respect for the individual, respect for national sovereignty and the spirit of self-government. The entertainment media and the press should all be used to teach these ideals' (Hirano 1992: 38).

Films demonstrated to the Japanese people the apparent pleasures of democracy compared to the older system of imperial rule and the American lifestyle was presented as a model of success and happiness. In terms of older cinema, the occupiers destroyed over 230 films from the wartime period that were 'deemed to be dangerous relics of the military era' (Hiroshi Komatsu in

Nowell-Smith 1997: 421). The occupation government issued an edict stating thirteen areas for which films were forbidden to show approval. Films would be prohibited if they were deemed to offer, 'approval of suicide either directly or indirectly', were 'anti-democratic', 'chauvinistic and anti-foreign' or 'nationalistic' (Hirano 1992: 44–5). One of the key points the occupiers wished to convey was the new standing of women. In 1946 women were allowed to vote for the first time and the most important element in terms of gender relations, the 1947 Japanese constitution contained the forbiddance of 'discrimination in political, economic, or social relations because of creed, race, sex, social status or family origin' (direct quote from Article 14 of the Constitution). Films such as *No Regret for Youth* (*Waga Seishun ni Kuniashi*, 1946, Kurosawa Akira), *Victory of Women* (*Josei no Shōri*, 1946, Mizoguchi Kinji) and *Morning of the Ōsone Family* (*Ōsonneke no ashinta*, 1946, Kinoshita Keisuke) all offered visions of strong independent women fighting against the odds. Despite this, as will be examined in closer detail in the chapter on Kawase Naomi, women remained marginalised in all aspects of society especially film production.

Two elements that the CIE were particularly concerned about was the portrayal of 'revenge as a legitimate motive' or 'feudal loyalty or contempt of life as honourable or desirable'. With this in mind, the occupiers took particular offence with regards to the average filmic representative of the *jidai-geki* genre. The use of swords in films such as the classic tale of *Chūshingura* (*The Loyal 47 Ronin*), were seen as being against the ideals that the occupation government wanted the Japanese people to embrace and for the duration of the occupation this genre suffered.

Despite these restrictions cinema in this period flourished. The major studios competed on all fronts and this competition resulted in a large number of films getting made. Cinema continued to be a hugely popular pastime as it presented an ideal method of escape from the harsh reality of occupied Japan. Despite problems such as strikes, ideological disputes and financial turmoil inside the production companies, cinema continued to boom and the studios flooded the market with comedies, musicals and *haha-mono* (mother) melodramas. These genres did not contravene any of the occupation government's concerns and managed to provide people with a few hours away from the hardship of post-war Japan.

The end of the occupation in 1951 heralded the beginning of the 'Golden Age' of Japanese cinema. The mid-1950s saw 19 million cinema tickets per week being sold in Japan (see Thompson and Bordwell 1994: 462), and by 1959 there were over 7,400 cinemas in Japan with a record-breaking peak of over a billion cinema admissions in 1958 (see Ritchie and Schrader 2005: 177). A number of the most illustrious names in Japanese cinema made some of their best and most enduring works during this period. Kurosawa impressed international audiences with *Rashamon* in 1950, followed by notable successes such as *Seven Samurai* (*Shichinin no Samurai*, 1954), *Throne of Blood* (*Kumonosujō*, 1958) and *Yojimbo* (1960). Mizoguchi received a Silver Lion at the Venice Film Festival for *Sansho the Bailiff* (*Sanshō Dayū*, 1954) and just two years earlier his classic *The Life of Oharu* (*Saikaku Nichidai Onna*, 1952) had seen him share the award with John Ford. Ozu delighted domestic audiences with *Late Spring* (*Banshun*, 1949), *Early Summer* (*Bakuchū*, 1951) and *Tokyo Story* (*Tōkyō Monogatari*, 1953) and his films from this period are deemed to be the best examples of his quietly emotional directorial style. Kinoshita Keisuke's *Carmen Comes Home* (*Karumen Kokyō kaeru*, 1951) and *A Japanese Tragedy* (*Nihon no Higeki* 1953) gained him popularity and his anti-war sentimental melodrama *Twenty-Four Eyes* (*nijū shi no hitomi*, 1954) has continually been voted Japan's favourite film. Naruse Mikio, Ichikawa Kon and Gosho Heinosuke were also directors who achieved fame during this period. The five major studios (Tōhō, Shin-tōhō, Daiei, Shōshiku and Tōei) presented the audience with a seemingly never-ending supply of melodramas, *kaidan* (ghost stories), *shomingeki* (lower-class) drama, musicals, *haha-mono*s and comedies. Free from the occupation edicts *jidai-geki* experienced a come-back and 1954 Honda Ishiro presented the enduring icon of *Godzilla* (*Gojira*) to the world.

The 1950s had not been as kind to Korean cinema. The end of Japanese colonisation had not heralded freedom for the small nation. The period immediately following the Japanese defeat saw the Korean peninsula become a divided and occupied territory, the Americans below the 38th parallel and Russian influence and military activity above. There was limited film stock in the country and most of the films that were shown in South Korea during this time were American imports. The Korean filmmakers were generally divided into those who supported the anti-communist military government and those that leaned towards supporting the Communist North. Many of the latter would later defect to North Korea in the early part of the 1950s. The American military government abolished the Chosŏn Film Regulations but then replaced them with some of their own. Censorship continued but the Korean film industry did try to establish itself in its own right. Colour arrived in the cinema and Hong Sŏnggi's *The Women*

Diary (*Yŏsŏng Llgi*) became the first Korean colour film in 1949. There were some Korean commercial successes from this period, most notably *Hurray! For Freedom* (*Chayu Manse*, Ch'oe In'gyu, 1946) whose anti-colonial, anti-Japanese and highly nationalistic approach delighted the audiences. Any developments the film industry had made, however, would soon be obliterated by the Korean War.

Starting in 1950 and continuing for three years the Korean War left no person or part of the country untouched. The Communist and anti-imperialist North supported by the Chinese and the Russians faced the rabidly anti-communist American and South Korean army. Families were divided, cities were razed and the conflict was used by 'both regimes in the North and South to eliminate their political enemies and strengthen their political bases' (Lee 2000: 103). An armistice between the two sides was declared in 1953 and thirteen centuries of a united Korea was ended with the division of the nation, very much in place to this day.[4] Bruce Cummings notes that the South Korea of the 1950s was 'a terrible depressing place, where extreme privation and degradation touched everyone: cadres of orphans ran through the streets … beggars with every affliction or war injury … half-ton trucks full of pathetic women careered onto military bases' (1997: 303). The war had destroyed nearly all South Korean filmmaking equipment and a huge proportion of the early Korean cinema. The cinema would need to start practically from the beginning and by the mid-1950s South Korean cinema was attempting to totally rebuild itself.

A series of measures were put in place to try and aid the industry. In order to compete with the American products that were imported into South Korea, South Korean films were exempt from tax in an effort to revitalise the film industry. These methods succeeded and the Golden Age of South Korean film was born. This Golden Age, lasting from 1955 to 1972, saw Korean filmmakers produce a prolific volume of work that was as 'historically, aesthetically, and politically significant as that of other well-known national film movements such as Italian Neorealism, French New Wave and New German Cinema' (Ablemann and McHugh 2005: 2).[5] This was the most productive and profitable period of Korean film to date. South Korea became one of the most active cinematic industries in Asia with over 200 films a year being produced from 1968 and 1971 (see Kim 2002: 25). Cinema attendance was at a record high and domestic films were produced in remarkable numbers. Films such as *Madame Freedom* (*Chayu puin*, 1956, Hyeong-mo Han), *A Stray Bullet* (*Abalt'an*, 1960, Hyun Mok Yoo) and

The Housemaid (*Hanyŏ*, 1960, Kim Ki-young) achieved huge levels of popular success.

During the 1960s Japan was beginning to consider in greater depth and with a new critical insight Japanese development since World War II. This will be examined in greater depth in the chapter on Fukasaku Kinji but it is important to note here that concurrent with the stream of popular studio-based genre films, the 1960s also saw directors who began to call for a new type of film that could challenge generic structures and aesthetics. The Japanese *nūberu bāgu*, or 'new wave', personified by directors such as Hami Susumu, Teshigahara Hiroshi, Masumura Yasuzō, Shinoda Masahiro, Oshima Nagisa and Imamura Shōhei began to demand more artistic licence from the rigid structures of the studio system. They broke stylistically and politically with their predecessors and offered challenging and unique films such as *Cruel Story of Youth* (*Seishen Zankoku Monogatari*, 1960, Oshima Nagisa), *Gates of Flesh* (*Nikutai no Mon*, 1964, Suzuki Seijun) and *Double Suicide* (*Shinjū Tneno Amijima*, 1969, Shinoda Masahiro). Films such as these offered a nihilistic, angry, unsentimental vision of post-war Japan – a 'counterculture repudiation of both militarism and humanism' (Nygren 2007: 17). Many films of the 'new wave' focused on those marginalised by this new and modern Japan. Women, prostitutes, the mentally ill and members of the various subcultures that began to spring up in the 'new Japan' were all examined. The noble army officer was no longer the hero and now films were focused on the anti-hero; often violent and tortured individuals who were unable to connect fully with the world around them. Standish notes that the characters from the 1950s to early 1960s films are often marked by a desire to rebel and this rebellion 'marks the point of departure on the hero's quest for an authentic identity, which will lead him to an alternative society and sense of connectedness based on homo-social structures' (2005: 293). A new generation was emerging that felt disconnected from the traditional structures and ideals of that nation, and cinema became a method through which they began to express their dissatisfaction.

Since the 1970s there have been huge changes in the cinemas of both Japan and South Korea. The 1970s and early 1980s saw Japanese cinema struggle in the face of the arrival of mass-marketed television and declining ticket sales. By the 1970s a number of prominent studios had collapsed or had turned to the production of soft porn. Known as *Pinku Eiga*, or pink film, these low-budget sex narratives accounted for forty per cent of domestic production by 1965 (see Standish 2000: 268) and this trend would continue into the 1970s. Despite the downturn, Japan still remained one of the key producers of cinema throughout the 1980s. It was during that decade that feature-length animation pictures based on Japanese comic books (*Manga*) emerged. Although animation had been domestically popular in Japan since the 1940s with propaganda films such as *Momotarō: Umi no Shinpei* (1945, Mitsuyo Seo) being greeted with great enthusiasm by Japanese audiences, films such as *Nauisica of the Valley of the Wind* (*Kaze no tani no Naushika*, 1984, Miyazaki Hayeo) and *Akira* (Otomo Katsuhiro, 1988) became popular on a global scale. Since then Studio Ghibli has achieved critical and popular success world-wide with film such as *Howls Moving Castle* and *Spirited Away*.

V-Cinema (straight to video) would transform the production and distribution of low-budget cinema by directors such as Miike Takashi and the tremendous success of Japanese horror films, exemplified by the work of Hideo Nakata, which, together with the critical success of films by directors such as Kore-eda Hirozaku and Kitano Takeshi, has resulted in Japanese cinema maintaining its place on the national and international market. In South Korea the legacy of the war lived on and, as will be examined in the chapter on Im Kwon-taek, South Korean cinema would struggle under decades of military dictatorship. It would be only in the late 1980s and early 1990s that South Korean cinema would come to global attention. Despite the economic crisis that hit East Asia in 1997 South Korean cinema would grow from strength to strength, as this book will explore in relation to four of the directors who have contributed to the critical and popular recognition of South Korean film. The relationship between Japan and South Korea has also undergone some subtle changes in the last few years. The legacy of the events of the Japanese occupation and World War II continue to mark the interaction between the two nations as the conflict regarding comfort women illustrates. What has taken place is, however, 'the entry of Japanese popular culture into Korea but to an even greater degree the advent of Korean popular culture into Japan' (Chua *et al.* 2008: 251). The success of Japanese television shows, music and art in South Korea has in turn led to South Korean culture and cultural products gaining unprecedented admiration in Japan. Although both nations maintain unique identities and still continue to struggle to resolve their past experiences on a socio-political level, the interaction between the two nations on a media/cultural level has never been so strong.

The next two chapters will offer an examination of the Japanese director Fukasaku Kinji and South Korean cinematic stalwart Im Kwan-taek. They both began working in the 1950s and their careers highlight many of the important developments in their respective film industries since that time. Through the chapters on the individual directors, together with the work of the respective individuals, the history and background of the South Korean and Japanese film industries will be explored further.

At this stage perhaps it is appropriate to just say a few further words about North Korean cinema. This isolated, mysterious and extremely secretive nation is one of the last bastions of radical communist thought and as a result there is comparatively limited information about this country or its people. Whilst it remains a relatively unknown cinema, for those interested, Hyangjin Lee's excellent overview of Korean cinema provides several interesting insights into North Korean cinema. He states that there are three major genres that can be seen: 'films on the revolutionary tradition of class struggle', 'films on the Korean war and unification' and 'films on the development of the socialist economy' (2000: 42–4). As with the cinema of Soviet Russia, the cinema produced in North Korea is totally controlled by the state and seeks to enforce the dominant ideology of the regime. Whilst South Korean cinema has gone from strength to strength in the last few decades, North Korea has made no notable contribution to cinematic history. This may change as the political and cultural situation of North Korea alters; however, the death of Kim Jong-il and the succession of his young son Kim Jong-un has not heralded an improvement in relations between North Korea and the wider world. Events such as public missile testing, the bombardment of Yeonpyeong and the sinking of ROKS ship Cheonan means that the state of the North Korean film industry has been ignored and it seems unlikely that North Korean directors will any day soon share the acclaim that is given to their southern counterparts.

NOTES

1   Although these terms are not without debate (see Thornton 2007), they serve as a general background structure and as the cinema in Japan developed into an established and vertically integrated industry they served to offer an easy way of classification.
2   For more information on the cinema of this period see High 2003, Thornton 2007 and Baskett 2009.

3   Yamanaka Sadeo has been often cited as the father of the Japanese humanist film. His films often debunked national myths such as the *Bushido* code. In the era of military-based nationalism this was not appreciated and he was sent to the Chinese front and died there in 1938 (see Buehrer 1990).

4   From this point on this book will only deal with the cinema of South Korea. There is a limited overview of North Korean cinema at the end of this chapter.

5   Unlike theses other movements however, the Korean Golden Age has been neglected by English-Language scholarship with a few exceptions such as Abelmann and McHugh's collection.

Im Kwon-taek and the March of Time

Godard said that if German music is Mozart, German cinema is Fritz Lang. Likewise if Korean music is the *pansori Chunhyangjeon*, Korean cinema is Im Kwon-Taek. (Chung 2006: 3)

It would not be hyperbolic to say that in charting the career of Im Kwon-taek one is also charting Korean national cinema. As the longest working director in South Korea, Im's films have featured and referenced nearly all of the major political and cultural events that have shaken the Korean peninsula over the last hundred years or so. Beginning as a director in 1962 and with an *oeuvre* that contains over a hundred films, Im is a vital element of South Korean cinema 'not because he stands apart from Korean cinema's contradiction but because his films demonstrate the film director's inability to escape the contradictions embodied in the national cinema' (Kim 2004: 22).

Im was born in 1936 in Jangseong, 30km south of Kwangju in South Chŏlla province, a notable area of South Korea for a variety of reasons. The arts and crafts from this region are renowned world wide and it is the 'birthplace' of the Korean tea ceremony. Less appealingly, however, the region has long been imbued with the legacy of a strong feudal class system and historically has been the site for various uprisings and subsequent retaliations, the most famous in modern times being the Kwangju massacre in May 1980. Im was born into this turbulent region 25 years after the occupation agreement. He grew up under the harsh Japanese colonial system that sought to repress and destroy Korean culture and language. The occupation ended when Im was twelve with the defeat of Japan by the Allies in 1945. As the tension between North and South Korea grew, the region of Chŏlla became a political flashpoint. People who had left during the Japanese occupation to study abroad returned and brought with them various elements of Marxist-Leninist thought and the desire for social, political and economic change. Chŏlla province became categorised as 'the North Korea within South Korea' and Im's father was one of many that joined the communist partisans in the mountains. His father's membership of a partisan group resulted in the sometimes violent ostracism of his family and Im's bitter memories of his home town.

> A few years ago, people in my home town said they would like to make a statue of me. I objected very strongly because I was terrified of my hometown. All the cruel acts between the left- and the right-wing at the time left persistent memories. (Im quoted in Chung 2006: 65)

Unlike many of his contemporaries who made their name during the 'Golden Age' of South Korean cinema, Im received a very poor education. He did not even finish school and suffered, as a result, of intellectual snobbery in a time when education was seen as one of the most important elements for success (see James and Kim 2001: 24). By the time all of the parties were engaged in the Korean War, Im had fled to Pusan and worked in various menial and badly paid jobs. It was there, however, that Im first became interested in the film industry. Pusan, a thriving port area, had temporarily become the capital during the Korean War and was, for a time, the place where the remnants of the film industry gathered. Yet with the end of the war the recovering film industry moved again to the Ch'ungmuro district in Seoul and it was here that Im began his apprenticeship in the production department. The process of apprenticeship was the key (or the only) way of entering into the film and entertainment industry. Apprentices learned the film business by following a mentor and gaining more and more responsibility until they could direct their own features. Im became apprenticed to director Chŏng Chang-hwa (primarily remembered for the Hong Kong action film *Five Fingers of Death* [*Tian xia di yi quan*, 1972]) and made the rapid advancement from very junior runner to director in only five years.

In order to place Im it is important to consider the period in which he began his filmmaking career. South Korea had moved from the much-hated Japanese occupation into a new form of American control. With the bellicose North Korea next door and the memory of the violent and destructive Korean War still very fresh in the memory, South Koreans were in desperate need of a reconsideration of their concept of nation and nationhood. The legacy of colonialism, war, division and economic and social hardship had left South Korea a nation uncertain of itself and its future. This uncertainty would swiftly become a part of the turbulent politics. The First Republic under the American-supported Syngman Rhee ended on 19 April 1960 after mass student uprisings and riots. The ill-fated Second Republic met its demise a year later with a military coup ousting Prime Minster Chang Myŏn in favour of the military dictator Park Chung-hee on 16 May 1961. Although Rhee had been becoming increasingly authoritarian throughout the late 1950s the military *junta* of Park was marked by two important elements: the tremendous, often forced, economic growth that led to the South Korean success of today and an unrelentingly harsh autocratic reign. Im would work though this period until the present day and his films reflect the progress and development of the Korean film industry since the 1950s.

The early 1950s had seen the Korean film industry destroyed but by the mid-1950s and under Syngman Rhee the South Korean industry was starting to rebuild itself. As already noted in the Introduction, the Golden Age was born then and this high point of South Korean cinema saw films produced on a mass scale and in a multitude of genres including melodrama, comedy, historical dramas and anti-communist propaganda. Im directed over 46 features between 1962 and 1971 so when one considers that of his hundred or so features he made almost half in the first nine years of his career the scale of the Golden Age becomes apparent. His debut feature *Farwell to Tunnam River* (*Dumanganga jal itgeola*, 1962) proved to be a huge success and focused on the Manchurian attempts to gain independence from Japan during the 1940s. The nationalist sentiments echoed throughout the film and the stirring action sequences resulted in Im becoming a recognised name in an ever-growing industry. Many of the numerous films Im made in this period are, however, unremarkable and highly formulaic with little to distinguish them as exceptional. What they did do was establish him as a capable and versatile director who was capable of producing films in any genre offered. Im states that, 'throughout the 1960s, I just considered directing as literally a job and made films as if I had to go to the office every morning. It was a method of earning a living. If I had followed my parents and hid in the mountains I would be dead already' (in Chung 2006: 71). What this statement makes clear is that for Im film was a form of escapism from economic hardship and social exclusion rather than a politically informed act. This approach would become key in his ability to survive as a film director in the next turbulent period of South Korean development.

The idyllic golden days were soon to end with the military regime of Park. This dictatorial regime quickly realised that control of cinema would be vital in attempting to prevent any dissent among the people. In 1973 the First Motion Picture Law came into action and forced a total restructuring of the film industry. The *Yushin* government under Park demanded that filmmakers and companies produced only films that were in keeping with the official state beliefs and ideologies. There was a drive to limit the number of production companies in the overcrowded market and this was enforced by the issuing of filmmaking permits. Without a permit you could not make a film and the issuing of permits became an increasingly corrupt system. Over twenty production companies went bankrupt in 1973 alone and the only filmmakers who saw success were those who were seen as loyal to the ideology of the state. The industry became controlled by a few powerful conglomerates or *Chaebeols*. From the 250 production companies that existed in 1968 only twenty remained by the end of the 1970s (see Chung 2006: 114). Imports of foreign products were limited and the lucrative (although highly taxed) screening licences were only granted to companies that had made the appropriate number of 'ideologically sound' features (known as Quality Films). In this way, the standard of the films often became irrelevant as it was more important to produce quick and cheap Korean product in order to secure the import licences for a lucrative Hollywood blockbuster (see Lee 2000: 50). Censorship was incredibly strict and the penalties for infringement could end in blacklisting or even prison, as the trial of director Yi Manhŭl, a leading name from the 1960s, demonstrated. Films underwent a 'double censorship' (Lee 2000: 51), first prior to actual production and then again before the film could be released to the public. Therefore films that in any way transgressed the government guidelines would never make it to the public arena.

Surprisingly under this harsh and unsupportive system Im managed to develop his career. He directed several Quality Films and was recognised as a director who would not deviate from the official ideology. Although the films made during this period are not especially interesting from a critical or aesthetic viewpoint

(Im himself made the comment that 'lousy films had to come first' [in Lent 1995: 86]), this period was one of the few times that directors could develop their technical skills free from box office pressures. In accordance with guidelines the Quality Films were divided into three main categories for government-issued awards: literary adaptations, anti-communist and *Saemaul* films promoting the government's economic model of intense industrial development (see Lee 2000: 49). Often literary adaptations, they always conformed to the anti-socialist, frugal, hard-working and non-complaining ethos of the *Yushin* government. The most important award for Quality Films was the Golden Bell award and Im received it in1973 for his anti-communist piece *The Testimony* (*Chŭngŏn*). Although conforming to the demands of the censors, Im's social policy films are by no means unskilled. Many of his films from this period show a more nuanced, subtle and questioning approach to the official rhetoric that was being presented. Despite the fact that his films from this period never deviate from the officially sanctioned narratives, Im's films over that time do show sophistication in style and content that would be developed further in later films.

One important film to have emerged from this time was *Weeds* (*Chapch'o*, also known as *The Deserted Widow*, 1973). Im has called this, his fiftieth film, his 'debut film as a real film director' (in Chung 2006: 115). This film was a box office failure but heralded a new awareness of Im as a director who could make a more varied and unique cinema rather than being merely a director for hire.

> Until then I had never made a movie that displayed life. From *Weeds*, I am talking about things that may not be my own experiences but things I was able to experience intuitively during the course of my life. For the first time in *Weeds* I wanted to start making films full of life, so I didn't have a choice but to abandon genre films. (In Chung 2006: 75)

Weeds tells the story of self-sacrificing widow Boon-rye who struggles to raise her two step-children after the death of her husband and her own son. The film references the destruction of poverty and the trouble that the pursuit of wealth can have on a family. Boon-rye opens a bar near the port and works long hours to provide for her children. Her adopted son, however, disowns her when he discover that in order to give him and his sister the best chance of success Boon-rye has also worked as a prostitute. Set during the occupation and then following the family through the trauma of the Korean War, *Weeds* closely follows Im's desire to 'display life'. The films sense of Korean history and innate humanism would become trademarks in his later films, and although it did badly at the box office *Weeds* remains a film of interest.[1]

The Genealogy (*Chokpo*, 1978) was another film that Im says was key in the development of a personal style. It controversially portrays a Japanese painter who is sympathetic to Korean independence and a large portion of the film is offered from his point of view. The film was an adaptation of a Japanese short story by Kajiyama Toshiyuki and *The Genealogy* offered the view that it was not only the Koreans that suffered under Japanese colonial rule. The focus is on the occupation government's attempt to eradicate Korean names by forcing families to adopt a Japanese surname. When Sŏl Chin-yŏng, the family patriarch, refuses to surrender his 700-year-old family name, his children and grandchildren suffer at the hands of the Japanese. The film's patriotic emphasis was in keeping with the time and indeed won Im his second governmental Grand Bell Award. What is remarkable about the film is Im's challenging of linear narrative and the focus on art and the artist as a method of examining Korean society and history. In *The Genealogy* Dani, the main Japanese character, is a landscape painter and Sŏl discusses Korean aesthetics as the camera moves over traditional ceramic vases. Quoting Japanese-Korean sympathiser Yanaki Muneyoshi he asks the question 'Where else in the world can you find so much beauty with so much sorrow?' This reference to 'sorrow', that is often referred to as *han* in Korean, is one of several concepts that are central to the Korean imagination concerning their national identity. *Han* is an elusive, slippery and often inconsistent term to define but it could be generally classified as 'the deep-rooted sadness, bitterness and longing sparked by prolonged injustices and oppressions' (Chung 2005: 121). Isolde Standish summarises it as ' the result of injustices perpetrated by, among others, parents, friends, siblings, a colonial ruler, an occupying army, past govern-ments, the present government, and those who in critical moments failed to display sincerity' (1994: 87). Im has been referred to as the 'director whose oeuvre brims over with *han*-centric films that aestheticise Korean history, tradition and culture in melodramatic modes' (Chung 2005: 121) and, as will be seen, the pre-sentation of *han* remains one of Im's key narrative and aesthetic features.

In *The Genealogy*, together with art, women also play a key role. Sŏl has a beautiful daughter, Ok-soon, that Dani falls in love with. When her father and fiancée refuse to obey the law it is Ok-soon who is most threatened as the vengeful district commander plans on forcing her to become a 'comfort woman' (a woman forced into prostitution for the Japanese army). She, together with the Korean landscape, becomes the site in which the *han* of the Korean people will be most clearly shown. In this way *The Genealogy* offers 'two privileged symbols on which the historical trauma of the nation will be re-enacted: the body of the Korean landscape and the bodies of Korean women' (James and Kim 2001: 56). This focus on women as the site of Korea's traumatic past and troubled present is referenced in many of Im's most renowned works. It is often through the trials and tribulations of his heroines that the faults of wider society are alluded to. This use of the female body in such a way is not without issue; it is one of the major debates in feminist film theory about the use of women as metaphor, particularly in terms of nation and nationhood. The alignment of women and nation, in, for example, terms and sayings such as 'mother of the nation' or 'rape of the nation', has been well documented (see Warner 1996, Hastings 1997, Yuval-Davis 1997). Writers who have considered the relationship between women and concepts of nationhood note that women are largely passive in nationalist discourse and movements, only being evoked symbolically by men to indicate an eternal virtue, as an object of defence or source of procreation. Anne McClintock states that 'women are typically constructed as bearers of the nation, but are denied any direct relation to national agency' (1995: 354). Women in this way are positioned as object rather than subject and are often presented as 'having things done to them' rather than being active in national and self-construction. The legacy of Confucianism that is dominant in a large part of East Asia, particularly South Korea, has seen women divided into stereotypes of the 'good wife, wise mother' or a woman of 'poor virtue' such as a prostitute. This dualism regarding women is something that will be discussed in greater detail in the chapter on Kim Ki-duk, but it is important to reference here in terms of the use of women as national symbols. The dual symbols of art and women as metaphors for the nation are something that Im would return to again and again. Later films such as *Mandala* (1981), *Gilsottem* (1985), *Ticket* (1986), *Come, Come Upwards* (*Aje aje bara aje*, 1989) and *Festival* (*Chukje*, 1996) would all feature women in key roles, and their bodies are often used as a site for the presentation of Korea's problems. The use of women in this fashion is problematic and feminist counter-cinema and theory has often tried to address and repudiate this particular type of representation (see Thornham 1999). In terms of Korean cinema, however, Im was attempting to raise particular social and cultural issues via his placement and treatment of women on film as a method of communication, therefore examination of his work must take this into account regardless of the problems which it raises in respect to gender and equality issues.

Women suffer in his work but it is not only women who are seen as a site of consternation. As David E. James and Kim Kyung Hyun note, even where 'the nation is gendered as female, the oppressions of women is commonly linked not simply to the oppression of Korea by invaders but specifically to the oppression of the working class' (2002: 59). Thus Im uses women and the female body as an ideal method to convey the very specific issues of class injustice.

The linkage of women and class references another key term in Korean culture: *minjung*. Standish states that '*minjung* are those who are oppressed politically, exploited economically, alienated sociologically, and kept under-educated in culture and intellectual matters' (1994: 86). In short, *minjung* will often exist in a state of *han*, and Standish argues that this word has direct reference to working-class culture. In Im's work from the late 1970s onwards the notion of *minjung* is vital in his presentation of characters who suffer as a result of their oppression, alienation and exploitation.

Surrogate Mother (*Sibaji*, 1986) focuses on a young woman who is chosen to act as a surrogate to a rich and powerful family. The family's economic and social standing renders her powerless to oppose them and she cannot prevent her child from being removed from her. Unable to regain her child or support herself, she commits suicide. In *Low Life* (*Haryu insaeng*, 2004) the main female character is tricked into prostitution by the promise of a job and then gang-raped and abused for 'debts' that she never knew she had incurred. Although several wealthy men say they will 'rescue' her they only seek to abuse and abase her further. The lowly class position of the women results in them being open to abuse and exploitation, and in his use of their stories Im offers a critique of the legacy of a feudal system that still continues to oppress those who are deemed to be lower or working class.

The oppression of the Korean people took a new turn throughout the 1980s which saw another radical change in the political structures of South Korea. In 1979 Park was assassinated as a result of a power struggle within the upper echelons of the government. Initially his death spurred a demand for democracy that saw student and labour unions mobilising themselves in a call for free elections, fair distribution of economic power and wealth and freedom of expression. These calls, however, known as the 'Spring of Seoul' were unanswered as in 1980 another military coup took place and saw the establishment of a hardline military dictatorship under General Chun Doo-hwan. The events that followed would mark South Korea until the present day. There was a mass arrest of labour unionists, student activists and anyone who opposed the government. The most terrible event of this period took place on 18 May 1980 when student protesters clashed with government troops. The Kwangju massacre resulted in thousands of dead and wounded (although the numbers have always been under debate) and left a lasting scar on South Korea. It has been, as will be discussed in the chapter on Lee Chang-dong, a continual presence in South Korean art and culture in the decades that have followed. Censorship and control of the film industry heightened at this time and even more directors found themselves on the government blacklist unable to make or produce films. Contrary to the fate of other directors, for Im Kwon-taek the 1980s saw a flowering of his filmmaking career. Despite a lack of critical attention from inside South Korea, his films had been the most successful Korean films on the international cinematic scene during the repressive 1970s (see James and Kim 2001: 31). The Chun government was anxious to see South Korea represented favourably on the international market and Im's nationalistic debate on Korean art, literature and history was exactly the type of image that the government wanted. This was also enhanced by the fact that he was one of the few experienced directors to be still making films after the turbulent 1970s. During the 1980s there was a series of initiatives to help South Korean films present at international film festivals and prizes for directors whose films were successful. In 1981 Im directed *Mandala* that won the Grand Prix at the Hawaii Film Festival and he was invited to compete in the prestigious Berlin Film Festival. *Mandala*, which focuses on the trials and torments of a young Buddhist monk, offered the audience a unique presentation of a lifestyle (orthodox Buddhism) that many, even inside South Korea, found exotic. *Mandala*'s focus on the sexual torment of the monks also added an incredibly erotic element to the narrative and the use of dramatic landscape shots framed the film as part of a unique Korean cultural heritage. In *Mandala* Im combined a narrative of Korean nationhood with popular cultural appeal and this pattern would continue in many of his future works.

Mandala was one of a series of films that celebrated various Korean cultural traditions. The term *minjok* is important to refer to here with reference to Im's work. *Minjok* can be defined as 'nation or people' in the sense of a bounded and unified group; it is based on the notion that the Korean people share a common history, culture, language and ethnicity. A patriotic sense of nationhood is vital in the presentation of *minjok* as the ideas behind it premise the concept of Korean 'uniqueness'. South Korean nationalism has often been articulated through this lens of a shared cultural history that has struggled to maintain itself, and in Im's films we see this via his presentation of various aspects of Korean culture and past. *Minjung* and *han* operate to provide a consolidated concept of *minjok*. In the sharing of a common sorrow and oppression the notion of a bounded nation united under a common experience can emerge. The focus in his films on cultural markers such as music, dance, Buddhism and Shamanism (seen in *Daughter of Fire* [*Bului dal*, 1982] and *The Taekback Mountains* [*Taebaek sanmaek*, 1994]), offers a shared sense of history and culture and a presentation of Korea as a nation that shares religion and historical traditions. This identity has been forged and maintained despite the myriad of traumas that have befallen it such as colonisation, occupation, division and the drive towards Westernised capitalism. Writing on nationalism in East Asia, Shin Gi-wook and Michel Robinson note the following in relation to South Korea:

> Placing the concept of the *minjung* at the centre of a counter-vision of national identity is an attempt to free Korean nationalism from its ties to a universalist path of Westernization and capitalism development as well. This vision posits that material progress linked to capitalist developments is antithetical to the 'true' nature of Korean identity, more appropriately centered on the culture and identity of the peasant-producers, the *minjung*. (1999: 16)

Films such as *Mandala*, *Ticket*, *Gilsotteum*, *Adada* and *Surrogate Mother*, through the referencing and presentation of various collective and individual experiences of *han* and *minjung* create an image of a shared notion of *minjok* or nation. In Im's films this sense of cultural unity often comes from being placed in opposition to a negative or destructive force. The Japanese occupation, economic hardship, the Korean war, are all referenced as key factors in the state of *han* that (South) Korea exists inside. *Gilsotteum* offers the tale of a woman seeking the son she lost during the Korean War and *Adada* features a mute woman who suffers continually at the hands of a dominant and repressive patriarchal system that has been inherited from the Korean Confucian past. The lead female character in *Ticket* is another working-class woman who suffers at the hands of the unforgiving economic and social system. *Come, Come, Come Upwards* offered the tale of two Buddhist nuns and their struggles to find spirituality and happiness in the face of personal and cultural hardship. Despite their desires to renounce worldly possessions and desires, both women find the path to enlightenment fraught with difficulties and torments. Both suffer from sexual assault at the hands of men they should trust and their pain, or *han*, is a reflection of the *han* that all those that surround them seems to be experiencing. In this way the nation is seen to be founded on the collective suffering of its members that leads to a notion of unity.

As an interesting addition to this litany of negativity, however, another interpretation of the concept of *han* is that while it is caused by negative sentiments or emotions, within the concept is an implication that these negative emotions can be transcended. Thus *han* has both negativity and transcendence of this negativity as an integral part of it (see Kim 2004: 65). Whilst the negative elements are very much represented, there is in Im's work an acknowledgement that this sadness can be overcome and defeated. This attempt to overcome negative emotions would be seen in his later films such as *The General's Son* (*Janggunui adeul*, 1990), *Festival*, and in the character of Kim Pŏm-u in *The Taebaek Mountains*. This change has a historical relevance: one of South Korea's key sources of *han* was being confronted during this period as the tremendously unforgiving autocratic rule of the early 1980s was challenged by the consolidated public support for democracy that grew after the Kwangju killings. In 1987 Roh Tae-woo, a colleague of Park, was elected to the presidency by the popular vote and in 1992 Kim Young-sam was elected as the first civilian president for over thirty years. South Korea took on a new lease of life and Im also opened a new door as in 1990 he rather unexpectedly made an action film. In the highly popular *The General's Son*, Im offered the story of a young gangster, Kim Du-han, who whilst living under Japanese occupation is fighting to gain economic and social power. Although Kim faces hardship and torment he still manages to have moments of intense triumph. *Han* in this way is always present but the struggles of an individual to overcome it become the main focus. *The General's Son* also saw a change in filmic style with fast editing, multiple shots and several intense action sequences. It became one of the most successful films of 1990 and its popularity resulted in two more high-action sequels following Kim as he struggles to sustain his position in the gangster hierarchy.

Despite his successful foray into the action genre it is for his films made from 1990s onwards that Im will probably be best remembered. The themes that he has explored throughout his earlier works would come together in a series of films focusing on aspects of Korean history and culture.

His work from this period onwards can be seen alongside the political and artistic '*Minjung* movement' which took place in the late 1980s and early 1990s. This nationalistic movement was a key voice in the demand for democracy together with a desire to reinstate Korean culture in the face of Japanese and American neo-colonialism (see Chung 2005: 113). Im's focus on Korean culture and traditions as part of a wider debate of nationalism and nationhood spoke directly to these ideals and although he was never part of the Korean New Wave personified by directors such as Park Kwang-su, his films can be seen as part of a wider debate on national culture.

Sopyonje, released in 1993, is arguable one of Im's most influential and popular films. This story of a *pansori* singer and his two adopted children not only explores one of Korea's most remarkable musical traditions but also offers a story of ordinary people facing the changes that history is forcing upon them. *The Taekback Mountains* was interesting for several reasons most notably for its desire to return to the hitherto neglected area of the Korean War. *Festival* charted the turmoil experienced by a family at the death of its matriarch. *Chunhyang* (2000) and *Chihwaseon* (*Drunk on Women and Poetry* [UK]/*Painted Fire* [USA], 2002) both took as their inspiration the traditional Korean cultural arts.

Returning to these films later, it is important to examine *The Taekback Mountains* as a film that allows many of the key ideas regarding national identity to come to the fore. The film's complex and often melodramatic narrative revolves around the 1948 Yŏsu-Sunch'ŏn Rebellion that was one of the many events that finally led to the outbreak of the Korean War in 1950. This traumatic period had until this film been largely ignored by cinema and since Im was the only working director to have actually *lived* through the war he was in a unique position of insight for a presentation of the actual realities of the time (see James and Kim 2001: 202). This insight was enhanced by the fact that *The Taekback Mountains* saw Im return to his home province of Chŏlla for the films setting. Although the book on which the film was based was a big hit in the 1980s Im had to wait until the implementation of a non-military government in order to make the potentially controversial film. The film has a huge cast but the key figures are two brothers, one a devoted communist (Sang-jun), the other a violent rightist (Sang-gu) and their intellectual nationalist friend Kim Pŏm-u. The division of the brothers, of course, directly references the division of Korea and the film offers images of the trauma and illogicality of this period. In one scene a village has men and animals taken away by the communists, the next day they are punished by the nationalists for helping the communists, 'collaborators' from the village are killed by the communists the next night, and then the nationalists come back and burn the whole village down. Rabid ideology and violence from both sides of the political line ruins the community and both sides are shown as destructive and impotent in providing stability and resources for the people. The debate about land ownership and reform becomes the focus of many of the tensions but it is only Kim Pŏm-u who fully understands the debate and identifies it as a legacy of the colonial period that neither side will be able to solve. Women are once again the site of intense suffering; both sides use the abuse of women as a means to punish their enemies. Sang-gu breaks into the home of Oesŏdaek whose husband is fighting for the communists, rapes her and forces her to become his mistress. His actions will eventually lead to Oesŏdaek's suicide. A young widow embarks on a passionate affair with a communist guerrilla only to be executed by him for being a traitor and nationalist spy when the communists take control of her town.

One of the female characters who best illustrates Im's focus on women and class is So-hwa, a young shaman who engages in a loving affair with Ha-sŏp, one of the guerrillas. She is arrested for this relationship and suffers a miscarriage after being viciously kicked by Sang-gu. The political situation caused her to lose her child but then Ha-sŏp's mother refuses to allow the pair to marry due to the girl's lowly class status. Even when Ha-sŏp confirms his desire to marry her he insists that she gives up her traditional shamanistic beliefs since as the future wife of an important member of the Communist Party she should not hold on to a 'poisonous' spiritual way of life. She will be marginalised not only by gender and class but also for holding onto her traditional beliefs. In short, she presents a Korean culture that is being destroyed through the clash of political ideals.

The divisions between peasant and landowner, tradition and modernity, women and men, private and public spaces are in constant flux throughout *The Taekback Mountains* and none of the characters escapes from the suffering. The turbulence presented in the film comes directly from Im's own experiences of living under occupation and then through the war itself; he states that, 'After living through that time, I couldn't take sides. Neither side took peoples lives seriously' (in Chung 2006: 110). His presentation of the conflict leads to a questioning of the future of Korea and how the traumas of the past infuse the national psyche.

Despite presenting horrific acts Im's film maintains a sense of humanism and hope via the figure of Kim Pŏm-u. Kim, a liberal nationalist son of a landlord, offers the melding of the various ideologies and combines this with his faith in the future of Korea to recover and to become whole again. It is interesting that the period 1990–93 had seen a slight thawing of relations between North and South Korea with various meetings of high-ranking officials and sport associations after the Beijing Asian Games. Although relations deteriorated again from 1994 (when *The Taekback Mountains* was released) hope had been generated for the nation's united future. Im's continual emphasis on shared culture and history operates within the desire that exists in South Korea for unification. The split in Korea continues to be a source of *han* to the present day and Im's humanistic approach to the topic in *The Taekback Mountains* (that disowns any allegiance to any political rhetoric) demonstrates that the hardship suffered by the Korean people has led to a fractured and problematic identity that they must seek to overcome through an mutual examination of their history and culture.

This examination of culture and history can be seen in the prominent place given to traditional Korean theatrical arts in several of Im's most successful films. Dance, song and music are central elements that consistently appear, enhancing the ideas that he has raised in other narratives about the need to focus on an essential Korean culture. *Sopyonje*, *Chunhyang*, *Chihwaseon*, and *Hanji* (2011) all base their stories on the arts and music of Korea's past.

Sopyonje was the first Korean film to draw over a million viewers in Seoul alone. The film was acclaimed critically both in South Korea and abroad and it was screened at the Cannes Film Festival and won six Grand Bell Awards (South Korean equivalent of the Academy Awards) and six Korean Film Critics' Awards. The film opens with Dong-ho searching the towns and villages for his lost adopted sister Song-hwa. The film is composed of a series of flashback as Dong-ho searches for Song-hwa and reminisces over the circumstances that led to his family being separated. Both Song-hwa and Dong-ho are trained *pansori* performers. They were taught by their adopted father and the art form plays a vital and central role in this film. The word *pansori* itself was developed from two separate words; *pan* means round, place or stage and *sori* means sound or song. The literal meaning can perhaps be summarised as 'songs performed in places of entertainment'. *Pansori* recitals and performances are several hours long and are performed by one singer, or *gwangdae*, who is accompanied by one *gosu* (drummer) playing the barrel drum. *Pansori* is notable for the vigorous training that takes place in the traditional apprenticeship system. The songs performed through *pansori* are often traditional folk tales and the idea of *pansori* as being 'folk' music as opposed to the more formal songs of the Korean court leads it to be aligned with *minjung*. *Pansori* is seen as especially important as a method for the poor and repressed to release their *han* (see Hoare and Pares 1988: 174). The linkage between *han* and *pansori* is quickly transposed into the idea of 'suffering for the art' and this idea is closely examined in *Sopyonje*. Believing that a state of *han* is vital to perfect *pansori* singing, the father deliberately blinds his adopted daughter by administering a poisonous herb. His desire for her to be the best *pansori* performer leads him to harm her in such a way that she will forever be marked by sorrow. He succeeds in this aim as one of the first things she requests after losing her sight is to learn the famous *pansori* song *Shimcheong-jeon*. His daughter's blindness is not the only *han* that the small family suffer for their art. *Pansori*, despite its high standing in the present day, was at the time that *Sopyonje* is set facing extinction. The arrival of cinema, Japanese colonisation and a desire for all that was modern, caused *pansori* to dip drastically in popularity. As Western music and cultural arts invaded Korea the more traditional 'local' arts declined. In *Sopyonje* the *pansori* singers are forced to perform in brothels, market places and bars. The art form they perform is ignored and the sufferings that they have undergone, the *han* that their music represents, is unseen by the people that watch them perform. The teenage Dong-ho can no longer suffer the poverty and the indignity and runs away, but his sister remains to suffer at the hands of their adopted father. In *Beyond Years* (*Cheonnyeonhak*, 2007) Im returned to the story of *Sopyonje* and shows the audience how Dong-ho continued to live in a state of *han* throughout the years he was separated from Song-hwa. In *Sopyonje* the final duet that takes place between Dong-ho and Song-hwa reaches heights of intensity as each brings their own *han* to the song. Their respective suffering has made them into ideal *pansori* players but despite this musical reunion they never formally acknowledge each other and after the song they separate once more. The film's lack of a 'happy' ending in the traditional sense has led to some debate about what Im was trying to convey (see Joang 2002). The ending can be seen more clearly when referenced against *Beyond Years*. Through that film it is clear that Dong-ho is maintaining an idealised and mythologised image of Song-hwa. When they finally meet in *Sopyonje*, acknowledgement of each other will lead to the past becoming reality. Dong-ho's image of Song-hwa is one that transcends all the traumas of the past. She remains an ideal image and one that would be destroyed if Dong-ho confronted her in the modern contemporary world, so instead they choose to enact their reunion by *pansori*. In the book devoted to the film Im states that 'the reason that they meet but can't bring themselves to reveal their identities is that they know all too well that neither can be of any help to the other in the future' (1993: 202). Kwak Han-ju summarises that:

> If she comes out led by Dong-ho's hands, to the present, modern world in which pre-modern and non-Western values are overridden by the materialist logic of capitalism, how is it possible to maintain her transcendence. (2004: 151)

This statement references a key element that has been seen in many of Im's recent films, namely the desire to maintain and promote traditional culture in the face of modernity and Western influence. His desire to promote a national culture is one that is tempered with the fear that many of the elements that make Korean culture 'unique' could be facing extinction. This is referenced clearly in *Sopyonje* with the decreasing popularity of the art been pointedly shown. Im states that:

> My personal desire has been to capture elements of our traditional culture in my work … the fear is, of course, that those aspects of Korean culture that are not favoured by the terms of this new international and more aggressive culture may be absorbed and in the end disappear. (Quoted in ibid.)

His desire was transformed into visible success since *Sopyonje* was in fact key in the revival of *pansori* as a popular art form in South Korea. In 2003 UNESCO proclaimed *pansori* as a 'Masterpiece of the Oral and Intangible Heritage of Humanity', and there has been a revival in young performers training to enter into the profession. Although criticism can be levelled against *Sopyonje*, especially in the use of the female body as *object* rather than an articulated and active *subject*, what the film does offer is a vision of Korean cultural heritage that until this point had been neglected in the modern era.

Pansori is a combined art in the sense it offers a novel-like storytelling quality as well as having a high degree of the dramatic in the interplay between singer, the song and the drummer. This notion of combined art forms is central in Im's later film *Chunyung*, which can be read as a companion piece to *Sopyonje*.

Indeed the two films share the same producer Lee Tae-won whom Im has referenced as being one of the sole reasons that the films were ever made (Chung 2006: 95). *Chunyung* has been rendered cinematically over sixteen times and has appeared in television format in over eleven different versions. Although the story itself varies slightly from region to region it is the most well-known of the major *pansori* operas that remain in complete entirety.[2] Whereas *Sopyonje* spoke of the trials and emotions of *pansori* performers, *Chunhyung* as presented by Im is a *pansori* song presented on film in its in entirety. *Chunhyung* is remarkable for its blending of film and theatre. The opening premise of some reluctant students going to see the most famous of all Korean operas becomes a dramatic and lush recreation of the classical story of the faithful wife Chunhyung. *Chunhyung* offers the tale of a young nobleman, Mong-ryong, who meets, falls in love with and marries in secret the honourable and virginal Chunhyung. The story's melodramatic imprisonment of Chunhyung by a lascivious and corrupt landowner, and her eventual rescue, is presented to the audience via fantastic visuals intermixed with the sweeping melodies and songs of the *pansori*. *Chunhyung*'s presentation of a traditional folk tale and art raises the question of Korean cinema on the international scale. In *Chunhyung* Im sought to present the 'distinctive uniqueness of cultural tradition', that is, as critic Sŏ Chŏng-nam notes, 'critical for global audiences to be aware of the notion of Koreanness' (quoted in Lee 2005: 66). In this way Sŏ makes the link between the national and the international markets' need for a consolidated image of Korea's culture and traditions. Films are no longer sold on a purely national level; the aim of any national cinema is to have its products recognised worldwide via success at festivals or in box office receipts. Im's idealised image of old Korea did not appeal to domestic audiences (see Lee 2005) but it did function perfectly in appealing to the international audiences' taste for a romanticised image of Korean culture. Lee Hyangjin states that, 'the creation of a new national identity for global audiences pursued by New Korean Cinema practitioners should be understood in this context. Since the 1980s Korean filmmakers and policy makers began to look for ways to present the national cinema as a new force of world cinema' (2005: 67). A vision of a unique and distinct Korean cinema is vital for its success on a global scale. Rather than attempting to produce films that imitate a universal (Hollywood) model, selling a unique culture allows for a cinema to emerge that can set itself apart from other national cinemas and use this as a commercial selling point. As the proclaimed *Kungmin Gamdok* (People's Director) and the grandfather of Korean film by virtue of longevity Im has been key in the selling of Korean cinema to a wider global audience. His long-standing presence at international film festivals and narratives that continue to focus on Korean history culture and traditions have resulted in Im being at the forefront of the new global Korean cinema.

An examination of Im Kwon-taek's films reveal several decades of engagement with many of the issues that have traversed modern South Korea. He has been one of the leading figures in South Korean cinema for over five decades and has shown an ability to transform himself to meet any political, economic or popular demand. In *Chihwaseon* (to be analysed in detail in the next section) Im once again offered the international audience his vision of classical Korean art and culture in his dramatisation of Korean painter Kang Sūng-ŏp. 2010 saw the Korean release of his 101st film, *Hanji*. In a similar fashion to many of his other films that focus on Korean art and music traditions, *Hanji* engages with the Korean tradition of papermaking. The film follows a low-ranking civil servant Pi-yong (Park Joong-hoon) as he struggles to organise a complicated project to restore classical annals from the Joseon Dynasty (1392–1897). This is simultaneous to trying to take care of his disabled wife and working with a documentary filmmaker as she interviews influential craftsman and makers of *hanji*. Pi-yong has little knowledge of *hanji* and therefore the film becomes an educational and celebratory experience as Pi-yong seeks to find out more about this tradition, not only to further his career but also to bring himself closer to his wife whose family had been paper manufactures for several generations. *Hanji* is familiar to Im's other features in that is seeks to celebrate a Korean tradition and try to find a way for this element from the past to find a way to exist in the present. As the audience follows Pi-yong we are shown the beauty and complexity of this tradition and the film's conclusion of several of the protagonists making paper in a river under the full moon to ensure that it will lasts a thousand years seems to point to a way to combine the past and present together without destroying either. The film's accessible and internationally popular celebration of another Korean art form and its debates on *hanji*'s place in the modern world reveals how Im has adapted his films to suit a global market whilst still maintaining a keen link to the concept of the Korean national. As Kim Kyung Hyun summarises, 'Im was never Korea's Mizoguchi. Rather he was Korea's Spielberg – but more versatile, radical and profound than Spielberg ever dreamed of being' (2002a: 40).

The release of *Hanji* was preceded by a two-month retrospective of his works at the Korean Film Archive paying tribute to the director's long-standing career and sought to introduce many of his older works to younger viewers. In 2013, a museum dedicated to Im opened in Busan at Dongseo University. His status as a man who deserves his own museum demonstrates how he plays a vital and important artistic role in the South Korean nation.

Whether *Hanji* will be the last film of the 78-year-old director remains to be seen, but one thing is certain: his place in Korean and world cinema is already assured.

NOTES

1 This interest, however, is unfortunately exasperated by the loss of the original print and the resulting reliance on images, film fragments and the contemporary writings on the film.

2 Five major songs of *pansori* have been passed down to the present day: *Chunhyanga*, *Simcheongga*, *Sugungga* (*Song of the Underwater Palace*), *Heungbuga* and *Jeokyeokga* (*Song of Jeokbyeok*).

Film Analysis

CHIHWASEON

취화선
Drunk on Women and Poetry (UK)
Painted Fire (USA)

2002

Director

Im Kwon-taek

Cast

Min-sik Choi (Jang Seung-up), Sung-kee Ahn (Kim Byung-Moon), Ho-jeong Yu (Mae-hyang), Yeo-jin Kim (Jin-jong), Ye-jin Son (So-woon)

International Film Awards

2002 Best Director, Cannes Film Festival

2002 Best Film, Blue Dragon Award

2002 Nominated Palme D´Or, Cannes Film Festival

2002 Nominated Best Camera Work, Camerimage

2002 Nominated Best Foreign Film, César Awards

Plot Summary

This film charts the life of Jang Seung-up, a nineteenth-century Korean painter who changed the direction of Korean art.

In the 1850s a young orphan's artistic talent is recognised by Kim Byung-moon, a leading artist. He decides to encourage the young boy in his artistic endeavours via a series of placements with prominent artists. Although he is a troublesome student, Jang Seung-up's skills are remarkable and he eventually gains a job as a painter in a prestigious household. He falls in love with the sickly daughter, So-woon, but the relationship cannot succeed due to his lowly origins. After she is married to another man he leaves the household and begins to study with a more superior master. His drinking and womanising become central to his life but his career does well despite his antics. He falls in love with a Catholic *kisaeng* (traditional entertainer) called Mae-hyang, but the couple are separated when she is forced to flee due to anti-Catholic persecution. So-woon dies and Jang is devastated. He decides to travel and continues to improve his painting style taking influences from all around him. He is given the prestigious pen name 'Oh-Won', but is often ridiculed by other artists for his poor origins. He goes to work for the king and horrifies the king's retinue by his manners and attitude. He eventually runs away from the palace when he is ordered to paint for a brutal Chinese general. During the peasants' revolt he is almost killed by the mob who regard him as an emblem of aristocratic power and influence. Oh-won takes to the road again and meets with his master Kim. Returning to Seoul he encounters Mae-hyang but his health is broken and he takes a job painting ceramics. Alone, he crawls into the furnace and the audience is told via subtitles that the fate of Jang remains unknown.

———

> For a long time, I had been thinking of doing a film about Korean painting ... Drawing and filming are two different genres of art but they are the same in the sense they both need to be agonised over to make a creative piece. (In quoted in Chung 2006: 101)

In 2002 Im released the film which would go on to achieve worldwide acclaim and win the Best Director Award at the Cannes Film Festival. *Chihwaseon*, also known by the title *Drunk on Women and Poetry*, tells the tale of the famous Korean artist, Jang Seung-up. Starring the vibrant Choi Min-sik in the lead role *Chihwaseon* gained a huge level of success on the international market but, as will be discussed, failed to inspire domestic audiences.

Chihwaseon charts the career of the highly talented but very difficult artist Jang Seung-op. The narrative of the film works on several different levels. The basic story is of the artist Jang, but Im's film aims to question wider issues with regard to Korean national identity. The opening credits inform us that the year is 1882 and the Korean people are fighting against foreign invasion and a corrupt government. As with many of Im's films the main protagonist is from a poor background. We see that Jang was born a beggar and it was only the intervention of kindly lord Kim Byung-moon that allowed Jang's talent to be nurtured and explored. The lowly status of Jang is continually referenced throughout the film and he struggles to fit in with the other art students who are generally presented as the spoilt sons of wealthy lords and landowner. What Jang lacks in breeding, however, he makes up for in talent and it is his development of his painting skills, concurrent with the history of Korea, which *Chihwaseon* seeks to present.

The film charts the period from around 1850 to 1897 and presents the persecution and killing of over 8,000 Korean Catholics in 1866; to the reformist revolution in 1884 where a Japanese-sponsored *coup d'état* was ended by Chinese military intervention. In his presentation of Korean history as intertwined with the history of Jang's painting, Im aligns the construction and development of national identity with art. The development of Jang's artwork can be read as the charting of a search for a Korean national identity. In his first place of study his tremendous ability for mimicry is established. He only needs to see a painting once and he is able to replicate it perfectly. Furthermore, throughout the film Im presents the history of Korean painting; how it was heavily influenced by Chinese traditions and the strict rules which dominated it (often developed from foreign ideals regarding aesthetics). This control meant that Korean artists were restricted in their ability to explore the medium. Working against the dominant painting traditions, his mentor constantly encourages Jang to look and experience as much artwork as possible, and then find his own voice and a uniquely *Korean* way of painting. Kim Byung-moon states that Jang needs to 'paint pictures which are infused with your spirit and soul'. In his rejection of Chinese styles, Jang (and Im in his presentation of him), can be seen as focusing on forging a new way of seeing Korean identity as a unique cultural artefact separate from the Chinese influences which had dominated for much of Korea's history.

The lush visual style of *Chihwaseon* is highly reminiscent of Im's earlier works. As Jang wanders around the ravaged countryside, the sounds of *pansori* fill the air reflecting his tortured soul in its melodies. Jang's love, the Catholic Mae-hyang, is a skilled musician and there are several musical interludes in the film presenting traditional music and song. Although the film's main focus is Jang we also see the torments and concerns of the poor peasants who are suffering under the hard rule of corrupt Korean officialdom and then later the Japanese. The *han* of the people is reflected in the various protests and calls for changes which we see taking place, all of which fail in their purpose. Jang himself is infused with *han*. He is a heavy drinker and womaniser and his search for perfection in his art drives most people away from him. Several times in the film we see him screaming at the sky in frustration at his almost-unachievable goals. Although he is offered a lucrative post at the royal court he wishes to be free to paint according to is own desires and as a result he flees the palace.

The film emphasises the connection between Jang's paintings and the role of motion. Compared to the older Chinese-based static style, Jang tries to discover a painting method which expresses movement and fluidity. His focus on motion is linked into the Korean people's desire for change. In one scene a young *kisaeng* comments that his painting of a hawk chasing a flock of sparrows is like the sorrow of the Korean people suffering under the tyranny of a corrupt government. This same painting will later be burnt by protesters calling for the overthrowing of the corrupt Joesen government. The peasant's revolt in 1894, however, rather than helping the Korean nation to develop, in fact made it easier for the Japanese to invade and colonise Korea. In the burning of Jang's artwork, a symbol of Korean culture and identity, it is implied that the nation is destroying itself by being unable to recognise the truth in the events which are taking place.

In a very poignant scene Jang asks a *kisaeng* to bear his child but in the process of having sex they are literally pulled apart by rioters and we see Jang's semen spill onto the leg of the woman. In this way the sterile nature of the protester's actions are perfectly illustrated. All the Korean political and social movements around this time were crushed and repressed by the might of the Japanese occupation force. It would be fifty or more years before Korea would gain its independence only to be then sunk into the Korean War and subsequent partitioning. Towards the end of the film a Japanese reporter tells Jang that 'night is falling on the Joseon dynasty' and that Jang's paintings are the 'last flicker of light in a dying nation'.

For the Japanese reporter, Jang's art is linked to the construction (or during this period, deconstruction) of the Korean nation. In the early part of the nineteenth century, the Korean identity was deeply under threat and Jang's unique approach to painting presents the best of the Korean nation which is struggling in the face of the encroaching colonial power.

Jang's final act of crawling into the kiln refers to traditional Korean cremation rites. His death by fire indicates that the search for artistic perfection has consumed Jang totally. As the pots are removed from the kiln the artisans comment on the perfect colour. One of the pots holds an image that we had earlier seen Jang working on. Jang has literally *become* his perfect artwork. The inter-titles then inform us that the real Jang disappeared without trace. An interesting historical cross-over in relation to the history of cinema is the year that the film denotes as Jang's death, 1897, is the same year which cinema was first introduced to the Korean Court. This link between the cinema and older Korean art forms is something which Im Kwon-taek would reference in many of this most popular works but it is in *Chihwaseon* that his vision is most clearly seen.

In the introduction to his book on Korean literature, Kwon Youngmin notes that 'the period after 1897 to 1910 has received a lot of attention … as the origins of modernity and the approaches to defining Korean modernity can be found here' (2005: 13). This period of time that *Chihwaseon* is charting can be constructed as the beginning of the modern age. In the film we see the origins of contemporary Korean modernity and in his presentation of this time period Im is making a direct link to the new era of transnational modernity where South Korea now resides. In this earlier period the Korean nation struggled to define itself by its traditions, culture and language, and in this current age of mass globalisation, South Korea once more needs to negotiate its cultural specificity.

Kim So-young states that *Chihwaseon* 'provides a framework through which the present South Korean problems under the globalisation era can be rethought' (2000). This statement refers to the perceived desire of Im to appeal to the international audience rather than focusing on the domestic one. His romanticised and historicised images of Korea speak to the wider world and offer a vision of a consolidated Korean identity which can survive in the face of foreign aggression. The presentation of the traditional arts of Korea that Im offers to the international audience is part of a wider drive to highlight Korean national cinema's 'cultural uniqueness from other national cinemas' (Lee 2005: 66). In order to succeed, smaller national cinemas need to gain footholds in the popular imagination of a global audience and it is via a process of self-orientalism that Im has proven most successful. In its original form proposed by Edward Saïd (1978), 'Orientalism' saw the East as being constructed and defined as an exotic 'other' to the Western imagination. Saïd focused on how the construction of 'the East' gave Western imperialism a source of power via the various discourses of knowledge which they utilised such as anthropology and linguistics in an effort to obtain 'knowledge of the other imposed from outside'. This imposition of knowledge allowed for the eradication of the oriental voice in favour of occidental pronouncements. In short, the West speaks for the other without allowing the other to articulate itself. With reference to the process of self-orientalism that Iwabuchi Koichi argues Japan has undergone over the decades since the war, he states that Japan become 'pleasurably exotic to the Japanese themselves' (1994a: 53). In the same way, Im's specific presentation of highly lauded, visually and culturally specific Korean art forms seeks to present a united vision of Korea that was desirable and unique on the international market. In his self-orientalism Im presents the international audience a vision of Korean art, culture and tradition and it is from this position that the global audience will engage with and construct a vision of the South Korean nation. He will provide for them a system of thought and understanding with which to process and define Korean cinema. As Lee states, films such as *Chihwaseon* 'return to history and traditions to satisfy the new, creative imagination of the contemporary audience' (2005: 76). In this way, the identity politics which have dominated Korean cinema for so many decades are now called on to interact with the wider global market. Here, films such as *Chihwaseon* performed well; however, this process of identity construction did not appeal to the Korean audience. Whilst on one level this self-orientalism could potentially operate as a method to resist Western hegemony (and thus be a positive development for a historically repressed South Korea) for Iwabuchi the inability to transcend the us/other binary resulted in self-orientalism falling into an unavoidable same trap. The South Korean domestic audience has no need to have their historical and cultural identity reconfirmed for them. They have no need for a system of knowledge with which to evaluate their past since they are already living in the reality of a global South Korea. There is no desire to self-orientalise into a binary subject positioning and as a result the film has generally been rejected in the home market. Iwabuchi notes that:

> We have simultaneously to debunk reciprocal imaginings of other communities and monolithic entities, and recognise the fragmented, multiple and mobile nature of all identities. We have to ask 'what process rather than essences are involved in cultural identity'. (1994a: 76)

As a nation, the younger Korean audience is drawn more towards films that present Korean themes but also provide the level of spectacle that the Hollywood blockbuster offers (see Lee 2005: 76). This approach as seen in films such as *Shiri*, *2009 Lost Memories* (*2009 Losteu Memoreejeu*, 2002, Lee Si-myung) and *JSA* (2000, Park Chan-wook) which present to South Korean audiences a vision that is more aligned with their experiences of a global South Korea reflecting 'notions of hybridity, heterogeneity and mimicry' (Lee 2005: 76).

This does not preclude films such as *Chihwaseon* reflecting a South Korean cinema but rather it proves that a national cinema operates on a variety of levels to a multitude of audiences. As Jinhee Choi notes, the recent changes and development in South Korean cinema (which Im has been a key part of) 'demand a careful delineation of the relationship between the local media industry, the government and the audiences (2010: 16). Heritage films such as *Chihwaseon* can be seen as part of this narrative in that they are located somewhere in the middle of these dialogues. In his presentation of older Korean traditions Im Kwon-taek is demonstrating a knowledge of the international film market that South Korean national cinema is now part of. Whilst the appeal to the domestic market was more limited, his success on the international stage has helped to expand and promote the still growing South Korean cinema industry.

Fukasaku Kinji and Beginning With a Bomb

Since many experts and victims of the blast have published articles on the military might of atomic weapons, and the cruelty of the harm which they inflict, I have no intention of speaking about this. But from my position I believe my task is to encourage absolutely everyone to think freely about these photographs and form their own criticisms on the basis of this date starkly recorded on camera. (Fukasaku quoted in Yamahta 1959: 23)

In January 2003, when Fukasaku Kinji's funeral took place at the Tsukiji Hongangi Temple in Tokyo, the crowds that surrounded the building were incredible to behold. The same area had a few weeks earlier experienced the arrival of David and Victoria Beckham and the comparable numbers of people that turned out to see Fukasaku laid to rest as appeared to catch a glimpse of *Beckham-san*, illustrated how highly regarded the 72-year-old director was at the time of his death. The director was still in the middle of directing *Battle Royale II* when he succumbed to the cancer he had been fighting for several years.

Fukasaku was born in 1930 and grew up through the period of intense nationalist fervour that marked pre-war Japanese society and culture. This period was the unlikely catalyst for contemporary Japan as defeat saw the country move from an emphasis on war and military developments into the peaceful industrial society it has become today. The 15-year-old Fukasaku was working in a munitions factory when the atomic bombs were dropped on Hiroshima and Nagasaki, resulting in the end of the war in the Pacific. Like many of his peers, Fukasaku spoke later in life of the trauma of this period and the death and horror that he saw daily around him during the Allied bombings, and these experiences, and the question of post-war construction of Japan, would be something that would mark much of his film work. The position of Japan after the war is key in evaluating not only Fukasaku's work but also much of the cinema that was made in Japan from the 1950s onwards. Japanese society radically altered as a result of the defeat and the American occupation, and the constraints that had been placed on the cinema during this period saw a new type of Japanese cinema emerge. Personified by the likes of Naruse, Ozu and Mizoguchi, Japanese film achieved acclaim worldwide and presented to the world an image of an economically successful and developing post-war Japan. Many people inside Japan, however, did not agree with the direction that the post-war government was taking (see Igarashi 2000). In his writing on post-war Japanese society, literary critic Katō Norihiro formulated what Takahashi Tetsuya dubbed the 'after the defeat discourse' (2005: 193). For Katō the period after the Japanese defeat in World War II led to a 'personality split'. Basically a division between those who supported the post-war constitution and those that kept a highly conservative desire for the pre-war systems of government and therefore society. Katō saw the division along the lines of those who were 'outward looking' and therefore more willing to embrace external/foreign influences in the construction of the post-war state and those who were 'inward looking' and 'grounded upon such traditions such as the homeland, the Emperor, and the purity of the Japanese ethos' (in Teysuya 2005: 194). Katō's work is certainly not without its critics but the question of how to construct identity after a trauma such as war is key in an examination of Fukasaku's work. After experiencing at first hand the dreadful consequences of the construction of the Japanese state and culture, Fukasaku certainly did not look backward for inspiration but became a harsh critic, via his films, of the post-war reconstruction. Throughout his work from the hyper-stylised *Black Lizard* (*Kurotokage*, 1968) to the *Battles without Honour to Humanity* (*Jinginaki Tatakai*, 1973) series, to his final completed feature film, *Battle Royale*, we see a strong critical, indeed political, imagination being exercised.

Like many teenagers in the post-war period Fukasaku was a devoted cinemagoer. Under the US occupation American films were frequently shown and together with the development of a notable Japanese cinema (exemplified by the works of Ozu, Mizoguchi and Naruse) Fukasaku was inspired to enter Nihon University to study film in 1949. He joined the Toei studios in 1953 and under the system of training and apprenticeship that was common in the Japanese studio system (for more on this see the chapter on Kawase) he was able to take the director's chair in 1961. His first features were B movies, notable perhaps only for their inclusion of Sonny Chiba who would later go on to become an international martial arts star and frequent collaborator with Fukasaku over his four-decades-long career. Under the studio system of the period, the continuing emphasis was on constant economic turnover and this led to an institutionalisation of certain forms of cinematic narratives and representations. Like Hollywood the industry relied upon time-tested genres: *jidai-geki*, historical films, were filmed alongside *gendai-geki*'s set in contemporary surroundings. Like many periods of mass cinematic production some films from this time are good while others are very poor indeed. The sheer number of films made over this period is staggering, however, with Toei alone making over a hundred features in 1963. One of the formulaic *yakuza* films that Toei began to specialise in during the 1960s were *ni-kyo eiga*. These films were usually set in the pre-war period and offered audiences an image of a gangster protagonist who, rather than being a callous criminal, was a modern-day representation of the traditional values usually seen as personified by the *samurai*. Valour, bravery, honour, defence of the weak and a commitment to the quasi-familial and highly patriarchal structures of the *yakuza* were exalted. These films often pitched the 'old school' villain against a more Westernised and less honourable younger gangster generation. The *jingi* code that dominated the *yakuza* society was a rigid hierarchical structure that saw the young man (*kobun*) swear eternal loyalty to his older master and gang leader (*oyabun*). The *jingi* code directly referenced the *samurai* code of loyalty and fealty to the master, demonstrated perfectly in the tale of the 47 Ronin who swore revenge for the death of their leader. Isolde Standish makes the valuable point that this structure also relates to the Japanese 'corporate structure of intense loyalty and dedication to your company and more specifically your boss' (2005: 300). This notion of working for the common good was a key theme of the period; one of the key points that was emphasised by the government in the post-occupation period was that 'the individual must be sacrificed, must give himself or herself over to the collective and to the nation to rebuild the country' (Cazdyn 2003: 6). Commitment to the patriarchal corporate structure was one way to make sure that people would all be working towards the same goal. The new *shinkansen* (bullet train) and the stadium built for the 1964 Tokyo Olympics seemed to herald a new and successful Japan. Japan's 'economic miracle' seemed to have worked and the post-war days of hardship and poverty seemed to be a distant memory.

Not everyone in society, however, agreed with this new economic drive. The 1960s also marked a period of various political scandals, student protests and calls for an open debate on the future of Japan. By 1960 over a million students were members of activist groups and many of the young directors, writers and artists of this period were centrally involved in the movements calling for a re-evaluation about the direction Japan was moving in. The cinematic New Wave had began to experiment with exciting methods of narrative and filming, Japanese literature and theatre was offering similar challenges to the status quo and there were continual debates about the economic drive that was subsuming the country and the need for Japan to properly reassess the past. Fukasaku himself noted that:

> The government was very keen on and preoccupied with the reconstruction of Japan and rapid economic growth. But I had doubts. Under that kind of situation where would the government be taking the whole nation? What direction are they taking us? These were the questions I could never shake off and I even felt resistance to what was going on. (In Mes and Sharp 2005: 43)

Fukasaku's early films, *Greed in Broad Daylight* (*Hakuchū no Buraikan*, 1961), *Gang Alliance* (*Gyangu Dōmei*, 1963), *Wolves, Pigs and Men* (*Ôkami to buta to ningen*, 1964) and *The Breakup* (*Kaisanshiki*, 1967) often focus on those residing in poor areas on the outskirts of the developing cities. Gangsters, prostitutes, criminals and poverty-stricken slum-dwellers are presented as the often unseen results of Japan's economic drive. Rather than the heroes of the popular *ninkyō* Fukasaku offers central characters who are far from honorable and are often doomed to failure, death, imprisonment and pain. He presents the people that the economic developments were leaving behind – outcasts who are alienated from the wider society. In *Street Mobster* (*Gendai yakuza: Mitokiri Yota*, 1972), a *yakuza* is released from prison imagining that he will be welcomed into a world similar to the one he had left. He soon discovers, however, that his former associates and the criminal underworld structure, together with the socio-political landscape of Japan itslef, have changed dramatically. His subsequent attempts to reassert himself in this new landscape result in tragedy and death. In what is arguably his greatest and most enduring film *Battles without Honour or Humanity* (also known as *The yakuza Papers*) Fukasaku offers an almost neo-apolitical post-war Japan. The film's opening is highly striking. An image of the atomic bomb covers the screen to be followed by a voiceover informing us of the film's location: Kure City, Hiroshima. The narrator tells us that 'The great violence of the war has disappeared, but a new violence is raging in a country devoid of discipline. The hot-blooded young men back from the battlefields, although confronting this lawlessness; had nothing to rely on but their own violence.' This rather depressing statement is emphasised by the screams of a woman as she runs through a crowded market place chased by American soldier's intent on publically raping her. Their status as the occupying forces means that the local people are unable/unwilling to help her as she fights unsuccessfully with the aggressive foreign attackers. The only two men willing to face the Americans to defend her are identified by subtitles stating their name and their positions in the crime families that they affiliate themselves with. This film and the many others that followed it focus on various *yakuza* members and how their traditional structures of honour and obedience are rendered obsolete in the new 'corporate' and economically-driven approach that organised crime is embracing. The *jinji* code of *oyabun/ kobun* is overturned as often the boss is shown as corrupt and deceitful, the desire for economic wealth and power destroying any of the traditional codes. In the *Battles without Honour or Humanity* series, rather than facing individual problems or people as seen in the earlier *ninkyō* films, 'the principal characters' struggles are solely against monolithic organisations, which collude with the legitimate authority to destroy them' (Standish 2005: 308).

People saw that the economic drive, personified by these faceless corporations and government agencies, had a continual human cost and the characters from the series usually 'die a solitary death, and the system that caused his death remains unaltered, and if anything continues stronger than before' (ibid.). The collapse of the idealistic *jingi* code in Fukasaku's work can be read as a questioning of a society that is based on deeds and problems that the government and culture refuses to address. It was during the late 1960s and early 1970s that some of very negative aspects of the Japanese economic growth emerged. The Minamata affair saw several thousand people poisoned by mercury that had been knowingly released into the water by a company over a prolonged period of time (the devastating effects are now known as Minamata disease). The Miike coal-mine explosion of 9 November 1963 which killed over 430 miners and saw over 800 poisoned by carbon monoxide had been caused by a lack of investment in safety and emergency procedures. In 1969 there was the release of the '14 years later' report on the children who had been affected by arsenic-laced Morinaga powdered milk in the late 1950s, again caused by industrial negligence. All of these stories would be fresh in the minds of the audiences that flocked to the theatres to see the original films. The *Battles without Honour or Humanity* series, with its critical look at Japanese society, clearly touched a cord with the population. *Battles without Honour or Humanity* was one of the most successful and popular films in Japanese cinematic history. With 9 million cinema viewers and VHS/DVD sales close to 400,000, Masahi Ichiki notes that this information alone points to the fact that 'the images of modern Japan presented in this mega-hit film are shared by a large number of people' (2011).

It was not just the stories but the filmic style of the *Battles without Honour or Humanity* series that energised and excited. Often shot on the streets using hand-held cameras, the visual style gives the films a sense of documentary realism combined with fast-paced editing and slanted cameras angles. Fukasaku openly admitted to the influence of the French New Wave in terms of visuals and his gritty, dynamic style of filmmaking certainly compares with that of Jean-Luc Godard and François Truffaut from this period. Although the films themselves are often ignored as 'low-brow' action films they demonstrate an anarchic irreverence to filmic and social traditions and show a keen political and cultural questioning.

Many of the themes and ideas that can be seen in *Battles without Honour or Humanity* can also be found in a variety of Fukasaku's other features. Although he is primarily known for his *yakuza* features and his later mega-hit *Battle Royale*, he has worked in a variety of genres from science fiction (*Message from Space/Ushū Kara no Messēji* [1978], *Green Slime/Ganma 3 Gō: Uchū Saisakusen* [1968]) to emotional dramas (*The Geisha House/Omocha*, 1999)

It was four years after the Tokyo Summer Olympics that Fukasaku collaborated with performer Miwa Akihiro to produce two quite remarkable films: *Black Lizard* (*Kurotokage*, 1968) and *Black Rose Mansion* (*Kuro bara no yakata*, 1969). Miwa, whose real name is Maruyama Akihiro, is one of Japan's most notable male-to-female performers and is a highly acclaimed writer, psychic, actor, gay rights activist and singer. *Black Lizard* is the highly psychedelic tale of a famous female thief and her desire to steal a priceless diamond. She faces 'Japan's Number

One Private Detective', Akechi Kogorō, and the couple engages in a battle of wits, desire and seduction. The Black Lizard, who is identified by a tattoo on her arm, also collects 'beautiful people' and preserves them as lifeless living dolls in her island hideaway. Her desires turn towards the diamond owner's beautiful virgin daughter and Akechi dons various disguises in to order to defeat her. In this film and its counterpart, *Black Rose Mansion*, we are treated to colourful sequences of Miwa singing and dancing in a feather boa and diamonds against Aubrey Beardsley prints. People who are familiar with the original *Batman* television series (1968), *The Avengers* (1961–69) and even the *Austin Powers* films (Jay Roach, 1997, 1999, 2002) will be on familiar territory in terms of aesthetics but the films carry a far darker undertone.

Although *Black Lizard* is based on a novel by Japanese mystery writer Edogawa Rampo (an amusing nod towards American horror writer Edgar Allan Poe) the novels were adapted for the stage and screen by Yukio Mishima. Mishima is one of the most famous Japanese writers and cultural figures from this period and in terms of his literary pedigree he was nominated for the Nobel Prize for literature three times. Mishima held highly right-wing beliefs and was one of the greatest critics of the development of post-war Japan. His novels, particularly his *Sea of Fertility* tetralogy (written between 1969 and 1971), are indicative of his own political and cultural belief systems that Japan had been betrayed by the government during and after the war and that modern Japan left much to be desired (this criticism resulted in Mishima committing ritual suicide, or *seppuku*, in 1970 in the Japanese Diet Building). His involvement and presence on the screen in *Black Lizard* playing one of the Lizard's lovers is still controversial not just for his political beliefs but also due to the fact Mishima was a practicing homosexual and was reported to have been engaged in a long-standing affair with Miwa. Miwa himself, who was born in Nagasaki, was present when the atomic bomb was dropped on his home town and although he was relatively unhurt compared to many of his peers he continues to be vocal about the suffering that he saw and experienced during this time. The presence of a *hibakusha*, the term used in Japan to refer to those that suffered from the effects of the atomic bomb and the subsequent radiation, together with Mishima opens up the legacy of World War II, an event that Fukasaku refused to consign to the past. Even in the modern age *hibakusha* still suffer from discrimination and marginalisation. The reason for this is that the *hibakusha*, as well as personifying the terrors of radiation sickness, are also marked with a 'death taint' (Lifton 1991: 179). This 'death taint', a living reminder of the war literally embodied by the *hibakusha*, is something that the dominant society sought to repress and ignore; Fukasaku, however, chose to actively engage with these issues. These two films, his *yakuza* works, and films such as *Tora!, Tora!, Tora!* (1970) and *Under the Flag of Rising Sun* (*Gunki Hatameku Moto Ni*, 1972) all reference the war and the unevaluated legacy of this event. Some references are more overt than others; *Under the Flag of the Rising Sun*, which will be examined more closely later, follows a war widow as she tries to uncover the fate of her husband who was lost during the Pacific war. Fukasaku's sequences in the American/Japanese co-production *Tora!, Tora!, Tora!* offered a dramatic recreation of Pearl Harbor and the events that had led up to Japan entering the Pacific war. Together with Richard Fleischer and Toshio Masuda, Fukasaku offered a relatively accurate telling of the story together with some dramatic aerial footage debating the causes and effects of the Pacific war, particularly the atomic bomb.

Hiroshima in particular is a constant presence in the *Battles without Honour or Humanity* series. The films are set in and around Hiroshima and the Hiroshima A-Bomb dome is a dominant feature. In the second film in the series, *Hiroshima: Deadly Battles* (*Hiroshima Shito-he*, 1973) the Motomachi area, also known as 'A-bomb slum', features prominently. Motomachi was famous as the area where *hibakusha* would reside, unable to live anywhere else due to poverty and social stigma for their afflictions. The same film also charts the development of Hiroshima from a ravaged city into the sleek modern environment it has now become. Fukasaku, however, constantly reminds us that not all the people have benefited from this – many of the *hibakusha* still live in sub-standard conditions, an embarrassing living reminder of the war that the society would rather forget. In the fourth film, *The High Tactics* (*Chojo Sakusen*, 1974), a visit to a home in an A-bomb slum reveals a broken television being watched by a young woman with a visible keloidal burn on her face. Ichiki points out that a 'television, along with the washing machine and refrigerator, symbolised this newly-achieved economic prosperity as one of the three "Imperial regalia"' (2011: 114). The family's lack of a television, one of the key demonstrators of economic success, implies how the booming economy has excluded some and in this case the family's status as *hibakusha* (demonstrated by the woman's keloidal burn) evokes the point that the war is still an everyday event for some families.

In *Black Rose Mansion* the male protagonist who falls in love with the mysterious singer Ryoko (played by Miwa) sees her emerge from a red cloud and concludes: 'They say that a storm follows a beautiful sunset. It was such a beautiful sunset that it worried people. I was on my way to work and stopped to look and that's when it happened.' Compare this with the real-life testimony of a victim of Hiroshima: 'I had just entered the room and said "Good morning" to colleagues and I was about to approach my desk when outside it suddenly turned bright red … I went to the windows to find out where the bombing had taken place. And I saw the mushroom cloud over the gas company' (testimony of Hiroshi Sawachika, a survivor of the blast from the Portman Atomic Archive). The similarities are striking and the sequence shows people looking in panic towards the setting sun as many in the surrounding area (Miwa himself included) would have looked towards the mushroom clouds over Nagasaki and Hiroshima. Ryoko travels with her loyal mixed-race assistant called George who is presented as African-American/Japanese. As will be explored more in the chapter on Miike Takashi there is a commonly held understanding inside Japan that sees the Japanese nation as a homogenous, genetically and culturally similar entity and this was especially true during the war and post-war period. The presence of mixed race children, particularly those of Japanese-American ethnicity, acted as a constant reminder of defeat in World War II and the American occupation and thus, the *possibility* of interracial marriage and procreation. *Black Rose Mansion* was directed in 1969, which was also the year that the Japanese GNP became second highest in the world after the USA. Igarashi notes that 'the success of the Tokyo Olympics and the nation's ensuing economic growth promoted a linear image of history that reduced the war to nothing more than a necessary precondition for Japan's present-day prosperity. The hardship and starvation suffered by the Japanese people during and immediately after the war became an integral part of the narrative that everyone knew had a happy ending' (2000: 165). In this way, the past had become nothing more than an unhappy 'blip' in the path of Japan's economic success and the events of the war, and the reasons why it had taken place, could be ignored in favour of a concentration on new economic developments. The *hibakusha* victims and mixed-race children were 'embarrassing' for the key reason that they were a living reminder of the war and as such were deemed to be a problematic element in the new modern Japan. In his use of people and characters that deliberately challenge the dominant ideology of attempting to 'forget' the war, Fukasaku is a fore-runner of later directors such as Miike Takashi who would also use non-Japanese characters to make comments on the state of Japanese society. Igarashi states that:

> The desire to return to the original loss was countered by the forward movement of the narrative: articulation of the war experience would take place only in the form of repetition, trapped between the contradictory need to remember and to forget traumatic experiences. (2000: 167)

This approach renders an individual trapped as they are unable to progress forward but unable or unwilling to articulate and deal with the past. Images and events that act as a reminder of the past thus hold an uncomfortable position as the site of tension and unresolved fears. With writers such as Mishima and Nosaka Akiyuki, the formulation of the dialogue on this simultaneous remembering and forgetting would come through the body, which became the 'crucial medium to re-encounter the experience of war' (Igarashi 2000:168). This approach can be seen in the work of Fukasaku. The bodies in his film are living, often scarred reminders of the past and society's unwillingness to deal directly with it. Mishima, with his dramatic suicide and body-building physique would come to represent this tension *par excellence*. Miwa too, as outspoken pacifist and firm critic of the war, offered a body that was imbued with the anxieties and contradictions of the post-war society.

Even though *Black Lizard* does not deal directly with the war the presence of Mishima and Miwa would have offered a method through which the audience could consider their own personal relationship to wartime events and the subsequent reconstruction. In other films the tormented and damaged bodies of the *yakuza* protagonists act as a marker of a post-war society, where 'violence and sex provide an alternative libidinal economy through which these characters negotiate their lives in alien cityscapes' (Standish 2005: 330). The feelings of dislocation from the contemporary state and society become key narratives in a society that Fukasaku felt was unable to go forward or back since it would remain forever trapped in the unresolved space of 1960s development.

Fukasaku's most critical film with regard to the war came two years after *Black Rose Mansion*. Whereas his duo of films with Miwa had offered oblique and metaphorical allusions to the war *Under the Flag of the Rising Sun* was a damning criticism not only of the war itself but also of the post-war government. The film follows Togasi Sakie, a widow who has been consistently denied a pension from the war office on account of the circumstances surrounding her husband's death on the Pacific frontline. The official records state that he was shot for desertion only days prior to Japan's surrender thus not fulfilling the criteria of being an 'official' casualty of war. Sakie is determined to clear her husband's name not for the money but for the love and regard she still holds him in. She seeks out four remaining soldiers from her husband's unit and proceeds to attempt to discover the truth. The stories and events conflict from one solider to another but what is made clear is the appalling and inhuman conditions the soldiers were forced to live under during the war-time period. One story has her starving husband shot for stealing a sweet potato, dying ignobly with it in his mouth. Another presents him as callously resorting to cannibalism in the face of hunger. He is alternately presented as a murderer, a mutineer and a hero. Sakie hears how prisoners of war were brutally killed and how rank and file Japanese soldiers lived in fear of their deranged, corrupt and incompetent commanders. The officers, as the representatives of the government and Emperor, are shown as driving soldiers to horrifically barbarous acts and then punishing them if they protest. Sakie's husband and his colleagues are eventually shown as scapegoats for a system that was profoundly and insidiously flawed. In the scene of their execution they call out for the Emperor, not out of loyalty but as a cry of accusation. The film is bleakly anti-war and is one of Fukasaku's most overt demonstrations of the poor regard he held for governmental structures. The events in the Pacific are made all the more pitiful by the way that the present-day bureaucracy treats Sakie and the remaining soldiers. One soldier now lives on a large rubbish dump and tells Sakie that technically the area is classed as Tokyo. He, like many of the citizens in Hiroshima featured in *Battles without Honour or Humanity*, has not benefited from the Japanese economic miracle. This presentation of soldiers and governmental systems went directly against the dominant notions of Japanese soldiers as heroic and honourable and the post-war government as fair and equal and perhaps because of this the film did badly at the box office. Fukasaku had been forced to make the film under an independent label and the film's lack of success resulted in him having to return to Toei and continue making the more popular (and financially successful) gangster films.

Under the Flag of the Rising Sun was the last non-gangster film that Fukasaku would make for several years. One of the drawbacks to the studio system was that when a studio hit on a winning formula they exploited it as far as it would go. *Battles without Honour or Humanity* ran for over two decades and, including the 'New Battle' and 'Then Afterward' series, totalled fourteen films. Many of the later films were poor imitations of the originals and Fukasaku himself was only involved with the first eight productions but he continued to produce films in the same genre. Made in 1975 *Cops Vs Thugs* was made between films four and five of the *Battles without Honour or Humanity* series and presented another high-octane, flamboyantly visual, action-packed tale of *yakuza* and their police counterparts. Rather than the simple binary between good and evil, Fukasaku offered audiences a police force that was as corrupt, violent and unreliable as the gangsters. Once again, the post-war Japanese economic drive is shown as resulting in a situation where commercial business, *yakuza*, police and government officials are all equally destructive.

Yakuza Graveyard (*yakuza no hakaba: Kuchinashi no hana*, 1976) was Fukasaku's farewell to the gangster genre and ironically coincided with the collapse of the Japanese studio system (the film would also later be remade by another director discussed in this book, Miike Takashi). The arrival of television and continual pressure from the Hollywood market saw several studios declare bankruptcy or turn to producing low-budget soft-core pornography. The success of the *Battles without Honour or Humanity* series, however, stood Fukasaku in good stead to survive the downturn and he continued to make a variety of films throughout the 1980s and early 1990s.

In 1980 he made *Virus*, a multinational production starring a variety of international names such as Sonny Chiba, Chuck Connors, Stephanie Faulkner, Glenn Ford and Olivia Hussey. The film offers not one but two apocalyptic disasters. First a man-made virus wipes out most of the world's population except for a few survivors in Antarctic ice stations and then nuclear destruction threatens even this small community. Although *Virus* conforms to many generic conventions in its narrative and scenarios racial stereotypes abound (aggressive Russians face excitable Spaniards, and the honourable British and brave Japanese try to control the domineering Americans), it does have an interesting part to play in an examination of Fukasaku's work. The premise that a small group of people need to recreate a whole society after a catastrophic event is one that would be recognisable to those that had lived through the war. The devastating effect of nuclear power is found in many of Fukasaku's films and the criticism of the economically-driven governments that allow this armageddon to take place in *Virus* is familiar from Fukasaku's films as far back as 1961.

By the late 1980s poor heath was affecting Fukasaku's work and it was this that led him to decline the directorial chair of a film entitled *Violent Cop* (1989) starring comedian 'Beat' Kitano Takeshi. Kitano would eventually take over the directorial role and this would see the launch of his career as a director. After his recovery in 1992 Fukasaku directed *The Triple Cross* which offered the tale of three ageing criminals as they attempt to gain revenge on a group of younger men who have insulted them in a variety of ways. The film is once again a high-action extravaganza and demonstrated to younger directors that Fukasaku was still capable of thrilling an audience with his work. He even directed sequences for a computer game (*Clocktower 3*) in 2001 that made him possibly one of the oldest contributors to this type of product.

The Geisha House (*Omocha*, 1999) is one of the most gentle of Fukasaku's films but even this still offers a challenge to dominant expectations. *The Geisha House* details the apprenticeship of the young maid Tokiko and it is through her eyes we see the trials and tribulations of this world of women. For Tokiko the poverty of her family is the driving force behind her need to sell her virginity to the highest bidder. The film is set in the 1950s and we see the women facing the realities of the anti-prostitution laws that were implemented around this time. Although Tokiko initially holds some childish beliefs about the work she is preparing to do, she gradually becomes as hardened towards romance as the other women that share her geisha house. Whilst it is not as political as his other works the film still references many of the debates that had been seen in his films from over two decades earlier. The post-war reconstruction of Japan is harshly criticised. As the government encourages the economic regeneration of Japan, it hinders the economic life of a sub-section of society that is highly vulnerable, in this case women working in the sex and entertainment industry. Tokiko begins to realise that she cannot rely on social structures to protect and support her and she must, like Sakie from *Under the Flag of the Rising Sun* and the various characters in the *Battles without Honour or Humanity* series, fight for her own survival and well-being in the face of an uncaring and potentially threatening governmental bureaucratic system.

It was in 2000 that Fukasaku directed his last and most famous film. *Battle Royale* was a success domestically and internationally and proved that although the director was over seventy he was still a master of action cinema. It presented the gripping and very violent tale of a group of schoolchildren that are forced to fight to their deaths at their government's instigation. Despite various legal attempts to ban the film due to the concern over its potential encouragement of teenage violence *Battle Royale* was released worldwide to great acclaim. The film will be examined in detail in the next section but as Tom Mes and Jasper Sharp state, the film 'brought Fukasaku fill circle. With its fifteen-year-old protagonists forced into life-threatening crisis situations, the director returned to his own youth' (2005: 50). As a young man Fukasaku faced death and danger as Japan went to war and then lost. The teenagers in *Battle Royale* fight in a real-life war game that, like many of Fukasaku's characters, makes them 'victims of a society created by corrupt politicians and an acquiescent majority' (Standish 2005: 334). This view of the social state is one that Fukasaku clearly held for his entire life and rendered cinematically in his work across a variety of film genres and styles. With over sixty films to his name he was unusual in that he was a consistently successful director in a career that spanned over four decades.

Fukasaku died during the filming of *Battle Royale II: Requiem* (*Battle Royale II: Chinkonka*, 2003) and it was finished by his son Fukasaku Kenta. This film, although nowhere near as skilled as the first, takes place in the post-9/11 world and makes clear references to a global political structure that is as corrupt and problematic as the domestic one. Fukasaku's death resulted in the end of 'one of the final authorial voices from a dying avant-garde' (Standish 2005: 332). He had worked consistently since the 1960s and his films offer the charting of a continuing alternative viewpoint on Japanese society. Despite Fukasaku's general neglect by film academics his films remain some of the most exciting and interesting of modern Japanese cinema. New directors such as Miike Takashi, Kitano Takeshi, Isshii Takashi, Aoyama Shinji and Kurosawa Kiyoshi have taken over the role of directing challenging and controversial action cinema but Fukasaku's continuing legacy can be clearly still be felt.

Film Analysis

BATTLE ROYALE

バトル・ロワイアル

Batoru Rowaiaru

2000

Director

Fukasaku Kinji

Cast

Takeshi Kitano (Kitano-sensei), Tatsuya Fujiwara (Shuya Nanahara aka Boy 15), Aki Maeda (Noriko Nakagawa aka Girl 15), Taro Yamamoto (Shôgo Kawada), Masanobu Ando (Kazuo Kiriyama), Chiaki Kuriyama (Takako Chigusa aka Girl 13), Kou Shibasaki (Mitsuko Souma aka Girl 11), Yukihiro Kotani (Yoshitoki 'Nobu' Kuninobu)

Plot Summary

In Japan in the near future, fear of out-of-control teenagers has resulted in the government creating the 'Battle Royale' act. With this act, randomly selected school classes are taken to an island and forced to fight and kill each other until there is only one survivor. Refusal to fight will result in the activation of the exploding necklace that they have all been fitted with.

Shuya is struggling to come to terms with his father's suicide. His friend Noriko witnesses Shuya's friend Nobu stabbing their teacher Kitano-sensei in the leg and hides the knife to protect Nobu. Later the entire class is on a school trip when they are drugged and taken to the Battle Royale Island. Kitano-sensei is overseeing the 'game'. They are shown a DVD of the rules and issued with a kit bag which each contains a weapon of variable deadliness. During this session Kitano-sensei kills a girl that was talking during the DVD and activates Nobu's necklace – blowing off his head. There are two 'exchange students' who are part of the class for the duration of the game: Kiriyama and Kawada. They have both played the game successfully before. Once the game commences we see all the different strategies the students apply. Some commit suicide rather than fight, some immediately start brutally killing their peers (especially Girl 13), and others join together to work on an escape plan. Gradually they are all killed by the deadly Kiriyama or by each other as the tensions mount. Noriko and Shuya stay together and are gradually joined by the brave and resourceful Kawada who is haunted by the memory of his girlfriend whom he killed in the last game. Together they defeat the system, escape and kill Kitano-sensei. Kawada dies of his injuries and Noriko and Shuya, now wanted by the police, are forced to go on the run.

––––––

'The nail that protrudes gets hammered down': traditional Japanese saying.
'The nail that comes all the way out never gets hammered down': contemporary Japanese saying.

These two opening adages offer a unique insight into the main themes of *Battle Royale*. Set in the near future this violent tale of schoolchildren being forced to kill each other became a worldwide phenomenon. It was a fitting tribute to a director that had thrilled Japanese audiences for years with his high-octane action dramas. As with all Fukasaku's works there is an underlying message rather than just an exciting presentation of violence. The opening scenes set the tone for what is to come. With Verdi's *Requiem* dramatically introducing the intertitles we are told that Japan has suffered from economic and social collapse and that with 800,000 children boycotting school the adults took fright and instigated the Millennium Education Reform Act (known as 'Battle Royale'). The exact contents of this Act are not yet revealed but the next images are of a young teenage girl covered in blood and clutching a doll, being presented to the mass media under the cover of helicopters and army jeeps. She is the 'winner' of Battle Royale and her smile directed at the TV cameras is terrible to behold. The notion of 'winner' opens the images of game shows and quizzes but instead the blood-soaked child seems to hark at a totally different type of event.

We are then introduced to Class B of Zantsuji Middle School via a black-and-white class photo. The central face is a recognisable one, the actor/director/comedian 'Beat' Takeshi Kitano. It will be their teacher Kitano-sensei (the film keeps the same name for the character as the real-life person) who will run the brutal game that Class B will soon find themselves involved in. The use of Kitano serves several purposes: first, as will be examined in later chapters, Kitano is one of the most successful Japanese stars to have emerged in last few decades and as a result he has very high levels of audience recognition on both the domestic and the international stages. This can be seen in the poster that was used to advertise the film where several of the children's faces are crossed out but he remains a dominant central figure. Secondly, Kitano is clearly an adult male and placing him as the opponent makes the children's fights all the more tragic since they are competing against a figure who has a proven 'history' of violent behaviour. Thirdly, and perhaps more vitally, his role as iconic mass media figure opens up the notion that this game could actually happen. Kitano himself presents many TV game shows such as *Takeshi's Castle* (1986–89) and the use of a real game show presenter gives a depth and a potential realism to this outrageous new show concept.

We are introduced to the class via their literal absence. When Kitano-sensei walks into a classroom he is greeted by rows of empty chairs and a rude message on the board informing him of their decision not to attend class. It is only Noriko, the central female character, that attends class and even she is late. Noriko's role, however, as a 'good' student is immediately called into question when Kitano-sensei is stabbed in the leg by Nobu, Noriko's friend. Rather than helping the injured teacher Noriko hides the knife to prevent Nobu's arrest. This short scene immediately sets up the conflict that we are told inundates the whole of society. The adult, in this case personified by Kitano-sensei, has given up in the face of teenage disobedience. The children are seen to be running riot and the adults are seen to be unable to cope, and it is their insecurity that leads to the carnage that follows. As the film progresses we discover that Kitano-sensei has an estranged daughter and his decision to become involved in the game, rather than attempting to mend bridges with her, seems to indicate the pathetic level that adult society has sunk to. The other main adult characters are even less effective than him. Shuyu's father hangs himself and leaves his son alone, and Class B's new teacher is brutally shot by the army for protesting at the choice of Class B for the game. This teacher who had previously been seen giggling and laughing with a group of teenage girls at the back of the school bus is dubbed by Kitano-sensei as a 'bad adult'. His humanitarian refusal to force the conflict between adults and children results in his death and Class B are on their own without any adult advice or help.

After they are drugged the children are taken to a classroom on the island and introduced to the rules of the game. This is done via a mixture of an upbeat pop-aesthetic training video presented by an enthusiastic young woman (making direct reference to contemporary Japanese pop culture which the teenagers can directly relate to) and the more violent teaching methods of Kitano-sensei. Before the game commences he has killed one young girl and gained his revenge on Nobu. All the children have been fitted with necklaces that monitor where they are on the island and are fitted with a hidden microphone, and can be activated to blow the heads of the wearer. Kitano-sensei demonstrates the effectiveness of the necklace on Nobu and Shuya is left covered in his friend's blood and the dawning realisation that there is no help coming for Class B.

Each individual member of class B is given a kit bag containing a weapon, from a pan lid (Shuya) to a scythe (Girl 11) to an automatic assault rifle (which ends in the hands of the deadly exchange student Kiriyama). As the game commences we are shown how, faced with such an extreme situation, people respond in a myriad of ways. Some immediately embrace killing, others commit suicide rather than fight, and others just die quietly. Old passions, resentments and fears are reignited. One boy runs all over the island to tell a girl that he loves her only to be shot dead when she panics. Two girls attempt to unite the whole class but are publicly killed by Kiriyama. Others try to sustain a sense of community spirit but these attempts quickly fall apart due to fear, jealousy and the usual teenage concerns made all the more fatal by the presence of deadly weapons. One group of students, led by the inventive Shinji, attempt to beat the system. Although it looks like they might have succeeded, Kiriyama kills them all before they can complete their escape. He is an enigmatic character and we never get to understand his motivations; unlike Shogo, Kiriyama is a natural born killer and his previous experience on Battle Royale seems to have given him the taste for murder. He easily dispatches all the students he encounters until he is killed by Nobu and Shogo.

Shuya and Noriko decide to stay together and Shuya does his best to protect Noriko as he feels that he failed to protect Nobu. When the pair join forces with the practical and inventive Shogo they will learn that feelings of love can be ruined in the face of such extreme situations. In a previous battle Shogo and his beloved girlfriend were the last two to survive and he ended up killing her in self-defence when she panicked and shot him when their necklaces were activated. Her death deactivates them and left Shogo the winner but he is hunted by her last words of 'thank you', and her smile. It is Shogo who figures out how to beat the game so that he, Shuyu and Noriko all survive. Once the army has left the island the threesome confronts Kitano-sensei. He presents to them a painting that he has drawn of all the murders with Noriko standing as an angel-like figure in the centre. He says that of all the students, Noriko would be the only one worth dying with. His admiration for Noriko relates back to a dream that she had where she and Kitano-sensei were walking on the beach. When she wakes up she comments that Kitano-sensei seemed sad. The sadness of Kitano-sensei is the heart of the film's narrative impetus. *Battle Royale* is far more about these feelings of sadness than it is a violent action film. It is telling that he would die with Noriko but not for her. Rather than embracing a higher purpose of a meaningful relationship, Kitano-sensei has no desire to protect those he cares for, he just wishes to see everything around him eradicated and does not care if he lives or dies as a consequence. The motivation of Fukasaku is to reveal a real social problem that he sees as affecting contemporary Japan. For him the sadness of Kitano-sensei reflects the malaise and feelings of inferiority that Japanese adults have suffered in the last few years. He states:

The fact that adults lost confidence in themselves, that is what is shown in *Battle Royale*. Those adults worked very hard through the 1970s in order to rebuild Japan. They went through that period working for the national interest. Of course there was a generation gap between the young and the adults, even throughout that period, but consistently adults were in control in terms of political stability and whatever was going on in the nation. However, since the burst of the economy bubble, these same adults, many of them salary men and working-class people, were put in a very difficult position with the economic downturn, and all of a sudden most of them started to lose confidence in themselves. And the children who have grown up and witnessed what happened to the adults, their anxiety became heightened as well. So I set the film in this context of children versus adults. (2001).

For Fukasaku, the state of the nation has spawned this brutal game. Juvenile delinquency has been caused by a chronic lack of confidence and the crisis that has set in amidst the older social groups rather than any innate problem with youth. The children are not originally to blame but they will be disproportionately punished for the failures of the adults. This reflects a real crisis in Japan where there have been several well-documented cases of teachers and the school system showing an extreme approach to the disobedience of children. The fear of those in positions of authority is that their inadequacies will lead to them losing power and control, and as a result they conduct themselves in an overly aggressive fashion towards the children that most represent their fears. In *The Japanese High School: Silence and Resistance*, Shoko Yoneyama (1999) cites two examples of this effect. In May 1985 a student was beaten to death by his teacher for using a hairdryer on a school trip. The students were forbidden from using hairdryers but the student had not wanted to go out into the cold with wet hair. Five years later in 1990, a 15-year-old girl called Ishida Ryoko was late for school for the first time. There was a heavy iron gate that the school shut at 8.30am. The teacher shut the gate at precisely that time even though he could see that she was running through the doorway, and the heavy gate crushed her against the wall, killing her instantly. The principal, Nomura Atsuo, rather than mourning the tragic death of the teenager, claimed that 'tardiness and absence led to delinquency' and that after Ryoko's death the 'message' was not to be tardy or late in life. This appalling dismissal of a teenager's death demonstrates the motivation for the game in *Battle Royale*. The teenagers from Class B are not 'mad and bad' delinquents. With the exception of Kiriyama, we see that even Mitsuko, deadly Girl 11, is motivated by her own experiences and feelings of inadequacy ('I just didn't want to be a loser anymore') rather than any innate cruelty.

The presentation of the brutal government structures that are using a vulnerable group as scapegoats reflects the concerns that Fukasaku expressed for his entire filmmaking career. Fukasaku himself had witnessed the brutal effects of the war, including having to clear away the bodies of his own classmates after a bombing raid (see Antoniou 2004). He saw first-hand the damage that a government can cause a nation to suffer, and was always a harsh critic of the post-war reconstruction and the failures that he perceived in post-war Japanese social and economic structures. He was part of the 1960s movement to challenge the status quo and of course in *Battle Royale* we are told that Shinji's uncle was an activist in the 1960s and had taught Shinji how to make bombs. This evocation of an earlier attempt to challenge the social system (which failed) is seen as an encouragement for the children to attempt to fight back. Although Shinji himself will ultimately die, Shuya and Noriko survive and it is on them that Fukasaku places his hope for the future. His final call for them to 'run as fast as they can' offers hope for a future that will challenge the dominant structures and create a new type of society. The opening sayings reflect the changes that are taking place in Japanese society and culture. From a situation where any dissent from individuals would be repressed for the benefit of collective harmony, the situation in the contemporary age is one where more and more people are beginning to challenge the status quo and society is beginning to acknowledge that individual opinions cannot always be ignored (see Yoneyama 1999).

It is perhaps ironic that *Battle Royale* was seen as promoting teenage violence when in fact it was commenting on the system that caused children to feel so aggressive and dislocated from society. The Japanese government even debated whether to prevent the film's cinematic release. The motivation for this considered embargo seems to have been as a response to the government's concerns about out-of-control teenagers challenging authority. In the USA, the events at Columbine High School and other examples of teenage rage resulted in *Battle Royale* being restricted. In the UK, Anthony Antoniou notes that the film was released just three days after 9/11 and perhaps this was key to its success. It seemed to speak to people who were struggling to consider and rationalise the interplay between violence and social structures. It is via this questioning of the causes and results of social unrest and decline that *Battle Royale* continues to have political meaning and relevance to the current day. The continual stagnation of the Japanese economy since the 1990s, the devastating 2011 Tōhoku earthquake and tsunami and the subsequent Fukushima Daiichi nuclear disaster have seen an increasing sense of social unrest and unease about the future of Japan develop. March 2012 saw over 20,000 people take to the streets in anti-nuclear protests and these generally peaceful mass gatherings have become the largest displays of public unrest since the 1960s, and seem to indicate a shift in Japanese politics and the wider Japanese society (see Aldrich and Dusinberre 2011). As a film *Battle Royale* contains many of the themes that are present in Fukasaku's wider works, and the recent contemporary rise in political awareness and activism directly speaks to many of his film's themes and content, making them relevant again decades after they were first made. His continuing belief that governmental structures need reconsideration and amendment is an idea that he has maintained throughout his entire working career and is one that more Japanese people are now seriously considering. *Battle Royale* is not just an action film; although violence is always present, Fukasaku allows the fears and feelings of the teenagers to be clearly shown to make clear political and social comment. The film offers a melding of action, popular culture and political questioning and was a fitting end to Fukasaku Kinji's career as a director that always sought to challenge.

Lee Chang-dong and
the Trauma of History

Whether commentary … is built into a structure of a history or developed as a sep-arate, superimposed text is a matter of choice, but the voice of the commentator must be clearly heard. The commentary should disrupt the facile linear progres-sion of the narration, introduce alternative interpretations, question any partial conclusion, withstand the need for closure … Such commentary may introduce splintered or constantly recurring refractions of a traumatic past by using any num-ber of different vantage points. (Friedländer 1992: 132)

Lee Chang-dong is certainly the only director examined in this book to have held political office. Lee was South Korean Minister of Culture and Tourism, 2003–4, under President Roh Moo-hyun, and of all the directors featured here he has been most notable for his direct involvement in governmental policies with regards to filmmaking. Although he no longer holds office he continues to be an influential figure in the South Korean art and film policy debates and works closely with the Seoul Institute of Arts in the training and encouragement of young trainee filmmakers.

Lee was born in Daegu, the fourth-largest city in South Korea, in 1954. Historically Daegu, seated near the centre of the Korean peninsula, has always acted as an important transportation nexus and has been the focus of much un-rest and political disruption over the last few centuries. Under Japanese colonial rule Daegu was the site of several uprisings and continued to be a site of unrest after the Japanese defeat in 1945. It was the focus of the most serious uprising under American military rule and experienced very heavy fighting in the subsequent Korean War. The decades following the end of the war saw Daegu develop rapidly in terms of population, commerce and industry (something that has continued to this day). The city also has the unfortunate reputation of being politically the most right-wing city in South Korea; it was the base of the military dictator Park Chung-hee and the conservative right remains a powerful political force in the area today. Recent events have seen Daegu as the site of the worst South Korean subway fire with a total of over two hundred dead.

Unlike Im Kwon-taek he did not live through the horror of the war but he grew up in a country that was struggling to repair itself after the trauma of the previous decades. Son of a permanently unemployed father, Lee's family was notable for being one of the few left-wing families in the area and this sense of isolation and the poor relationship he had with his father were themes that are returned to again and again in his writing as well as his films. Lee graduated from Kyungpook University and began his career as a high school Korean literature teacher. It was during this time that his literary career took off with the publication of two volumes of short stories. One of these, *There's a Lot of Shit in Nokcheon* (1992) earned him the 25th Hankook Ilbo Baek-sang Prize. *There's a Lot of Shit in Nokcheon* is clearly influenced by the poor relationship Lee had with his father and the political background in which he grew up. The focus is on the pain and confusion felt by the main protagonist and his desire to escape his existence for a new beginning:

> At this moment, I would like to be born again. I want to write something different, and I feel the desire to live a new life. Like throwing off old clothes, I want to change into a different me. Although this desire has brought me failure so far it is also a desire that supports me. (Lee 1992: 4)

This image of the desire for change can be seen again and again in his films. In *Oasis* (2000), the mentally-challenged man and a woman crippled with cerebral palsy are, for brief moments, transformed into an active and healthy couple. In *Green Fish* (*Chorok Mulgogi*, 1997), it is the protagonist's desire to begin a new and glamorous existence that leads him to become involved with a group of gangsters. In *Secret Sunshine* (*Milyang*, 2007), the focus is on a woman who aims to start a new life with her small son after the death of her husband. *Poetry* (*Si*, 2011) sees an old woman diagnosed with Alzheimer's realising her life-long dream of writing a poem.

The legacy of Korea's turbulent past and the subsequent economic and social developments of the 1980s and early 1990s are very important in the work of Lee, both in his films and his writings. As mentioned in the chapter on Im Kwon-taek the 1980s, when Lee began working, was a period of intense economic growth but was also a dark time in terms of South Korean individual freedoms and human rights. Chun Doo-hwan succeeded as President in 1980 and quickly declared martial law and disbanded the National Assembly. Many opposition politicians and student and union activists were arrested, beaten and often killed. The most infamous event of Chun's regime is, of course, the Kwangju massacre that saw the armed forces open fire on crowds of protesters. The death toll remains unclear to this day with the official figures claiming that the incident resulted in 207 deaths, 2,392 wounded and 987 missing people (however, many claim that the figure is in fact a lot higher but that the government hid the real statistics). Concurrent with these terrible events, Chun's presidency oversaw a period of rapid economic growth and low interest rates, making affluence and a high standard of living the norm for many South Korean citizens. This growth continued long after Chun's demise into the early and mid-1990s. The lives of everyday Koreans radically improved and 'for the first time people found themselves living in a society no longer dominated by economic debates and economic imperatives ... the habitual tendency to view social problems through the prism of economic policy faded, and awareness of social problems and issues grew in ways that were unthinkable to the previous generation' (Buzo 2002: 157). Previous concerns about poverty and economics began to fade away with South Korean affluence and people began to focus their concerns on social problems such as crime rates, disability, equality and teenage pregnancy. The legacy of Korea's traumatic recent past once more came to the fore and the new era of democracy allowed people to begin to articulate their memories of how the past affected them as individuals. The new emphasis on the social is evident in much of Lee's work; especially the acclaimed *Peppermint Candy* (*Bakha Satang*, 2000). In his excellent book, *The Remasculinasation of Korean Cinema* (2004), Kim Kyung Hyun traces how contemporary South Korean cinema has had to deal with the legacy of colonialism, militarism, dictatorship and the quest for modernity. The cinematic method for the extrapolation of the

South Korean past has often been conducted via a violent exposition of the (male) individual in crisis. The male-in-crisis figure can be seen in many of the films to have emerged from South Korea over the last two decades. Many of the films by South Korean directors discussed in this book focus on an individual male subject as the site of the tensions and stresses that traverse South Korean society. Although Lee is one of the few in this book that offers narratives from a female perspective (as seen in *Oasis*, *Secret Sunshine* and *Poetry*), he also seeks to present the social and cultural through the experiences of an individual. His films focus on those whom society has marginalised in a variety of ways and are therefore rendered highly vulnerable to abuse and misuse. Throughout his films frequent motifs reoccur: the disabled, the poor, the mentally unstable and those who are perceived as 'different' from the majority. Lee is also an avid critic of South Korea's economic development and the economic growth of the 1980s which, combined with the intense economic crisis in Asia in 1997 and the slow process of economic rebuilding after the depression, all blend into the social preoccupations and examinations that we see in Lee's films, as well as the two films that he scripted prior to directing his own works.

Park Kwang-su's *To the Starry Island* (*Geu seom-e gago sipta*, 1993) and *A Single Spark* (*Areumdaun cheongnyeon Jeon Tae-il*, 1995), both written by Lee, are considered to be two of the most important films of the 1990s and contain many of the themes that would later mark Lee's filmmaking. *To the Starry Island* focuses on the wounds left by the Korean War and how the past constantly informs the Korean present when a man returns to his hometown to bury the body of a friend's father. His return sparks memories of how his friend's father was responsible for the massacre of innocent villagers during the war. The film negotiates the collective memory of the villagers regarding the event and the conflicting recollections of the individual. *A Single Spark* tells the tragic tale of a young labour activist who in 1970 immolated himself at the age of 22 to protest against the appalling conditions under which predominantly female South Korean garment-industry workers were forced to work. The focus on the interaction between the often alienated individuals and the wider collective society is something that Lee would continue to deal with in his own feature films. The success of Park's work made it possible for Lee to raise the capital to direct his own films, and his first feature *Green Fish* was released in 1997.

Green Fish tells the tale of Mak-dong, a young man who returns home from military service to discover that his family's circumstances have radically changed.

Military service is still one of the Four Constitutional Duties (along with taxes, education, and labour) for all South Korean male citizens. From the outset this commitment is shown as cruelly ironic as the state offers Mak-dong nothing in return after his period of service. He returns home expecting his family to be awaiting him but during the time he was away (military service is anything between 22–26 months) the socio-economic situation of South Korea has radically changed. The farm land that once surrounded the family home is now concrete apartment blocks, his mother is working as a maid and he discovers that his younger sister is working as a prostitute in a local bar. His older police officer brother is an alcoholic who abuses his wife and child. The state that demanded Mak-dong's physical and emotional commitment over the period of his military service offers him in return a broken and splintered family that is struggling to survive. The only person to show any real delight at his return is his mentally disabled older brother; for the rest of the family Mak-dong's return is little more than an inconvenience. He tells his mother of his desire and determination to gain a highly paid job to support her and bring the family back together again but his mother's response suggests that for her, the new and modern South Korea offers nothing more than hardship and disappointment and she expects nothing for her sons either.

The 'new' South Korea is wonderfully portrayed in the opening section as Mak-dong travels with his other brother, an industrious egg-seller through the streets of Ilsan. When stopped by the police for speeding the two immediately offer to bribe the officer. The two policemen that stop Mak-dong and his brother are shown as happy to take bribes and then rob the young men of their limited income rather than upholding the law. The desire for economic gain that the government and society is happily upholding is shown to have become so great that corruption has become commonplace and, ironically, financially worthwhile. The forces of law and order in the films of Lee are at best useless and at worst highly corrupt and brutal. This desire to succeed financially and provide material comfort for his family sees Mak-dong gradually become involved with a group of gangsters, seemingly the only people that are benefiting from this new society. For Lee the linkage between violence and economic development is clear:

> The theme of the film is the nature of violence. We have had about thirty years
> of economic development in Korea. A unique value system has formed around

modernization. The whole ideology is to get results at any cost. Of course there is a diversity of violence, from political violence to gangster violence. But I think violence is violence, regardless of who is committing it. I wanted to show the nature of that violence to my audience. (Lee 1998)

Mak-dong believes that the gangster way of life offers the economic and social benefits that society tells him that he should aim to achieve. Joining the gangster lifestyle allows him to enter into the discourses of modernisation and development that surround him. After rescuing the gangleader's girlfriend from rape Mak-dong is brought into the world of organised violence and he appears to be adopted by the charismatic gangleader Bae Tae-gon. For Mak-dong the link between violence and economics is clear. In order to intimidate a local official into obeying Bae, Mak-dong mutilates his own hand. This violence committed againts his own body gains him respect and therefore material gain as he moves up inside the gang's power matrixes. Bae was once a poor orphan but he is now a wealthy businessman with legitimate as well as illegitimate income sources. For Bae human life and society are based solely on economic value: he only sees individuals in terms of what they are worth; in essence he is the living personification of the economic drive that took place in South Korea in the 1980s and 1990s. People are rated according to their positioning on the economic scale and this scale is one that, in Bae and Mak-dong's world, is enforced by violence. Mak-dong's proximity to violence has temporarily enhanced his econcomic worth but the violence that he enacts on himself to gain respect will soon be enacted on his body by others in order to maintin their own economic and social positions. French anthropologist and philosopher René Girard (2005) has made the direct link between violence and material acquisition, where the driving force behind human interaction and development is the acquisition of wealth (although 'wealth' in Girardian terms can be anything from material goods and money to social status and parental love). In basic terms, the desire for wealth leads to an intensely violent and antagonistic feeling that grows inside a society/ group until an arbitrary victim is chosen to be sacrificed to appease the others. The elimination of the victim appeases the violence in others until the process begins again. In *Green Fish* (and indeed in his other works) a victim is chosen for the economic drive to continue. When another mob boss threatens Bae he hires Mak-dong to dispose of his rival. Reluctantly Mak-dong kills the other man but is then murdered by Bae to ensure that everyone remains unaware of Bae's involvement. Mak-dong becomes the sacrificial victim of the wealth acquisition that marks the society that surrounds him. Mi-ae (despite the fact that she appears to have developed feelings for Mak-dong) accompanies Bae to the factory where he will kill Mak-dong and watches him die against their car without any attempt to aid him. Having previously been forced to perform sexual favours for a corrupt government officer to aid Bae, the substitution of Mak-dong for her as a victim to Bae's continual drive for wealth and power is one that she accepts as a process of self-preservation. The economic driving forces are seen to isolate and alienate all human emotions and social traditions. As Lee notes in an interview, the economic drives of the 1980s resulted in a huge shift in the social organisation of local areas such as Mak-dong's home town of Ilsan:

> After moving to Ilsan I wondered, where have all the people gone who used to live here before? What traces are there of the people who used to live here? I started thinking about those people, and then about the people who remain, like the family of the main character. These people who lived there before the area became built-up are now running a restaurant for the new people who have moved in. The original people are now servicing the people who have taken away the land. I felt that was ironic. That symbolizes something essential about Korean society. (Lee 1998)

After Mak-dong's death his family manages to move back under the same roof and are seen running a small restaurant that, as Lee notes, is ironically serving the people that moved onto their old land. His family is an active part of the new dream of economic development; in short they are realising Mak-dong's deeply held dream. His death is rendered even more tragic when Mi-ae and Bae turn up at the family's restaurant. Mi-ae is heavily pregnant and as she stares at the family photos we are brought to the harsh realisation that all that Mak-dong desired came to pass but he is absent. He is not the father of Mi-ae's child, Bae is not his real brother and he dies before his family are reunited. Kim Young-jin notes that the end of the film is a 'self-mocking portrait of contemporary Koreans who have engaged in self-deception' (2007: 49). Where the self-deception lies is perhaps open to debate. For Kim it is in the tendency of both audiences and characters to see dreams and fantasy as achievable aims. Mak-dong's aim of a united family, wealth and a beautiful girlfriend turns to ashes in the face of the socio-economic machine that demands a sacrifice to be made in order for others to succeed. It is interesting that during the rapid economic and industrial growth of the 1980s union membership in South Korea was still remarkably low (only two per cent of South Korean workforce [see Buzo 2007: 157]). The lack of representation of the blue-collar workers (and although in an illegal industry Mak-dong certainly falls into this category) resulted in tremendous economic growth but at the sacrifice of individual needs and rights (something that *A Single Spark* references wonderfully). The political situation in South Korea during the 1980s enhanced this loss of personal freedom and human rights and the scars of this period are still felt on a personal and social level. Although *Green Fish* has many strong elements it appears to be uncertain exactly what *type* of film it wishes to be, uncertain whether to offer violent action or quiet introspection. Lee's nuanced and subtle directorial style that would come to be seen in his later films was lost in this film's desire to conform to the genre conventions of the gangster film and the mixed reviews reflect this.

Following *Green Fish* Lee made what has become his most famous film, *Peppermint Candy*. Whilst *Green Fish* clearly focuses on the gang underworld and was thus forced to deal with the genre conventions of this type of film, *Peppermint Candy* chose to deal with 'ordinary' Koreans and the effect that the past has, and offers a more radical and unconventional film narrative. A far more political film that *Green Fish*, *Peppermint Candy* deals directly with the legacy of Chun's time in office and how the prominent events of this period affects the lives of individuals to the present day. The film traces the fate of one individual, Yŏng-ho, backwards from 1999 to 1979 and shows how the political, economic and personal all combine to produce a tragedy. The film's backwards chronology would be echoed a year later in Christopher Nolan's *Memento* (2000) but the issue with *Peppermint Candy*'s protagonist is that he *can* remember events rather than permanently forgetting them like Nolan's. The film begins in 1999 with a drunken Yŏng-ho attending a reunion of an old youth group that he used to belong to. He is rude, offensive and is quickly chased away, and ends up standing on a railway bridge in front of an oncoming train screaming 'I want to go back'. The metaphor of a train is utilised throughout the film as the method through which we are transported back through Yŏng-ho's life. During the late 1990s the economic crisis of South Korea deepened to such a point that the IMF was forced to assist the government in sustaining the economy. Bankruptcy and suicide rates were at an all-time high and with this in mind we meet Yŏng-ho again. Bankrupt, divorced, unemployed after his business partner cheated him and living in a tent, he is on the point of shooting himself when the husband of his first love, Sun-im, appears. Sun-im is dying and whilst visiting her at the hospital Yŏng-ho presents her with the sweet from the film's title, peppermint candy. Yŏng-ho is overwhelmed by grief and as the film's narrative takes us *backwards* we see him experience the myriad of crises that propel him, starting (although this is the film's narrative ending) with his accidental shooting of a young girl during the Kwang-ju uprising when he was on military service.

Of all Lee's films *Peppermint Candy* has been the most discussed in academia. It is a still from *Peppermint Candy* that graces the front cover of *Remasculinization of Korean Cinema* and Yŏng-ho certainly fits the bill of an emasculated, narcissistic and deeply traumatised individual whose inability to engage with the forces of modernity and change result in him damaging himself and everyone around him. After Kwang-ju and his military service we learn that Yŏng-ho entered the police force. During the 1980s under military rule, levels of police violence and brutality grew and torture became a common method of information extraction as part of the intense crackdown on political freedoms. In the sections set in 1984 and 1987 we see Yŏng-ho gradually get pressured into, then actively choosing, to commit acts of extreme violence on suspects. In 1984 he rejects Sun-im and the gift of a camera she has brought him, thus beginning the long descent into oblivion and finally suicide. The camera offers him the ability to self-reflect, to consider his place in South Korean history rather than being swept away on the tide of militarism and then modernisation. The camera serves to preserve time and for Yŏng-ho remembering is something that he strives not to do. His desire to eradicate history is what leads him to stand in front of the train in the final section of his life (but the first in the film). He desires to return; to go back to the past so that he can re-live the experiences and make different moral and emotional decisions. Even his attempts to remember the good parts of his life goes wrong; at the end we see him buy a new camera to present this to the dying Sun-im, but it is too late as she is unable to receive or understand his gift. For Yŏng-ho the only way to return will be to die. In a similar fashion Mak-dong in *Green Fish* telephones his family prior to committing the murder for Bae (and later being killed himself). He speaks to his family of childish occurrences and happy memories but it is too late and returning to the innocent past is no longer possible. The past informs the present and creates the future and we see how the killing of the young girl that reminded him of Sun-im in Kwang-ju causes Yŏng-ho to reject the real Sun-im and strive to find a series of replacements for her in the various bar girls and women he sleeps with. Yŏng-ho is unable to evaluate his past as he refuses to engage in self-reflection and as such he is a victim of the passage of time. When South Korea is affluent in the early 1990s we witness an economically stable although morally redundant Yŏng-ho but when the economy of South Korea takes a turn for the worse in 1997 Yŏng-ho goes bankrupt. His desire to forget and his refusal to engage with his actions in the past (as the film goes backwards) is shown in his engagement with a man he tortured in custody. Meeting the man and his family in a restaurant in 1994 Yŏng-ho greets the man with no sign of embarrassment for the appalling way that he treated him. His economic success (which we know will be fleeting) seems to have given him a limited peace but this is one that is built on denial and therefore will quickly fail. This is paralleled with the economic rise and fall (and then rise again although that came later than *Peppermint Candy*) of South Korea. In a similar fashion he is unable/unwilling to accept his role at Kwang-ju and his accidental killing of the student. The legacy of this is a physical manifestation of his guilt. During his time in Kwang-ju he was shot in the foot and this old wound continues to recur at times that remind him of the past such as when he goes to visit the dying Sun-im or when he has sex with a Sun-im surrogate. He is the literal embodiment of recent South Korean history but this is embodiment without reflection since Yŏng-ho rejects any attempt at discerning meaning. It is only the outside (the camera/audience) that is able to see the truth. Unbeknown to him (but shown to the audience) Yŏng-ho acts as both the victim and the perpetrator in South Korean history. He is not exceptionally cruel, stupid or unlucky – he is just an ordinary Korean resident who is swept along by history and is unable to place himself in historical events, and thus does not learn from his experiences. As he states in an interview Lee's aim was to present a character that the audience could both identify with and simultaneously stand back from.

> The audience project themselves onto the character whilst watching the film. Through this act of projection we can either absorb a character or take objective distance and reflect on ourselves … I neither wanted full identification or objectification … that was my intention in the case of *Peppermint Candy*. (In Kim 2007: 65)

This concurrent process of association and dissociation serves to highlight the aim of the film to examine historical events via the personal history of one individual. In the 1994 section, when encountering the man that he tortured in a restaurant toilet, all Yŏng-ho says is 'life is beautiful'. Yŏng-ho is referring to the sense of success and happiness he feels at the precise moment in time, however, as the audience is aware that this will be fleeting. The process through which the film alienates us from Yŏng-ho means that we, as the audience, are able to view the truly beautiful moments in his life that Yŏng-ho himself misses. The prime example of this is his relationship with Sun-im. Throughout the film we see Yŏng-ho systematically destroy and reject the relationship that offers him positive benefits. The reverse nature of the film allows the audience to see the numerous 'what if' scenarios and this lends the film a poignancy that would have decreased if the film's narrative had been linear. We are already aware that there is no happy ending to this tale since we have witnessed Yŏng-ho's death in the opening scene.

Between each of the segments is a shot of a railway line and the camera moving over the tracks in the manner of a train. These segments achieve several purposes; to link once more in our minds the fate of Yŏng-ho beneath the train wheels but also, more importantly, the metaphor of the train and the continual journey that is undergone is a recurring reference to the recent history of South Korea. We are watching the tragedy of one man but the film refers to a much wider history of a nation that exists in an almost constant state of trauma due to the legacy of a terrible past (*han*). The Kwang-ju massacre not only ruined the life of Yŏng-ho but also scarred the national psyche of South Korea. This was not a foreign invading force that caused the deaths but rather South Korean troops killing South Korean citizens. The legacy of Kwang-ju is seen not just in this film but in scores of other films, artworks, photographs and writings to have emerged since the 1980s. The *minjung* art movement referenced in the work of Im Kwon-taek was keen to embrace the legacy of Kwang-ju as the ideal means to convey the legacy of all the various traumas that have befallen the Korean people. Lee's embrace of the legacy of Kwang-ju references the notion that all Korean people suffered as a result of the past, but that the refusal to engage correctly with common history has resulted in a situation where the desire to forget the past has caused a state where is it *impossible* to forget the historical events. We see in the case of Yŏng-ho the soldiers that fired on the crowds are also left to deal with the legacy of the dictatorship and the effects that this has on their individual lives. Yŏng-ho is failed by the wider South Korean society rather than an aggressive or malevolent outside force. He is unable to fully articulate his pain and need for forgiveness, and as a result he destroys himself. The desire to forget

Kwang-ju imbues Yŏng-ho's entire life. He attempts to find ways to alleviate his pain. He drinks, womanises and aims for economic triumph. However, in the end, all of these displacement activities fail him and he attempts to return to a point of innocence that he and the audience find at the end of the reverse narrative.

> The reverse chronology is not only a narrative manoeuvre to undermine the hegemony of a linear progressive temporality but also a subversive ideological apparatus to retrofit two decades of South Korean social history from a contemporary critical perspective' (Chung and Diffrient 2007: 126)

In this way Lee utilises the narrative form, not only to challenge dominant filmic expectations of a linear narrative but also to allow a critical revelation of South Korean history and society. Lee's films are highly critical of contemporary South Korean society and the refusal to correctly evaluate and come to terms with the events of the past. He offers a society whose economic and social development has resulted in a multi-layered society that seeks to exclude any persons who do not conform to dominant ideologies. In many of Lee's works, Seoul is an alien cityscape that offers an unforgiving backdrop to the narratives. *Green Fish*, *Peppermint Candy*, *Secret Sunshine* and *Oasis* offer visions of the tremendous development in buildings and infrastructure that has taken place in the last couple of decades in South Korea. Apartment blocks and huge building sites dominate the skylines and the rail and road systems traverse this modern metropolis. However, underneath we are shown the negative side to this development. In *Oasis* Gong-ju's family resides in a luxurious modern apartment block but this is contrasted with the poverty-stricken slum where she is left. In *Green Fish*, Bae shows Mak-dong a run-down factory which he has just forcibly bought from the owner, with the indication being that he will turn this into prime real estate. He is in a position to profit from this economic development not only in terms of the building but also in that his economic dominance allows him to exercise power over others. He tells Mak-dong that the previous owner had insulted him as a child so over the years he has slowly forced him into bankruptcy. In comparison Mak-dong's family have been physically separated due to their financial circumstances and he will become a victim of the economic processes that surround him. He will die in the factory grounds and metaphorically the buildings that come after will have been built on his grave. *Peppermint Candy* shows Yŏng-ho move from being a successful business owner to sleeping in a slum on the outskirts of Seoul. As Hagen Koo notes, 'economic inequality in South Korea has grown significantly over the past decade, and the growing disparity is manifested in every aspect of social life from consumption patterns and lifestyles to residential segregation and educational opportunities' (2007: 1). The desire to interact with global capital culture has seen South Korea develop at a remarkable rate but for Lee, the Age of Globalisation has led to a structure of inequality that marks all aspects of the social space.

Lee's focus on those who are social, economic and cultural minorities continued with the 2001 film *Oasis*. Also an award-winner, it focuses on the relationship between a mentally-challenged man and a woman with cerebral palsy. Unlike *Green Fish* and *Peppermint Candy* this relationship is not marred by the lovers themselves; their respective disabilities are not a problem for each other. Their love is real, honest and has the potential to succeed; however, wider society, as personified by their families, refuses to understand or allow their relationship. The male protagonist Jong-du has recently been released from jail after serving several years for a motor accident that we later discover was actually committed by his older and more successful brother. Jong-du took the blame at the behest of his family since his brother is the most economically successful of his siblings and has a young family. His sacrifice is not appreciated and his family repay him by moving from their home and not leaving a forwarding address. His lack of money and registered address result in him being arrested once more when he cannot afford to pay for a meal. The police reunite him with his less than enthusiastic family and he gets a menial motorbike delivery job. Jong-du has a child-like attitude to the world and his impulsiveness and inability to communicate with people effectively, combined with this lack of mental acuity, lead him into trouble. He is an annoying, occasionally repulsive character but he shows a great ability for love that is constantly rejected by his family, including his own mother. His delivery job leads him to meet Gong-ju, a women profoundly disabled by cerebral palsy who has been abandoned by her family in a run-down poverty-stricken two-room apartment. Her family have stolen her benefits and live in a luxurious government apartment which they gained through claiming that they are her full time carers. Jong-du quickly falls in love with Gong-ju but his initial demonstrations of love are horrific to behold. In the most disturbing scene in the film he rapes her whilst telling her how much he loves and desires her. He cannot see her distress and pain and when she passes out with fright he runs away in panic. Despite this start it is Gong-ju who then approaches Jong-du for a second meeting when she phones the number she has found on his business card. It is not implied that Gong-ju is any type of masochist but rather, despite his clumsy and violent initial actions, Jong-du is the only person that is seen to treat her as a desirable adult women rather than little more than an animal. The rest of society refuses to grant Gong-ju any recognition: her family ignore her, the neighbours hired to take care of her openly have sex in front her and restaurants refuse to serve her. The only element that society sees with regard to Gong-ju is her disability; it is only Jong-du, as flawed as he is, who is able to see her true nature. The desire of mainstream society (South Korea in this case but the same argument can be made for most social groups) to marginalise and ignore those who do not conform to its roles and expectations is painfully shown when Jong-du decides to take Gong-ju as his date to his mother's birthday party. Although he sees her as beautiful and intelligent his family react with horror and see her presence as an insult to them. When her family find out the true nature of their relationship they have Jong-du charged with rape and refuse to listen to Gong-ju as she attempts to articulate the true nature of their relationship. The relatively conventional narrative structure is interrupted by fantasy sequences that allow the audience to see the world through the eyes of the two protagonists where they are transformed into a healthy, happy couple. Jong-du is an intelligent upstanding member of society and Gong-ju is active and able-bodied. In one striking scene Gong-ju's empty room with its dirty mattress on the floor is transformed into an exotic Eastern abode equipped with elephant and small slave boy. The metaphor of this non-specific Eastern paradise evokes the film's title; for Gong-ju and Jong-du the only 'oasis' that they can find in the hard and unforgiving landscape of Seoul is their own imaginations. The use of the image of an exotic otherness demonstrates how alienated they feel from their own culture and society. Unable to fulfil the cultural demands of economic success (Jong-du) or feminised beauty (Gong-ju) their marginalisation cannot be resolved. What the film highlights is the neglect that marginalised people suffer at the hands of dominant social structures. Gong-ju is at best ignored and at worst abused by the people who surround her. Her disability means that people are unwilling to look beyond her twisted body to her active intelligence. The idealised concept of a shared national identity, or *minjuk*, that was so exalted in early periods is now shown to be a highly problematic concept with the consistent social exclusion of those that are perceived as 'different', not because they are from without the culture but in their inability to conform to perceived social norms. Slavoj Žižek notes that 'the national cause is ultimately nothing but the way subjects of an ethnic community organise their enjoyment through national myths' (1993: 202). In this way, paradoxically, 'one enjoys one's membership of a national identity through experiencing that identity as being threatened or lost' (McGowan 2007: 181). In terms of Lee's work, the threatening 'other' is not the Japanese occupiers or the American neo-colonials but rather 'otherness' has been transferred onto selected members of the South Korean society. He demonstrates the process through which those who do not conform to dominant social structures and modes of behaviour will often be unfairly punished. Jong-du is arrested and sent to jail while Gong-ju is left isolated once more. With the troublesome couple dealt with, their families return to their lives without any risk of disturbance.

Yŏng-ho will die beneath the wheels of the train since he is unable to forget and 'move on' from the traumas that have befallen South Korea over the last two decades. His body has become 'other' to the idealised concept of a new and modern South Korean state. In the body of Yŏng-ho, Lee has offered a critique of the illusions of nationhood via both the actions he commits but also though the 'break with the conception of temporality that serves as a foundation for national identity' (McGowan 2007: 188). *Peppermint Candy*'s refusal to move forward illustrates how the concept of 'nation' operates to potentially repress and destroy. Lee's films rarely end with a narrative conclusion in the traditional sense. Compared to Im Kwon-taek's lush offering of cultural traditions that link to a firm sense of nationhood, Lee's films seek to illustrate how the consolidated idea of nation can fail to offer a solution to the debates that traverse modern global society.

Despite his concerns surrounding notions of South Korean nationhood, Lee has never wavered in his desire to promote and develop a strong and successful national cinema industry. As previously mentioned, Lee served under Roh Moo-hyun as Minister of Culture and Tourism in 2003–4 and in this role he was a keen advocate and supporter of the South Korean film industry. During his time in office Lee was vocal about the need for small nations to defend their national cinemas from the onslaught of Hollywood. Lee was a fervent defender of the quota system that sought to protect domestic film product by restricting the amount of foreign imports, stating that:

A nation whose mass media is controlled by foreigners cannot be called a nation … without the quota system, South Korean film could be thrown into a spiral of decreasing investment and production leading to an irreversible quagmire. (Quoted in Paquet 2003)

The quota system went against free trade agreements and Lee found himself fighting a losing battle. Eventually he was forced to resign from his ministerial post in 2004. For Lee, a balance between national and global needed to be maintained. Whilst South Korean blockbusters such as *Shiri* (1999), *Oldboy* (2003) and *The Host* (2006) have done well on the international market in recent years, the well-financed Hollywood machine is an ever-present threat to smaller national cinemas and Lee felt the quota system would provide a method of support for South Korean products. Lee's stance concerning this issue saw him receive the French Legion of Honour medal for his efforts to promote cultural diversity through protectionism.

His resignation gave Lee the time and space to return to filmmaking and in 2007 he made *Secret Sunshine* (evaluated in closer detail in the film analysis section that follows). Beautifully shot and framed, the story focuses on a young widow and her small son, and the mental collapse of the woman when tragedy strikes her again after her son is murdered. This film certainly maintained his reputation as a Korean director who can garner international attention as well as appealing to home audiences. *Secret Sunshine* was nominated for the Palme d'Or at Cannes in 2007 (with Do-Yeon Jeon winning the Best Actress award) and won four of the top awards at the Korean Annual Film Awards including Best Film and Best Director. *Poetry*, released in 2011, returns to his literary roots. This was also successful on the international stage; winning at Cannes for Best Screenplay and was triumphant in the Grand Bell Awards winning Best Picture, Best Screenplay, Best Actress and Best Supporting Actor.

The film keeps to many of Lee's previous preoccupations with those who are marginalised from mainstream society; the current state of South Korean society and the negative relationship between money and social justice in the modern South Korean state. Mija (played by veteran actress Yun Jung-hee) is struggling to cope with her recently diagnosed Alzheimer's and facing the truth that her grandson that she raises was part of a group of six youths who repeatedly raped a female classmate over a six-month period until she ultimately committed suicide. The fathers of the other boys involved in the rape and suicide decide to pay the mother of the dead girl a vast sum of money to keep her quiet and to prevent the matter from been reported to the police. Like Jong-du and Gong-ju (*Oasis*), Mak-dong (*Green Fish*) and Yŏng-ho (*Peppermint Candy*), the young girl here is a silent and defenceless victim, not only in the empty school class-rooms where she was repeatedly raped but also in the school principal's and the boys' parents' desire to keep her sad story a hidden secret. Her mother is a poor widow with other young children, and in one scene the five fathers surround her in an attempt to 'encourage' her into agreeing to a settlement. Their power as socially and economically domineering figures leaves the woman silent in the face of their pressure. The question of the literal value of human life is raised. For the fathers of the rapists it seems clear; their sons' actions can be undone in the payment of cash to the grieving mother. Only the often-confused Mija realises the shameful and appalling acts the boys have committed; made worse by her grandson's refusal to show any remorse or willingness to atone for his crimes. Alongside struggling to cope with her grandson's actions and her own mental decline (all whilst still working as a carer for an elderly man), Mija is also fulfilling her life-long ambition to write a poem and is attending a local class. This linkage between art and life is made clear via the film's frequent trips to the classroom where we see the participants speak passionately about key movements in their respective lives and Mija's continual focus on her poetry, despite the actions going on around her. Communication is once again a troubled and problematic process. Mija's mental decline results in her often unable to remember simple words; the man she cares for has been affected by a stroke and struggles to make himself understood; her grandson is unable/unwilling to articulate his actions and feelings and the dead girl's mother is silent when confronted by the parents of the boys. Mija will soon be unable to remember the actions that have taken place and her one and only poem will be dedicated to the dead girl. 'Agnes's Song' (the dead girl's name) creates a permanent remembrance of the girl via Mija's art and constructs an unbreakable link between her and Mija. Like the girl Mija will soon vanish from life (mentally if not literally) and her poem will be the last words we have from her (in the world of the film) and she chooses to present Agnes's experiences and feelings rather than Mija's own. present Agnes's experi-ences and feelings. This linkage between the dead girl and the vanishing woman evokes the notion of the narratives of life, and although this story was a tragic one the film does not end on a sad note, rather we see Agnes face the camera with a slight smile. This open-ended conclusion can be seen in Lee's other films from *Secret Sunshine* to *Green Fish* and *Oasis*. Despite the tragedy that marks the characters in Lee's films, life will go on and develop; change, whether positive or negative, will continue to take place.

Although Lee has directed only a limited number of feature films (when compared to the prolific Kim Ki-duk who has had a career of similar length) his films have been central to world recognition of contemporary Korean cinema. His postmodern, fractured, alternative narratives and his focus on those who are marginalised by dominant social structures offer a personal view of South Korean society that speaks to cinematic audiences on both a national and international level. With his outspoken views on film policy, combined with the critical and popular success of his films, Lee Chang-dong has become a figure in South Korean cinema that cannot be ignored.

Film Analysis

SECRET SUNSHINE

밀양
Miryang

2007

Director

Lee Chang-dong

Cast

Jeon Do-yeon (Shin-ae), Song Kang-ho (Jong-chang)

International Film Awards

2007 Nominated Best Film, Cannes Film Festival

2007 Best Actress: Jeon Do-yeon, Cannes Film Festival

2007 Best Picture, Asian Film Awards

2007 Best Director, Asian Film Awards

2007 Best Actress: Jeon Do-yeon, Asian Film Awards

Plot Summary

Shin-ae moves with her small son to her deceased husband's hometown, Miryang, for a new start. On the way to the town her car breaks down and mechanic Jong-chang comes to her aid. Jong-chang falls in love with Shin-ae and although she makes it clear she does not have romantic feelings for him he continues to try to get close to her. Gossip with regards to her situation abounds in the small town; especially about how much money she has. Shin-ae encourages these rumours and even tells people she is thinking of buying land and building a house. One day her son is kidnapped and a ransom demand is made but Shin-ae does not have enough money. She hands over all the money she has but the boy is later found dead in a river. The murderer is caught and is revealed to be the local school teacher who had kidnapped the boy to try and gain enough money to escape his monotonous and unhappy life with his teenage daughter. Shin-ae is devastated by the loss of her son and, watched by the ever-loyal and loving Jong-chang, she spirals into depression. Her depressive state leads her to join the local evangelical Christian Church. Shin-ae fervently embraces God and Christianity as means of emotional escape. She is convinced by the Church to go to the prison and forgive her son's murderer and despite Jong-chang's pleadings, she agrees. The experience is a traumatic one for Shin-ae and she turns against the Church in a series of disruptive acts, such as replacing prayer music with an angry pop song and the seduction of a married Church member. She eventually tries to kill herself and is committed to the local mental hospital. When she is released Jong-chang takes her to a hair salon where she meets the daughter of her son's murderer. She discovers that the girl had been sent to a government reformatory. Unable to face the girl further, Shin-ae runs away with an incomplete haircut. She returns home where she is eventually joined by Jong-chang who helps her to complete the haircut. The film ends with images of her shorn hair blowing in the wind.

Secret Sunshine is Lee Chang-dong's fourth film and this touching tale of a young woman facing tragedy saw Lee gain even more recognition as one of the key directors to have emerged from South Korea in the last two decades. Lee's role as a government minister made him a well-known figure in South Korean politics but the nomination for Best Film at Cannes helped enhance his reputation as a South Korean director that could succeed on the international stage as well as charm local audiences. Secret Sunshine charts the emotional results when a kidnapping goes wrong. Unlike in Park Chan-wook's Sympathy for Mr Vengeance (2002), there is no dramatic resolution to the trauma; instead we are shown how a bereaved mother is forced to deal with her son's tragic death.

Secret Sunshine contains no dramatic action sequences, visual trickery or dramatic editing techniques. Lee's film offers a meditative and gentle approach to what is, in essence, a violent story. The people involved are ordinary members of society; Shin-ae is a young piano teacher and Jong-chang is a mechanic. They are unexceptional people who are caught up in a tragically exceptional situation; the kidnapping and murder of a child.

Like Peppermint Candy there is a cyclical nature to the film as we see a similar point returned to again and again. Each time, however, there is a difference, a slight change. The opening shot of the film offers the audience a view of a beautiful blue sky through the front windscreen of a parked car, and this shot is returned to later in the film to powerful effect. The first time we see this shot the camera turns to show the tired face of Jun, the small son of recently widowed Shin-ae. Jun sits listening to his mother as she yells to a mechanic down the phone from the side of the road where they have broken down. It is clear that Shin-ae loves her son as she plays with him by the roadside but we are quickly alerted to the fact that Jun's father is not around and they are retuning to the father's hometown under sad circumstances. The mechanic that comes to collect them is a familiar face to recent Korean cinema: Song Kang-ho (Shiri, Green Fish and JSA). Song plays Jong-chang as a self-confessed 'good Samaritan' who shows absolute and unreciprocated devotion to Shin-ae and remains a pivotal character in the film. Shin-ae settles into the town as a piano teacher and faces down the curiosity of those that surround her.

The film takes a dramatic turn when her son is kidnapped for money that she does not have and then is found dead by the local river. The murderer turns out to be the local school teacher. As mentioned, the film opens with Jun looking at the sky through the car window. When Shin-ae is called to identify the body the same shot is repeated; however, this time when the camera turns around, it is Shin-ae, not her small son who is staring at the sky. The question arises: why the repeated shot at two very different times in the film? For Lee, the view of the world from the eyes of the vulnerable is a key feature in his work (in particular, in *Oasis* and *Poetry*). As a small boy entering a new town having just lost his father, Jun is in the highly vulnerable position of a child whose life is changing beyond his control. The repetition of the shot enhances the vulnerability of Shin-ae. The shot aligning her with her child not only emphasises their link but the intense vulnerability and terror which she is feeling in the face of having to identify her son's body. The actions of the police further enhance her as a minority female subject in the face of the male majority of the police investigators. Rather than showing her any real concern the police point her to the body with the words, 'he's over there – will you be alright?' The men stand back and let her approach the body with the camera maintaining a distance from the tableau. They are unable to respond to her grief with any sort of empathy or help. Although the murderer is caught very quickly there is no sense of satisfaction in the solving of the crime. As in *Poetry* and the suicide of the abused girl, the death of the child is nothing more than a simple tragedy without any real meaning. The identification of her son's killer only grants Shin-ae more pain as she discovers reasons for the mistake. She had only made the comment about buying land to stop people prying into her private life. This means that her casual actions and another's misunderstanding of them resulted in her son's pointless death.

This inability of people to effectively communicate is portrayed constantly throughout the film. When Shin-ae first moves into town she tells a local shop owner that she should redecorate her business to make it more appealing to customers. Her intentions are good but she naturally ends up insulting the shop owner. Shin-ae's attempts at friendly communication misfire and she gives the impression of rudeness and arrogance. When her son is kidnapped Shin-ae runs to the garage where Jong-chang works and watches him dance around to music. Shin-ae is in clear need of human contact and yet she cannot manage to cross the threshold of the doorway and make her presence felt. In this way words are seen as a method of miscommunication rather than effective communication. Jong-chang is frequently clumsy and awkward in his interaction with Shin-ae and she finds it impossible to convey her real feelings about the death of her husband and then her son. The need for communication and the desire to convey her pain at her loss is what leads Shin-ae to her brief but disastrous alignment with charismatic Christianity. When she first arrives at the town she is dismissive of the attempt by the local chemists to convert her to their belief system but after the death of her son Shin-ae makes the decision to attend church and quickly becomes a passionate convert.

The presence of charismatic Christianity in the film references a key development that has taken place in South Korea over the last few decades. Pentecostal and Evangelical Christianity in South Korea has experienced a huge rise in popularity (see Kim 2000) and has raised several issues in South Korean society about its role and purpose, as the unfortunate incident of the church group kidnapped in Afghanistan demonstrates.[1] The Church in *Secret Sunshine* is presented in a very ambivalent light. Shin-ae is suffering and the Church uses her pain as a method to convert her. The chemist tells her that the Church will take away her distress and provide her with comfort, yet this seems almost cruel given the trauma that Shin-ae has undergone. The appeal that Christianity holds for Shin-ae is seen in her first visit to church. Under Jong-chang's concerned gaze Shin-ae howls and sobs her heart out to an accompaniment of hymns. What the church space seems to do is to allow her to express the pain that she had not been able to voice on the outside. At her son's funeral her mother-in-law had accused her of being 'hard' since Shin-ae had refused to cry but in the space of the Christian church she finds a brief emotional release. This event is misunderstood by Shin-ae as the mark of the Church's ability to aid her in her grief rather than seeing her experience as part of the normal pattern of coming to term with loss. This is quickly pounced upon by the Church elders and they continue to encourage her fanatical devotion to God as it represents their desire to convert people to their system of belief. In prayer groups Shin-ae is shown as a success story about the power of God to heal and yet we are aware that in her home environment, away from the eyes of others, Shin-ae is clearly unable to come to turns with her son's death. Her relationship with the Church, except for the first demonstration of release, is actually constraining her natural desire to grieve. Since she is 'in Gods hands' and part of His wider plan, she is told she must accept her son's death and the Church encourages her to go and forgive her son's murderer.

It is a trip to the prison that causes Shin-se to realise the false sense of comfort that the Church is offering her. When she goes to forgive her son's murderer she discovers that he has already converted to Christianity and achieved a sense of peace and reconciliation with the crime he had committed. He tells Shin-ae that he is happy she has embraced God and that he is aware that God forgives all sins. For Shin-ae the notion that the man believes that he has already being forgiven for his actions before she, the child's mother, has forgiven him, hits her newfound faith hard. She turns against the Church through a series of telling and considered acts. She breaks into an outdoor prayer meeting and replaces the church music with an angry pop song that informs the churchgoers that everything said is 'lies, lies, lies'. For Shin-ae the Church represents a hypocrisy which has contributed to the magnification of her pain. She tries to highlight this hypocrisy even more by seducing the chemist's husband. Although he is initially a willing participant, before he commits himself fully to the act of sex he panics and exhorts her to pray with him for forgiveness. Shin-ae, however, has rejected the notion of forgiveness or hope for the future. She is on a self-destructive path that ends in her trying to commit suicide. Her inability to find a suitable and effective method of communication to articulate her grief, and a supportive and appropriate outlet for her emotional distress, has resulted in Shin-ae utilising the last method she has left to enact her grief: her own body.

Shin-ae's suicide attempt results in her being placed in a secure mental unit and we see her friends and family withdrawn from her in embarrassment over her distressed and very public mental breakdown. The social state is unable and unwilling to cope with Shin-as as a living embodiment of the tensions and negativity that is clearly present through wider social structures, and as a result she is ostracised and removed from the public sphere. Only the loving and loyal Jong-chang remains, and it is he that collects her from the hospital on her release. From here Jong-chang takes her to the hairdresser where she meets the daughter of her son's murderer. We learn that she was placed in a reformatory after her father's incarceration. The crime committed by her father had many victims, not just Shin-ae's son; however, the notion of divine forgiveness has been rejected and Shin-ae still cannot face or forgive the daughter of the man that murdered her son, and she runs away from the hairdresser with an incomplete haircut. Lee rejects an overly sentimental ending which would see her reconciled with the past by forgiving and embracing the daughter of the man that murdered her son and becoming romantically involved with the loyal Jong-chang. Instead Lee demonstrates the complexity of human emotion by showing that there will never be a complete conclusion to Shin-ae's grief. Her feelings will change and be less painful, but they will never be eradicated. Her personal tragedy will mark her and those around her for the foreseeable future. There is, however, a sense of hope that is maintained throughout the film. Although the legacy of the tragedy will not leave, there is still a chance that Shin-se will gradually manage to put her life back together. It will never be the same as it is impossible to return to the past, but what is offered is the notion that there is still a future in some form. As Jong-chang cuts Shim-ae's hair the camera pans to her shorn hair blowing in the wind. Rather than looking towards the sky as the film and Shin-ae had previously done for answers to questions that cannot in fact be answered, the film now focuses on the ground and the literal steps that Shin-ae will have to take to begin her life anew despite the tragedy. The new haircut and the subtle change in Shin-ae that allows her to let Jong-chang help her without protest opens the option of a new future. As with all Lee's films there will not be a happy and easy ending. The hair blowing in the wind does not provide the audience with the complete answer; it only points to a myriad of possibilities.

Secret Sunshine contains many of the developments that have marked modern-day South Korea. The presence of Christianity is a key part of the modern nation. Lee's film questions the role that this institution plays in wider society. His film is not, however, anti-Christian; although the Church does not succeed in offering permanent comfort to Shin-ae, Jong-chang continues to go and enjoy services even after Shin-ae has left the Church. What *Secret Sunshine* offers is a questioning of the motivations of certain individuals related to the Church and how there is no such thing as a quick and easy solution to emotional turmoil. Yet the Pastor, the chemist and his wife are all seen as hoping to define their own purity and love of God via their conversion of Shin-ae; they are not genuinely interested in helping her, as their reaction to her sudden dismissal of the Church illustrates. Rather than attempting to understand her distress and grief they berate her for her lack of faith. The Church is seen as part of a wider social problem based on a lack of empathy for others. Most people are seen as so embroiled in the narratives of financial, social and personal desires that they are unable to fully relate to those around them.

Economics evidently plays an important role as it is financial crisis which leads to the kidnapping. The small town is marked by a process of infrastructure building which is taking place across South Korea. When Shin-ae goes to view a plot of land we see a large motorway development in the distance, and Shin-ae is perceived by the kidnapper as the personification of a rich Seoulite who has moved to the countryside. We learn that this is a false impression but it speaks to the notion of social aspiration which marks the small community. Surrounded by economic development and change, the schoolteacher seems to fear being left behind and resorts to drastic methods to try and achieve the economic dream. Shin-ae is a piano instructor and this role speaks to the new social aspiration that marks South Korean society as she teaches music to a series of middle-class children.

The presentation of a recognisable landscape of South Korean development gives *Secret Sunshine* a powerful sense of realism. The film does not offer trite explanations or conclusions, and the lack of melodrama makes the events of the film even more poignant as we become aware that these are ordinary flawed human beings having to face a tragic occurrence and trying to overcome it. *Secret Sunshine* rejects over-sentimentality in favour of a narrative that presents real emotional depth. We believe and care about the characters and it is this sense of the 'real' which perhaps explains the success of the film around the world.

NOTE

1   South Korea sends more missionaries abroad than any other nation and in 2007 eighteen missionaries were kidnapped by the Taliban and accused of illegally preaching Christianity. After the execution of two members, the rest were eventually released when Seoul promised to withdraw troops from the region (something which was later reneged upon resulting in more attacks again South Korean military bases in the country).

The Legacy of a Violent Man: Kitano Takeshi

Japan is a reinventing superpower – again. Instead of collapsing beneath its widely reported political and economic misfortunes, Japan's global cultural influence has quietly grown. From pop music to consumer electronics, architecture to fashion and animation to cuisines, Japan looks more like a cultural superpower today then it did in the 1980s, when it was an economic one. (McGrey 2002)

Film scholars have often asked following question: 'how do we draw the boundaries of a career and impute meaning into it?' (Polan 2001: 161). This approach, moving away from the all-encompassing notion of the *auteur*, focuses on the need to examine, not just the individual director, but also the producers, cinematographers and actors that they consistently work with. Many directors have long and sustained relationships with people who clearly contribute a large amount to their respective films. Notable examples of a symbiotic working relationship include the French director Claire Denis who traditionally works with cinematographer Agnes Goddard; Kurosawa maintained a long and successful (although tumultuous) working relationship with actor Mifune Toshiro and Lee Chang-dong and Park Kwang-su have collaborated on several projects. Kitano Takeshi is almost unique in that he often fulfills multiple roles in his own films under distinct personalities. We have 'Bīto' ('Beat') Takeshi the actor and occasional director, working alongside Kitano Takeshi the director, editor, writer and producer. At the same time as international film festivals are screening his thoughtful, often subtle works, he delights Japanese television audiences with slapstick comedy routines on one channel whilst presenting a talkshow dressed as a clown on another. His star persona is remarkable in its breadth, depth and diversity and as Darrell William Davis sums up, 'Kitano as a media figure is not just an auteur writ large across disparate media, but a cultural production, a little industry in his own right' (2001: 58).

Born in 1947 in Tokyo, Kitano was the youngest child of four. His father Kitano Kikujirō was a failed businessman and occasionally violent drunk whilst his mother Saki had deep social aspirations for her children. Growing up in a lower-class neighborhood he developed an understanding and appreciation for those that were marginalised and excluded from mainstream society. The working-class suburbs (*shitamachi*) of his childhood were disliked by Kitano and remembered as a place of discrimination and hardship (see Bitō 1999: 82–99). The figures that surrounded him, however – *yakuza* members, unsuccessful criminals, the handicapped and poor – would frequently and sustainably emerge in his comedy routines and then later in his films. Unlike Miike Takashi who grew up in a similar setting, Kitano did not see the gangster lifestyle as a genuine career choice since Saki encouraged all her children to do well at school, and eventually Kitano entered Meji University to study engineering. He would soon quit however, and, after a series of menial jobs, he ended up on the Asakusa comedy circuit. Historically Asakusa was the entertainment capital of Japan; dominated by a huge temple and crafts market, it was also the site of *France-za*, a strip and comedy club where Kitano began working. His success as a comedy performer would quickly lead to his television debut in 1975 and by the late 1980s he was a huge star; Kitano's success as a film director is based on the tremendous success he continues to enjoy on television.

Kitano first emerged on Japanese television as part of a *manzi* comedy duo known as 'The Two Beats'. Together with partner Beat Kiyoshi (real name Kaneko Jirō), Beat Takeshi offered the audience chaotic, often highly offensive comedy routines. *Manzi* is based on the interaction between two roles; the *tsukkomi* or straight man versus the *boke* or funny man. In his role as *boke* Beat Takeshi excelled in dazzling the audience with streams of anarchic, subversive, often cruelly funny observations on a variety of topics and individuals. *Manzi* went through a period of increasing popularity in the early 1980s and people such as Kitano pioneered a new style of *boke*, one that was increasingly chaotic and disruptive and focused on a harsh critique of Japanese society and social norms. Japanese cultural critic Yoshimoto Takaaki makes the statement that the audience 'laughed because they realized that this painfully poisonous tongue expressed all the poison that everyone had clogging up their throats but could not spit out even if they tried. Another reason was because this artistry was soaked in a friendly expression and tone, a gentle weakness that could dissolve the poison. It was supplied with the power and the timing that would take the black, prejudiced feelings of offence and turn them into smirks and wry smiles, diffusing them into roaring laughter' (quoted in Gerow 2007: 24).

Kitano offered a criticism of society via a method that did not alienate or irreparably offend the audience. A Western figure analgamous to this alternative and sometime cruel truth-telling method would be *King Lear*'s fool who tells the truth that no one else dares to state. In relation to the notion of entertainment as social critique, it is interesting that Kitano's first film acting job was one of the leads in Oshima Nagisa's *Merry Christmas Mr Lawrence* (1983). Oshima as one of the lead figures of the 1960s counter-culture (discussed in the chapter on Fukasaku) was a director whose work aimed to challenge and alter society. Oshima and his peers focused on film as an ideal method to critique and subvert contemporary dominant cultural, political, historical and social trends (see Desser 1998, Turim 1998). Unlike Oshima, Kitano has never claimed to have a serious political agenda but his star persona, together with his films, opens up a variety of issues that reflect many aspects of contemporary Japan, such as a notion of a society in decline and the role of the ever-present mass media.

Kitano's screen popularity began to grow and in the case of the Two Beats the straight act of Beat Kiyoshi was increasingly sidelined by the acerbic narratives of Beat Takeshi and gradually Kiyoshi faded and vanished under the full force of Kitano's rising star. By the 1990s he was appearing in a multitude of shows and commercials; he frequently wrote for magazines and newspapers and published books of poetry and fiction. The NHK Television poll voted him Japan's favourite television personality for six years in a row (1990–95).[1] After all this success it was ironically the ill health of another director featured in this book, Fukasaku Kinji, which led Kitano to direct his first feature film. When Fukasaku had to quit the directorial role on *Violent Cop* (*Sono otoko, kyobo ni tsuki*,1989) Kitano surprised many people by taking on the joint role of lead actor and director.

The title of Kitano's debut film, literally translated as 'That man, being violent', references one of the key themes in his work, namely that of violence and hostility.

His aggressive comedy routines and TV drama roles that had included a mass-murdering serial rapist (*The Crime of Kiyoshi Ōkubo/Ōkubo Kiyoshi no Hanzai*) had created in the public imagination an image of 'Beat' Takeshi as himself a violent man. This image was enhanced by a series of real-life events involving Kitano and his 'Army' (*gundan*).[2] The violence inherent in Kitano's directorial debut is immediately presented to us by the vision of a homeless man being viciously beaten by a group of high-school boys. Motivated only by a sense of casual violence as 'fun', the situation is reversed when police detective Azuma arrives at the lead boy's home shortly after the attack. Going to the teenager's bedroom Azuma proceeds to mercilessly beat the cowering boy and concludes with the demand that the boy and his friends go to a police station and confess.

Compared to other films noted for their violence, *Violent Cop* actually features a relatively small amount of graphic brutality. What the film does do is establish a society where violence seems ingrained in all aspects of life. Children maliciously throw cans at a passing barge; a police officer is stabbed without a second thought and another is beaten up with a baseball bat accompanied by music. In one scene the chief villain, Kiyohiro, whilst attempting to kill Azuma, fires a gun at him but shoots a woman standing innocently at a bus stop in the head. The film does not linger on this, we hear her companion's screams but the camera does not stop to examine the tragedy; instead it focuses on the conflict between Azuma and Kiyohiro. Aaron Gerow notes that 'the reason violence does not stand out is because the everyday is so cruel and violent' (2008: 68). There is a sense of nihilism that imbues the whole of society, from the teenagers considering the near-murder of a man as a suitable social activity to the indifference shown by the police chief to the murder of his officers.

The cruelty and indifference of society would emerge again and again in Kitano's work via the casual violence that permeates them. In *Kakijuro* (*Kakujirō no natsu*, 1999), a gang of teenagers bully and rob the young child protagonist; in *Boiling Point* (*3-4X jugatsu*, 1990), an argument at a petrol station leads to two teenagers attempting to buy guns in Okinawa and then later committing suicide as a final method of gaining their 'vengeance'; in *Sonatine* (1993), an aging yakuza slowly moves towards his inevitable death; in *Dolls* (*Dōruzu*, 2000), one man blinds himself; a woman is disfigured in a car crash and another woman attempts suicide, all under the dispassionate eye of society; and in *The Kids Return* (*Kidzu ritān*, 1996), two teenagers each try to gain success in their chosen intrinsically violent professions of boxer and *yakuza*, respectively, but both fail miserably at their goals. Even in the chaotic comedy *Glory to the Film Maker*, (*Kantoku Banzai!* 2007), the world and everyone in it ends in a ball of flames when a random meteor crashes into Earth.

For Isolde Standish, Kitano's films mark a current trend in Japanese cinema which is entwined with the discourse on the negative side of postmodernism. She states that 'the films, all drawing on similar thematic concerns and employing the vast array of visual registers which are possible in the digital age, are symbolic of an allegorical shift from the modern to the "post-tragic" realm of the "post-moral" of postmodernism' (2005: 332). She goes on to cite Terry Eagleton, claiming that the films of directors such as Kitano show a 'world in which there is no salvation. This is the post-tragic realm of postmodernism' (2003: 57).

The aims and concerns of the post-war generation, personified by directors such as Fukasaku and Oshima, have been replaced by an amoral consideration of Japan's position in the globalised economy. Critics of post-modernism see it as offering little more than a 'society of the spectacle … of reproduction and recycling, so rather than producing the real it reproduces the hyper-real' (Bruno 1987: 63). The concept of the hyper-real refers to the idea that the real 'is not what can be reproduced', but rather it is 'that which is always reproduced, which is essentially a simulation' (Bruno 1987: 67). For many the post-modern is the 'age of simulation' and there is no longer a gap between the original and the copy. The question of reproduction is caught up in the star body of Kitano himself. Throughout his career there exists an emphasis on how each film references not only his other films but also his television work, star persona and acting credentials. This can all be read on a national and international level since he operates worldwide. This is made additionally complicated by the fact that Kitano Takeshi is also Beat Takeshi, demonstrated in the fact that *Getting Any?* (*Minna-yatteruka!*, 1995), technically Kitano's fifth film, was actually billed as Beat Takeshi's directorial debut. This slapstick comedy about a young man who will go to any extremes to try and have casual sex is highly indebted to Kitano as the TV star rather than referencing his early film works such as *Violent Cop*. In particular Abe Kashō (Casio in some English-language publications), a prolific writer on Kitano, has focused on how the body of Kitano becomes imbued with the often contradictory narrative of Beat Takeshi, the popular TV personality and Kitano Takeshi, the established film director. Kitano has spoken often of his almost schizophrenic split identity and in the film *Takeshis'* (2005) he focuses on the relationship between the TV star Beat Takeshi and an unsuccessful film actor called Kitano Takeshi. Playing both roles, *Takeshis'* offers a self-reflective musing on the multiple identities that 'Takeshi' in his myriad forms embodies. Originally entitled *Fractal*, hinting at the fragmented individual that is Kitano Takeshi, the *Takeshis'* film poster summarises the essence of the film (and perhaps Kitano's whole being). In it many small images of Kitano combine to create a larger figure of the bleached-blond Kitano that will star in *Takeshis'*. The numerous 'Kitanos' that make up 'Kitano' is probably the most decisive comment on how he is unable to fully reconcile all aspects of his life. He once stated:

> I'm having fun with Beat Takeshi and Kitano Takeshi. If I'm asked who I am, I can only answer, 'I'm the man who plays Beat Takeshi and Kitano Takeshi'. Every once in a while I call out to myself, 'you must be tired', and ask, so what should we do Take-chan? It's a classic case of split personality. (Kitano 1995: 27)

His body now bears the scars of another key event in his life. In 1994 Kitano was involved in a near-fatal motorbike crash that fractured his skull and left him scarred and partially paralysed down one side of his face. Although he has recovered his later acting roles all contain the marks from this event on his facial features. In this way Kitano the actor can never be fully split from Kitano the man; the two co-exist inside the same physical space but neither can they ever be fully disassociated or sublimated. This split personality manifests in *Takeshis'* as we struggle to fathom whether the successful Beat Takeshi is dreaming of being Kitano Takeshi or vice-versa. The film cuts between the two as each appear to see or imagine what the other is experiencing and concurrently experience it themselves. The film offers us a walk through Kitano's past work: *manzi* comedy routines, a trip to the seaside, a dramatic *yakuza* shootout, an armed robbery and a return to the World War II territory of *Merry Christmas Mr Lawrence* all appear, referencing key aspects of Kitano's television and film career. The film does not offer any indication of how we are supposed to reconcile all these different images and narratives; instead we are given a post-modern identity rendered large.

Takashis' was the first in a trilogy of 'autobiographical' films which focus on the personality and history of Kitano himself. In *Glory to the Filmmaker*, a documentary-style narrator charts for the audience the trials and tribulations that face the filmmaker as he decides what *type* of film he wishes to make. The film offers a comedic and highly chaotic vision of 'Kitano' as he tries to reinvent his filmmaking style again and again. We see him try various genres such as romantic tearjerker, J-horror, science fiction, ninja action and an Ozu-*esque* 1950s black-and-white family saga, all in an attempt to find a perfect film style with which to define his career. We are told that the director achieved great success in the gangster genre and made a rash statement that he would not make any more similar films, and now has to find a new genre to work in. This is clearly very close to the real-life Kitano's career where his work as a director has often been defined by his earlier films such as *Violent Cop* and *Boiling Point*. In *Glory to the Filmmaker* Kitano attempts to (re)write his own narrative history but we are faced with an anarchic rendering of his life where his desire to achieve cinematic triumph sees him attempt multiple film styles with little or no success. Just as the myriad of Takeshis' refusals to reconcile themselves to form a consolidated narrative in *Takeshis'*, in *Glory to the Filmmaker* we are left confused about what the film actually *is*. In his presention of all the various genres that we see the director Kitano (the one who the film is following) attempt, we are presented with exact genre conventions which are then suddenly overturned. Such as the black-and-white Ozu homage 'Retirement', where the low-key action, sparse sets and family-focused narative mirror perfectly the style of the older Japanese director. 'Retirement', however, ends abruptly in midflow when the narrator announces that the film was halted since people were 'bored with tea-drinking'. The instant dismissal of the film takes place just as the narrative was starting to develop and the audience is then transported to the world of a romance between a blind artist and his student which, in turn, is just as suddenly ended when it is made clear that the filmmaking team could not figure out what 'art by a blind man would look like'. Kitano's own ability to defy any attempt to label or constrain him to a particular genre takes a comedy twist as it is implied that it has been a process of trying (and failing) rather than a consolidated and considered career plan. All aspects of Kitano's life are engaged with since the film is filled with references to his Japanese television roles and shows, films and his media persona.

In *Takeshis'* he was faced with the myriad images of himself; in *Glory to the Filmmaker* Kitano's doppelgänger is a life-size plastic dummy that is clearly meant to be Kitano. Throughout the film this non-speaking, non-moving inanimate body of Kitano is frequently used as a stand-in for his physical presense. In the opening scene we see the dummy undergo a series of medical tests, including an MRI scan, only for the Doctor to conclude that next time 'he will have to come himself'. Throughout the film, whenever the Kitano character is bored or being physically assulted, the dummy is suddenly and without explanation inserted in his place. Kitano himself seems to offer a vision of his body being 'emptied out', leaving a plastic shell though which the characters in the film, and the audience watching, can focus their opinions. If *Takeshis'* enacted a 'politics of fluid identity' (Gerow 2008: 225), in *Glory to the Filmmaker* Kitano goes one step further and offers a vision of his identity that has no notion of a real or solid basis – he can literally be replaced by a empty dummy.

In *Achilles and the Tortoise* (*Akiresu to Kame*, 2008), Kitano completed the final part of his trilogy and presents the journey of an artist called Machisu (played by Kitano) as he devotes his entire life to art, despite his lack of commercial or critical success. The film is filled with Kitano's own artwork and it meditates on the tension between commercial art and 'art for art's sake'. Zeno's Paradox, from which the title is taken, argues that 'in a race, the quickest runner can never overtake the slowest, since the pursuer must first reach the point whence the pursued started, so that the slower must always hold a lead' (Aristotle, Ivi). Ironically, therefore, no matter how hard the fastest runner tries s/he can never overtake the slower runner. This paradox is seen in the film as Machisu visits his art dealer who constantly encourages him to follow the latest artistic trend, only to reject his work as 'imitation' as soon as he returns with the requested artwork. The notion of imitation is key in all three of the 'autobiographical' films. Kitano's image is constantly reinterpreted, transformed and (re)presented in a multiplicity of different situations and scenarios. All three of these films engage with various aspects of Kitano's persona; rather than offering a clear division between 'Beat' Takeshi and Kitano Takeshi, all his multiple personaes are offered to Japanese and global audiences for consumption. Every time he offers himself for consumption, however, he once again subverts any attempt to firmly label or constrain him.

The power of Kitano's multifaceted persona lies in its ability to be non-essentialist; it does not provide fixed meanings but rather its pluralism results in its ability to be read in a variety of ways, both negative and positive. Kitano's films reflect this star persona. These are not narratives that offer any essential truths or ideals; rather, we are offered a transcendence of boundaries that is open to multiple readings. This is simulation *extraordinaire*. We struggle to find any essence of the real but all that seems to be presented is a hyper-real notion of Kitano in all his forms. The perceived nihilism that is inherent in his films open up hidden conflicts and questions regarding our own perceptions of the modern state by forcing us to engage with the darker side of life.

This fractured presentation of the individual (the characters in the films as well as Kitano himself) can be read as a vision of a Japan that is in a state of crisis as it struggles to articulate its identity in the face of globalisation. Rather than seeing this as a reflection of a nation in decline, however, Kitano's work can be seen as part of an ongoing debate and interrogation about the realities and structures of this post-modern existence.

Often in Kitano's films this post-modern narrative, a narrative of reproduction, can be seen to be circular. In *Violent Cop* Azuma may be dead but his younger sidekick, Kikuchi, has replaced him. He dresses, walks and approaches policing in the same way as Azuma (he even gets the same theme tune – an updated version of Erik Satie's *Trois Gnossiennes, Lent*). In *Dolls* the film begins and ends with the *bunraku* puppet show. The three individual tales contained within the film all concern the notion of returning to the beginning. Masumoto runs away from his wedding on hearing that his former fiancée Sawako has attempted suicide. They end up wandering aimlessly together tied by a red thread; reunited until their sudden deaths on a mountain. After the accident of pop star Haruma, her most devoted fan will blind himself so that her perfect image will remain forever engraved in his brain. A *yakuza* chief who once abandoned his loyal girlfriend tries to go back to his youth and reunite with her. Even in the slapstick *Getting Any?* the narrative is dominated by the fact that pathetic, sex-obsessed Asao never actually 'gets any'; he just moves from one extreme situation to another and he seeks a sexual gratification which he will never achieve. In *Kakujiro* the protagonists literally move in a circle as they end up back at their starting point. *Sonatine*, together with many of Kitano's other films such as *Hana-bi*, *Dolls* and *Kikujiro*, feature a flower motif representing a circular narrative of constant decline and revival. In *The Kids Return* the two protagonists start and end in the schoolyard, giving a vision of a narrative that does not allow them to escape; although time has passed they both have ended up cycling in circles. Abe states that 'the film seems to subscribe to the shape of a zero' (1994: 236) and there is constant repetition as both boys engage in the same activities: they cycle the same routes, and run the same pathways. A 'zero', as Abe describes it, implies a lack, a space, a nothing. This nihilistic sense of 'zero' is manifested in the range of Kitano's characters and situations that all lead towards death. In *Violent Cop* Azuma seeks out Kiyohiro with the tacit knowledge that this will lead to both his and Kiyohiro's death. In *A Scene by the Sea* the deaf protagonist finds a broken surfboard and decides to learn how to master the waves, an act which will lead to his death by drowning. In *Hana-bi* the character played by Kitano actually commits suicide. In *Boiling Point* we also see two teenagers commit suicide by driving a petrol truck into a building. Many of the characters in the films do not seem to want to actually die but they do not try very hard to live. Several of the targets, in films such as *Boiling Point*, stand up prior to death presenting an even greater target, and the respective characters' actions seem to run counter to normal sensible survival techniques. Rather than seeing these deaths as a tragedy, Kitano's usage of the desire for death is presented as an alternative method of reconciling oneself to life. He states: 'It seems to me that life and death have very little meaning in themselves, but the way you approach death may give a retrospective meaning to your life' (in Abe 1994: vi). This is linked to the concept of Kitano as caught in the post-modern matrix of repetition and reproduction. The endless copies of a non-original entity results in a state of emptiness that, ironically, can best be examined in the drive for death.

This need to approach death in a particular fashion is perhaps the reason behind the many scenes of childish play that exist in Kitano's films. This notion of play refers to the scenes of childlike innocence that occur with regularity. In *Kikujiro*, after Masao has seen his mother and discovered she has remarried and has another child, Kikujiro and some people they have met along the way attempt to cheer the small boy up. In a series of stupid slapstick games they run naked, act in a play, chase each other, juggle and dance. The scene allows the characters to have a few moments of childish fun before they return to Tokyo and their respective 'real' lives. These comedy moments also serve to remind the audience of Kitano's TV origins and at the end of film when Masao asks for his new friend's name the repose is telling: 'Kikujiro you idiot!' Giving the character the name of Kitano's own father implies that for the director, this idealised image of a boy spending time with a father figure is, for him, an idealised return to the past. The figure of death is not present in *Kikujiro* but the film offers a space for the adult man to return to the past and play. In *Sonatine* the gangsters jump, play and wrestle in the sand. In *Boiling Point*, as he collects flowers with which to hide a machine gun, Kitano's character Uehara also creates for himself a crown of flowers in a very childish and playful moment. Later in this film whilst holding the flowers the machine gun will accidentally go offer spraying the ceiling with bullets. In a wonderful moment of deadpan comedy Uehara will barely react to the event.

The use of slapstick comedy (referring directly back to the world of 'Beat' Takeshi) and the employment of Kitano's own life story in films such as *Kakujiro* and *The Kids Return* is part of the self-referential processes that many of Kitano's films participate in. In this way Kitano's oeuvre itself can be seen to be circular in nature. As already mentioned, his works are heavily inter-textual with constant references to the previous work of Kitano Takeshi (as well as Beat Takeshi together with his own star persona and personal history).

In many of Kitano's films the beach and seafront become the space where this post-modern dialogue will take place. *A Scene by the Sea*, *Sonatine*, *Boiling Point*, *Dolls* and *Kajijuro* all feature the sea/beach as an integral part of the narrative. The sea therefore acts as an extended metaphor for the process of life and death that his protagonists are going through. Kitano states himself that:

> I do live by the sea, but at the same time, something tells me to keep a distance
> from it. We all know our origin is in the sea and it feels to me that Mother Nature
> is calling us home. But on the other hand … we know we no longer belong there.
> (Quoted in Smedley 2000)

For Kitano the sea acts as the focus for the desire to try and return back to an original state and yet, as he observes, this original state is no longer a possibility, so many of this characters remain trapped in this liminal space. It is on the beach in *Dolls* that Haruna and her 'number one fan' will meet. She has placed herself in self-imposed isolation after a car accident has disfigured her face and he has blinded himself to prevent the eradication of her perfect beauty from his mind. They meet on the beach but we are aware that both of them are actually seeking a means to return to the past rather than to progress into the future. His remembrance of her perfect face allows her to maintain the illusion that she still looks the same way and in return her physical presence gives credence to his idealised vision of her. In *Sonatine* the characters play on the beach as a method of alleviating their boredom whilst waiting for the death that they know is coming. They set up a wresting ring, dance around and play frisbee. They will also, more tellingly, play a game of William Tell, taking turns to shoot a can from each other's heads. It is during this game that the lead gangster Murukawa will offer the audience an indication of his drive for death. He picks up the gun and plays an impromptu game of Russian roulette, pulling the trigger against his own temple. We find out later that there are no bullets in the gun but the image of the smiling Murakawa with a gun to his head re-emerges throughout the film and is a precursor to his own suicide. In *Hana-bi* Horibe will face the sea contemplating his existence and the question of whether or not to commit suicide. In *A Scene by the Sea* the young man is desperate to learn to surf and together with his loyal girlfriend, they attempt to succeed at a surfing competition. The beach and the sea become a site of play and development but it will also become a site of death. After his drowning, his girlfriend will paste an image of them together onto the board and throw it into the sea. It will come and go with the tide, trapped in a circular and perpetual narrative.

In 1998 Kitano published an essay criticising the ultra popular *Tora-san* series (directed by Yamada Yōji). Kitano stated that he felt that the formulaic and over-sentimentalised *Tora-san* films (along with the popular films of Itami Juzō) had destroyed Japanese cinema. For Kitano, Yamada's films old-fashioned, overly romantic tales were purveyors of clichéd morality and the 'over-explanation' that can be seen in a large amount of Japanese film and television (see Bitō 1998: 87–8). According to Kitano, Japanese cinema suffered from its aesthetic and narrative links to television. He was openly critical of the amount of close-ups that were used claiming that it was sufficient to have 'no more than two' in any film (see Gerow 2008: 41). He stated that the constant need to over-elaborate and offer clear and obvious explanations to the audience was ruining Japanese cinema. His filmic vision and desire not to offer the audience clear and easy reading can be seen in the lack of dialogue in many of his films. Silence dominates *A Scene by the Sea* where the two lead characters never exchange a word. In *Dolls* the young couple ceases to communicate with words and walk mutely tied together. In *Hana-bi* disabled police officer Horibe paints as a way to explore his unarticulated emotions. Azuma in *Violent Cop*, Nishi in *Hana-bi* and Murakawa in *Sonatine* are all men who remain silent for huge parts of the film, leaving the audience to ponder their actions and feelings without any explanation from the director. Compared to the loquacious TV personality Beat Takashi, Kitano Takashi the film actor is nearly unreadable in voice and manner. When Azuma shoots his mentally ill and drug-addicted sister after she has been kidnapped, raped and abused by violent criminal Kiyohiro, only the briefest of inclinations of the torrent of emotions that he is experiencing are shown to the audience; Kitano's still, almost emotionless features give very little away. In *Hana-bi* we are aware of Nishi's deep love for his dying wife through the small moments of interaction we are shown, such as the division of the cream-cakes that he gives her. Kitano does not need to offer any confirmation of Nishi's feelings for his wife; rather, his actions speak for him. The robbing of the bank to fund their last trip together indicates an emotional depth that belies his lack of dialogue. There is focus on contemplation and stillness which marks Kitano's work, and Tim Smedley offers the view that 'the less the characters react, the more scope the viewer has to read emotions and significance' (2003). He cites the case of *Sonatine* when Murakawa's friend Ken falls dead at his feet. Murakawa's face is almost expressionless but there is an innate sadness and recognition of a shared fate that is conveyed via his *lack* of hysterical response.

It is not only dialogue in Kitano's films that is sparse. He often utilises static compositional shots that frame, rather than support and interact, with the action. In *Zatoichi* (2003) the camera stays still as the people move down the hill towards the rest stop. In *Kakujiro* the camera frequently frames an object such as a bus stop and is static allowing the characters to provide any action or movement. His desire to move away from the traditional close-up that Kitano believes is over-used in television productions results in films that are primarily filmed in medium or long shot; this approach seeks to distance the audience from the actions taking place. Gerow labels this the 'detached style' (2002: 2) and it can be seen in the work of other contemporary directors such as Kawase Naomi. Kawase's films have arguably, however, a warmth and a sense of positive emotion that Kitano's sometimes lack. The camera remains distant and detached that makes the incidents of violence that take place with frequent alacrity in his work all the more jarring and disturbing. In *Violent Cop*, as we watch Azuma beat up first the teenager and then later an informant, the camera remains distanced, allowing us to watch the entire scene as if detached. Violence is not used as a dramatic spectacle, Kitano does not utilise close-ups or fast editing to make the experience more 'filmic', instead the lack of camera movement gives the violence a disturbing realism. His comments on his filmic style in *A Scene by the Sea* are telling:

> I wondered if it couldn't just be a story of a guy who hated humanity dying at sea, so I made sure the camera did not get emotionally close to the characters. If emotion enters the picture then you have to do a whole bunch of things, so I though it was best to do it like filming animals, like viewing animals in a safari park. (Quoted in Gerow 2007: 91)

This approach can be seen through the lack of editing that takes place in the surfing scenes. We are shown the surfers and then those watching the surfing event; there is no interaction between the two. The camera moves back and forward from those on the beach to those at sea offering us an experience similar to being in a zoo. This is returned to at the end of the film as the camera shows us group shots of all the respective elements that have been seen in the film, from the local football team to the surf shop staff. They are presented face-on in medium to long shot and the audience is left to decide on the relevance of these last scenes. In *Dolls* the end of the young lovers sees them dangling over the edge of the cliff, but the camera keeps its distance and offers no sentimental emotional close-ups. The face-on, flat and restrained film style, allows the audience to invest whichever qualities they desire in the figure that we see on the screen. In this way, although the films can seem distant and remote, the audience's interaction with the images and scenario is in fact enhanced. In his refusal to offer easy and recognisable emotions, Kitano is forcing the audience to draw its own judgements and values into the equation.

In 2003 Kitano once again surprised audiences by deciding to remake a Japanese classic series about a blind swordsman, *Zatoichi*. His previous challenges to older Japanese cinema concerning narrative and visual styles seemed to argue against him being the ideal director for this project but, once again, Kitano presented a challenge to those who wished to constrain him. The film does contain many of the dominant features of the *chambara* swordfighting film: the noble hero defending the poor villagers from an evil villain, dramatic martial arts displays and corrupt government officials. The difference between Kitano's presentation of the film and earlier versions is that for Kitano the notion of performance is central. He stated in interview that he wanted the film 'to be a frame for all sorts of entertainments: comedy, action, dance, music … for me the spectacle in *Zatoichi* was as important as the central narrative problems for the protagonist' (in Ciment 2003: 19).

In *Zatoichi* the notion of performance permeates the film not only in terms of the narrative of the cross-dressing geisha and the fact that it is implied that Zatoichi may not actually be blind; but also in the way that the film is presented. There are a series of theatrical performances throughout the film and the end sequence involves a huge mass dance with all the cast members, including those who had been killed throughout the film. The constant referencing of the notion of film as performance acts to destabilise our relationship to the narrative; we are distanced from the characters since we are always aware of the performative nature of the entire film. There is no attempt at realism; instead Kitano shows us the artifice of film and performance.

In *Dolls* performance and theatre is referenced even more closely with the usage of *bunraku* puppets that demonstrate that, like them, all the characters in the films are puppets performing for the director. The idea of performance is something that relates to the success of Kitano's films on the global stage. As his work has gained more critical appreciation from global audiences, the notion of how Kitano's films fit into the idea of Japanese cinema came to the fore. For many, Kitano's stark, violent and surreal films have become the embodiment of Japanese cinema and Japan as a nation. He has consistently represented Japan at international film festivals and his star persona is one that operates on a transnational level. In 1997 the cinema journal *Eureka* (*Yiriika*) presented a special edition on Japanese cinema that was literally entitled 'After Kitano'. For many people Kitano symbolises a new generation of Japanese filmmaking that transcends national boundaries and offers a new aesthetic and narrative approach which is free from the structures of older cinema.

There is a dual discourse taking place here, however, since Kitano's films do clearly sell a sense of the national. As his career has developed we see more and more culturally specific elements entering into his work. In *Brother* (2001) Kitano focuses on a Japanese *yakuza* boss who goes to America, and in his placement of Japan against America the cultural specificity of both nations is closely illustrated. *Zatochi*, *Dolls* and *Hana-bi* all feature Japanese locations, arts and traditions, offering the international audience a notion of Japan as a national space while simultaneously disavowing the notion of 'Japaneseness'. Gerow offers the idea that Kitano aims to 'latch onto the national as an abstract but still serviceable frame for making sense of a globalised world (2008: 64). Davis concludes that in his mediation between national and international, Japanese television star and international film director, Kitano, 'domesticates the national for export in his films … he could also be "salvaging" it at home, throwing it into a pit of antagonism in which it cannot help but fight for its life' (2001: 75). Thus whilst challenging domestic ideas and stereotypes, Kitano is forcing the nation to debate its place and construction on the global stage.

His success on the international market and his continuing popularity inside Japan means he maintains a unique position in Japanese media. His company, Office Kitano, is a multinational institution that covers all aspects of the media industry from production to distribution to advertising; from film to television to internet. Kitano has produced all his films with Office Kitano since a dispute with Shōchiku after *Sonatine*'s failure to recoup at the box office. Its subsidiary company, T-Mark, specialises in the acquisition and distribution of up-and-coming Asian film talents. Chinese filmmaker Jia Zhangke (*Platform/Zhantai*, 2000) and Iranian director Samira Makhmalbaf (*Blackboards*, 2000) are just two of the directors that T-Mark has funded. The company invests in potential filmmakers and operates by selling low-budget films to a variety of international markets. Film festival success, limited releases, and the gradual building of international Asian links have resulted in a company that avoids taking big risks but is 'a picture of informal vertical/horizontal integration in motion' (Davis and Yeh 2008: 73). Office Kitano is not simulating the film giants that collapsed in the 1980s but allows a flexible approach to media production that operates on all levels of the industry.

The heart and soul of the organisation, Kitano himself remains a dominant force in Japanese film, a position strengthen by his continual television presence. For over two decades Kitano has lived in the glare of the media spotlight. All aspects of his work, life and personality are of keen public interest and he holds a unique position in that he has comparatively unlimited freedom to develop his films in any way he desires. His international reputation as a director is buoyed by his financial and popular success in Japan. His multifaceted persona means that he can operate on a multitude of media levels, and television and film work are, if only by the nature of shooting schedules, heavily interlinked. He will often start a film and then have to take time off for television commitments and it is only the sheer scale of his critical, popular and financial success that allows for such a flexible approach that few, if any, other media personalities can demand.

As a media entity he remains an incredible mass of contradictions. His writings, films, performances, television shows and artworks all reveal a personality that is impossible to define or to contain; as Gerow states 'he can be seen as both a product of the mass media, and yet perpetually shifting his identity to become the genius managing the mass media itself' (2008: 2). His ability to manage the media can perhaps be seen in a *Sankei News Thursday* internet poll from 2010 which stated that Kitano was the most influential person in Japan, ahead of the Japanese Prime Minister, and Kitano's ability to rank higher than all the leaders of Japanese industry, banking and politics is a reflection of the status which Japan accords to him. Also in 2010 Kitano returned once more to familiar territory with the *yakuza* film *Outrage*. This is Kitano's biggest domestic box office hit since *Zatoichi* and once again returns to questions of the cycles of violence and destruction that exist inside the criminal underground. *Outrage Beyond*/*Autoreiji: Biyondo* (2012) continues in the same vein, focusing on a violent *yakuza* war which breaks out between North and South factions of the organisation. Premiering at the 68th Venice Film Festival, *Outrage Beyond* has achieved acclaim and popularity at both national and international levels and it has been indicated that *Outrage 3* is now being considered. The success that both films have enjoyed inside Japan, as well as on the international stage, indicates that Kitano is still capable of drawing local, as well as international, audience approval.

On a global stage also Kitano maintains a high profile. In 2010 the French Ministry for Arts and Culture awarded him the prestigious *Chevalier des Arts et des Lettres* (Commander of the Order of Arts and Letters) at the same time as the Pompidou Centre presented a retrospective of his film works. This was simultaneous to the Fondation Cartier pour l'Art Contemporain (Cartier Foundation for Contemporary Art) in Paris exhibited a selection of his art works and installations. The exhibition, entitled *Gosse de peintre* (literal translation: 'Kid of the Painter'), toured internationally and was billed as the work of 'Beat' Takeshi Kitano. This new identity combined both the moniker of 'Beat' as well as the full name he uses to direct films, and perhaps indicates that Kitano the painter and sculptor will be another facet of this already highly complex entity.

NOTES

1   NHK is Japan's National Broadcasting Association.
2   Takeshi's *gundan* consist of several comedians that have appeared in many of his television shows and films. The most notable famous event involved the storming of a tabloid newspaper's head office that had published reports of Kitano's rumoured extra-marital affairs. Five newspaper staff were injured and Kitano was arrested for assault.

Film Analysis

HANA-BI

はなび
Fireworks

1997

Director

Kitano Takeshi

Cast

Kitano Takeshi (Yoshitaka Nishi), Kayoko Kishimoto (Miyuki, Nishi's wife), Ren Osugi (Horibe), Susumu Terajima (Nakamura), Tetsu Watanabe (Tesuka)

International Film Awards

Hana-bi *won 21 awards and received 16 nominations; only included the most prestigious ones are included here.*

1997 Golden Lion, Venice

1997 Critics Award, São Paulo International Film Festival

1997 Screen International Award, European Film Awards

1997 Best Film, Kinema Junpo

1997 Readers Choice Award Best Film, Kinema Junpo

1999 Best Director, Blue Ribbon Awards

1999 Best Film, Blue Ribbon Awards

1999 Nominated for Japanese Academy Best Director, Best Actor, Best Film, Best Screenplay Awards

Plot Summary

Detective Nishi finds two teenagers sitting on his car eating their lunch and, after a brief struggle, he makes them clean the vehicle before he drives away. Nishi and his partner Horibe discuss their wives whilst on a stakeout. Horibe tells Nishi to go and visit his wife at the hospital. Horibe sits with two younger detectives, Nakamura and Tanaka, and they ask whether it is true that Nishi has recently lost a daughter and his wife has leukaemia. Horibe lets the younger detectives go home and stays on the stakeout by himself. Nishi goes to the hospital and is informed by the doctor that his wife's cancer is terminal and he is advised to take her home so she can die in peace.

Horibe is shot by the violent *yakuza* they are following and ends up in a wheelchair. Nishi goes to visit him and Horibe tells him that since his wife and daughter have left he feels he has nothing left to live for, but is considering taking up painting as a hobby. Nishi goes to see Tanaka's widow who is struggling to manage after her husband's death. Nishi is harassed by a couple of *yakuza* over money that he owes. Nishi attack them and walks away. He encounters the two teenagers who sat on his car and after another fight he goes to the hospital to collect his wife. The doctor advises him to take her on a trip. Horibe attempts suicide but survives. He receives a large box of painting supplies and a beret. There is a flashback to the arrest of the *yakuza* who shot Horibe; we see that Tanaka is killed and Nakamura injured, then the man is shot multiple times by Nishi.

Nishi robs a bank by painting an old taxi to resemble a police car and using his old police uniform. We see the robbery via the CCTV footage in the bank. Nishi then goes on holiday with his wife but he is pursued by the *yakuza* who demand payment. Finally Nishi kills them all. Nakamura finds him and his wife at the beach and tells him that the police know about the robbery and the dead *yakuza*. Nishi asks for a little while longer and goes to stand on the beach with his wife and they play with a little girl and her kite. His wife says thank you to Nishi and the camera focuses on the sea and the sky as two shots ring out.

———

The main themes of *Hana-bi* can be summed up in its actual title, which is literally the amalgamation of two words: *hana* that translates as 'flower', representing life, and *bi* that means 'fire', and therefore death. Thus life and death are brought together as the two parts of a 'dichotomy that turns out to run through the film' (Rayns 1997: 28). For Japanese critic Abe Kazushige the emphasis should be placed on the hyphen rather than the individual composite elements. The two words are intimately linked and in *Hana-bi*; we see the characters as continually balanced between the two poles.

The film opens with a series of artworks; actually painted by Kitano himself, in the world of the film they will later be seen as the artistic outpourings of the disabled police office Horibe. The art is colourful and bright with a family standing watching a bright firework display in one and a field of bright flowers in another. From these happy scenes we are then transported to present-day Tokyo and the silent exchange between two teenagers and Detective Nishi (Kitano). The camera focuses on Nishi's deadpan appraisal of the situation, cuts to his hand delving into his pocket and then a sudden cut to the teenagers cleaning his car. There is another cut to the shot of the parking space that Nishi's car has just vacated and the bold red words, 'drop dead' emblazoned across it.

Hana-bi contains many of the themes that mark Kitano's other works. The opening sign of 'drop dead' and the car driving off along the road refers to something that dominates *Hana-bi*: the spectre of death. We learn that Nishi's daughter died and now his wife is dying of leukaemia. In the first part of the film we see one policeman killed and another crippled. By the end of the film we realise that Nishi had never intended to outlive his wife and so the entire narrative of *Hana-bi* is one charting his slow move towards death. Suicide is referenced, and indeed occurs, several times in the film. Horibe attempts suicide and then later paints images with the word emblazoned on it. Nishi and his wife will die in what seems like a suicide pact; she knows she is dying and he does not wish to live without her.

Controversially, alongside this narrative of death and suicide, *Hana-bi* is a film which evokes many national images of Japan, such as Mount Fuji and the snow fields of Hokkaido. Stereotypical images such as cherry blossoms and temples are also all present alongside this narrative of death. The linkage between suicide and the Japanese imagintation goes back many centuries but it was World War II that made Japanese soldiers notorious for their willingness to commit suicide for the nation, personified in the figure of the *kamikaze* pilot. In the presentation of national images and the notion of suicide, what is Kitano referencing? Is he making a retroactive statement about the question of seeing suicide as a honourable way to die? In response to critics that raised this question Kitano answered that:

> When forced under oppressive conditions it could be like the spirit of *kamikaze* pilots … when it is not forced but is done on an individual basis, I think it's romanticism worth admiration. But romanticism for the nation is bad, that's why I call it poison. (1998: 70)

Kitano therefore appears to feel that the actions of the individual outweighs wider national and historical issues. Throughout *Hana-bi* the question of the individual versus the wider social group is seen in the decisions which Nishi makes to refuse to conform to dominant expectations. Although he is shown as a devoted police officer he actually robs a bank using his old police badge and uniform. Nishi acts on his belief that his duty to his wife outweighs his commitment to the state and he confirms his individualism and continues to operate according to his own moral compass rather than to social constraints.

Like many of Kitano's lead characters Nishi is marked by his silence. He rarely speaks and his face is nearly expressionless. This is not, however, a film lacking in emotion. On two occasions when Nishi returns home he is confronted by items that evoke the memory of his dead daughter; one a child's tricycle which he calmly moves out of the way and the other a small pair of shoes which he stares at for a few seconds before moving upstairs.

Although his reactions are minimal the audience is left to ponder the depth of feeling that is taking place beneath his passive exterior. In his relations with his wife there are no dramatic declarations of love and devotion but their tremendous care for each other is shown in dozens of small details. When Nishi brings home some sweet treats we see a family ritual as she takes his cake away from him and presents him with the strawberry from the top of hers. As they travel around Japan together we see several scenes that evoke the idea of the unarticulated love they hold for each other; such as when his wife holds up cards for him to guess. She is initially amazed by his ability to guess each card since unbeknown to her he can see the cards in the rear-view mirror. Finally figuring it out she holds up something else; 'crunchy chocolate' he says, laughing. Just because she wishes to see the snow they drive a considerable distance and when she gets stuck in a snow drift he rushes in panic to her aid. Nishi sends money and paint to Horibe as well as to Tanaka's young widow. Although he never voices his feelings it is clear that he desires to take care of and support those he loves. When Nishi's wife says thank you to him on the beach before they commit suicide, we are aware that this is for the many years of happiness they have clearly enjoyed.

On one level Nishi is the very image of a gentle man; however, throughout the film we are aware that he is able to suddenly commit acts of great violence. Nakamura states that although Horibe was the more violent, when Nishi was set loose he was the more frightening. We see him stab a man in the eye with a chopstick, kick another in the face and shoot several more. When a random stranger insults his wife on the beach as she waters a bunch of dead flowers, Nishi brutally beats him and nearly drowns him. When violence occurs in *Hana-bi* it is quick and brutal, such as when the *yakuza* shoot a businessman who refuses to pay. The film does not linger or focus on the actions but, instead, Kitano the director pulls us away from the violent acts. When Nishi and his wife commit suicide we only hear the shots and visions of the sky and sea followed by a return to a child's face staring in shock.

The final scene of Nishi and his wife playing with a child is marked with particular poignancy since we are aware that the couple have lost their own daughter. The binary of family versus loneliness is a constant presence in *Hana-bi*, and we see many fractured family units throughout the film. Nishi and his wife have lost a child, Horibe's wife and child leave him when he is crippled and he proceeds to paint images of family groups enjoying firework displays. For Horibe his painting becomes a release for his feelings of loneliness and isolation. He comments that although Nishi's wife is dying, perhaps Nishi is in a happier situation than him. Tanaka's young widow is struggling to cope, raising her son without his father. The film offers no solution to their grief but there is the indication that this is part of the 'circle of life' that all people are engaged in. The focus on death also, by extension, offers a vision of life. *Hana* is combined with *bi* to produce the two poles of existence. Flowers, which emerge throughout the film, illustrate a blending of nature and life with this narrative of death. Horibe paints images of animals with flower heads and this seems to speak to the notion that all living creatures are part of an ebb and flow of existence. As with many of Kitano's other works, the sea plays an important part: Horibe paints by the sea shore, and it is on the beach front where Nishi and his wife will die. The sea acts as a space of circularity; a place to return to, the site often of death and of conclusion. Just before he attempts to commit suicide we see Horibe sitting on the beach with the waves lapping against his wheelchair. His failure to kill himself seems to inspire him in his art and although death seemed an appealing option, unlike Nishi, Horibe chooses to go on living. One painting that the film focuses on is a bright snow scene with the word 'suicide' written across it in red paint. Later in the film Horibe throws paint across the words as a symbol of his desire to choose life. We see that inside the film the balance between death and destruction and life and living is maintained.

As with all films that contain Kitano in the lead role, the notion of his star persona enters into the discussion. Nishi is one in a long line of violent, silent men that Kitano has presented in his films. The idea that Kitano himself is a violent man was referenced in the previous chapter and characters such as Nishi only enhance this image of him. As with other films, the legacy of Kitano's comedy past is shown in small humorous incidents throughout the film, such as when Nishi and his fake police car are waved down by an irate civilian. The car is, of course, an old taxi and, as all Japanese taxis have automatic doors, Nishi merely activates his to knock the man down. When Nishi tries to light a firework for his wife to enjoy, it misfires and knocks him over in a moment of pure slapstick. The paintings throughout the film are all by Kitano himself and reference once more the notion of his star persona and the interaction with the filmic process. One painting of a group of gangsters is seen on the wall of the *yakuza* meeting place, and the camera returns to it a couple of times placing an 'element' of Kitano in every scene. The film opens with the paintings that we will later see Horibe 'paint'. Thus the film becomes infused with the idea that this is a 'Kitano' film through and through.

Hana-bi achieved tremendous success on the international stage with 21 awards and six nominations from film festivals and competitions, and it confirmed Kitano's place as one of the leading Japanese filmmakers in the eyes of the global audience. The film is violent and often sad, but it also offers a sense of the love and care that can exist even in death. As David Kehr states:

> Ozu and the other great Japanese classicists concerned themselves with the sad
> acceptance of the world full of pain and disappointment; in the 1960s, Oshima
> and Imamura arrived at an angry rejection of a world now ruled by violence and
> horror. Kitano, the great equilibrist, balances these two traditions; in *Hana-Bi*, his
> characters achieve a furious peace. (1998)

This notion of 'furious peace' perhaps summarises the entire film as Kitano creates an exposition of sadness, violence and anger amidst an often beautiful, funny and musing on the nature of life and death. The vibrant and dynamic figure of Kitano himself infuses the whole work and renders *Hana-bi* one of the most representative works of his filmmaking career to date.

Twisted Histories: Park Chan-wook and the Legacy of Personal Trauma

The purpose of waiting
Does not have to be reunion.
If my heart is heavy.
So be it.
A distant smile flies
As I hold my shoulders back
Against the wind.
Where can they be?
Those days of wandering
In search of wandering
In search of part of myself.
If that part existed
From the moment I was born,
I want to meet it now.
(Excerpt from *Standing Alone* by So Chong-yun, 1988)

In the last decade very few Korean film directors have made such an impact on the international scene as Park Chan-wook, and the key to his fame is perhaps summed up in one film title: *Oldboy* (2003). Although his previous works *JSA* (*Gongdong gyeongbi guyeok JSA*, 2000) and *Sympathy for Mr Vengeance* (*Boksuneun naui geot*, 2002), did well on both national and international levels it was *Oldboy*'s macabre, violent and highly transgressive narrative that saw Park become one of the most well-known and popular South Korean directors on the international circuit.

Park in many ways personifies what has come to be known as the Korean New Wave. Although the term 'New Wave' is something that has been applied to several other filmmaking groups across a variety of time periods (including the other 'new' Korean wave that took place in the 1980s), this 'New Wave' can be seen to emerge from 1997 onwards. This new has presented to the world a series of films that have had domestic and international success. Films such as *The Ginko Bed* (*Eunhaengnamoo chimdae*, 1996, Kang Je-gyu), *Christmas in August* (*Palwolui Christmas*, 1998, Hur Jin-ho), *Attack the Gas Station* (*Juyuso seubgyuksageun*, 1999, Kim Sang-jin), *My Wife is a Gangster* (*Jopog Manura*, 2001, Cho Jin-gyu) and *Family* (*Ga-jok*, 2004, Lee Jeong-cheol), have all been part of the development of a strong and successful South Korean cinematic moment. Although the films and directors have been very varied in their approaches there have been several common elements that have marked this period of South Korean cinema. These include a level of technical sophistication that has allowed them to compete with Hollywood productions and a tremendous creativity, combined with the desire and courage to take risks with and explore film genres, styles, narratives and aesthetics.

Born in 1963 Park was part of the generation who grew up in post-partition Korea. A child through the turbulent 1970s, Park lived in Seoul and eventually decided to study philosophy at Sogang University, one of the leading liberal arts colleges in Seoul. After graduation from University, Park began working as a director's assistant, most notably for Kwak Jae-young who would later go on to direct the hugely popular *My Sassy Girl* (*Yeopgijeogin Geunyeo*, 2001).

Park had an inauspicious start to his filmmaking career; his first film, *The Moon is What the Sun Dreams of* (*Dal-eun … haega kkuneun kkum*, 1992), was a box office and critical failure. It's attempt to challenge and distort the gangster genre received resoundingly negative reviews and for a few years after the release he instead concentrated on becoming a film critic. He became a regular contributor to film magazines and published a collected edition of film reviews, entitled *Videodrome: The Discreet Charm of Watching Films* in 1996. In this he presented his critical analysis of a variety of films from *Le Mepris* (1963, Jean-Luc Godard) to *Alien 3* (1993, David Fincher). In *Videodrome* Park offered controversial admiration for the master of screen violence, Sam Peckinpah, and his approach to storytelling can be seen as an influence in Parks works, especially in the way that violence becomes ingrained in all layers of society (something that will be examined below). Despite some critical appreciation of his film-reviewing skills, his second feature film, *Threesome* (1997), a black comedy road movie, received similar negative responses to his debut film. One critic dubbed it 'the impossible dream of a cinephile' (Gu 1997: 135), relating his comments not only to Park's standing as a critic but also with negative regard to the film's over-stylisation.

During this time, however, and despite his directorial failures, Park became closely acquainted with producer/director Lee Joon-ik, founder of Cineworld, a leading production and film import company and more recently, director of *The King and the Clown* (*Wang-ui namja*, 2005). His relationship with Lee saw him write the colonial-era adventure film *The Anarchists* (2000, Yu Yong-sik), a co-production with a Chinese film company, a trend that is becoming more common in South Korean cinema as a method of gaining finance and opening up the possibility of wider East Asian markets. Park was even offered the director's chair for the film but he declined, deciding instead to direct *Joint Security Area* or *JSA*. This was to prove a wise decision as *The Anarchists* performed poorly and *JSA* achieved phenomenal box office and critical success for Park.

Released in 2000 *JSA* came one year after the massive South Korean action blockbuster *Shiri* (1999). Kang Je-gyu's tale of undercover North Korean agents, betrayed love and high-tech weaponry had broken box office records with 2.5 million admissions in Seoul alone (breaking the record set by Im Kwon-teak's *Sopyonje*). The film dealt directly with the controversial question of Korean re-unification but offered the action aesthetics of Hollywood films such as *Lethal Weapon* (1987, Richard Donner) or *Die Hard* (1988, John McTiernan). *Shiri* was notable for another reason – one directly related to finance. For many decades the Korean film industry had been dominated by the large conglomerates known as *chaebals*. These giant corporations came into existence during the 1980s and had continued to be major investors in films throughout the 1990s. These conglomerates sought to produce films with a constant eye on the television, cable and DVD markets and as such had developed wide-reaching systems for production and distribution on a national and global scale. Companies such as Daewoo, Samsung and LG all produced and distributed films and in the early 1990s over three-quarters of all South Korean film distribution was controlled by the *chaebals* (see Paquet 2005); between 1992 and 1995 Samsung alone produced 22 feature films (see Davis 2008: 14). Films were now being made for purely commercial benefit and attention focused on the best way to maximise profits through the use of well-known actors, popular and recognisable genres together with the high production values that aimed to compete with American imports. *Shiri* had not benefited from the government film quotas or subsidies, and had been targeted as a Korean blockbuster – a role it filled admirably. The aesthetics are pure Hollywood but the narrative and the use of Korean reunification as the central story made it a unique addition to the action genre. In this way '*Shiri* conforms to the notion of high concept; a recognisable, digestible idea that can be extended and intensified by marketing formulas' (Davis 2008: 16).

In 1997 a financial crisis hit Asia and as the giant *chaebals* faltered, film needed to turn to a new source of funding, and venture capital stepped in. Unlike the *chaebals* venture capital was not so interested in video and cable rights; rather, what was wanted was high returns from theatrical runs (see Davis 2008: 17). This meant that quantity would be key (*chaebals* had been limited in production numbers) and as a result venture capital offered many more opportunities for young and first-time directors to produce work in order to meet the numbers of films desired. This venture capital funding was thus a key element in the development of the Korean New Wave as companies were willing to invest in films that did not conform to conservative filmic traditions. Films that spoke to popular teenage culture began to be made as investors knew that box office success would follow by appealing to this comparatively time-rich generation and its disposable income.

Unique film financing projects, such as 'netizen' funds where anyone with internet access can invest in future productions, has encouraged a variety of films that would not have gained finance through more traditional means. A key example of the success of 'netizen' funds was the gangster film *Friend* (*Chingoo*, 2001, Kwak Kyung-taek) that raised over US$90,000 from 190 online investors in one minute (see Pacquet 2002). Success of films such as *Shiri* drew interest from overseas investors and distributors helping to develop the popularity of South Korean films in territories such as Japan, China and Hong Kong.

JSA was also a success story of venture capital funding. It broke *Shiri*'s box office record and propelled Park into the spotlight. It achieved huge national and global success, winning the Best Film at the Blue Dragon Film Awards; Jury Prize, Audience Price and Best Actor Prize (Song Kang-ho) at Festival du Film Asiatique de Deauville, the Blue Ribbon award for Best Foreign Film (Japan) and the Korean 38th Grand Bell award for Best Film, Actor, Sound and Art Direction.

Like *Shiri*, *JSA* offered a narrative that focused on the tensions between North and South Korea, personified by a group of soldiers who form an unlikely friendship across the de-militarised zone between the two countries.

When an incident occurs that results in the deaths of both North and South Korean soldiers, a UN representative, Sophie-Jean, is called in to investigate. She is ethnically Korean but her father fled North Korea after the Korean War and relocated to Switzerland, and she struggles to understand the tensions that continue to imbue her home nation. Throughout all of his films it is the tensions that exist in all aspects of South Korean society that Park is interested in exploring. With *JSA* it is the legacy of Korean partitioning, whilst *Sympathy for Mr Vengeance* examines the negative, dark side to South Korean economic growth and the downturn in 1997. *Oldboy* offers a dark tale of one man's quest for a terrible revenge for an inadvertent 'slip of the tongue' in high school. *Sympathy for Lady Vengeance* questions the notion of vengeance and the ability and desire to torture and kill that Park sees all people as having the potential for. *I'm a Cyborg and That's OK* (*Saibogujiman kwenchana*, 2006), in many ways the least violent of Park's films, still manages to interrogate the notion of 'normality' and the role of the individual in a collective social group.

The questioning of boundaries, either physical or mental, is key in Park´s films. In *Sympathy for Mr Vengeance* the central protagonist is a deaf mute, constantly reminded with his physical disabilities which make him unable to communicate with the outside world. Park shows us several scenes from his point of view, as people mouth words and yell at him despite the fact it is clear he cannot hear them. He is unable to communicate and engage with the wider society and is restricted in his interactions to a few people (primarily those who know sign language). He is rendered separate from the world around him and his attempts to engage usually end badly for him. His girlfriend is another character separated from the rest of society; although unlike her boyfriend she has no physical reason to be separate from those that surround her, she chooses to put herself in opposition to mainstream culture and society. She works for a 1980s-style anarchist group in the hope that she will be able to disrupt the social space through her acts of minor terrorism. She openly transgresses various social codes and is the primary instigator behind the kidnap in the film. We also discover she had pretended to be deaf for several years in order to attend a local deaf school. In *Oldboy* Oh Dae-su is kidnapped and forced to spend sixteen years in one room. In *Sympathy for Lady Vengeance* the heroine Lee Guem-ja spends a large portion of her life in jail for a crime she did not commit. In jail she meets a series of people, from a woman who has killed and eaten her husband and his mistress, to an armed robber and a prostitute, for all of whom transgression of social and legal boundaries has resulted in their incarceration. The protagonists in *I'm a Cyborg...* are restrained inside the mental institute. They are not only constrained by physical boundaries but their respective mental states render them unable them to function in a wider social space without danger to themselves or others. In *Thirst* (2009) the various characters are constrained in a variety of religious, social, physical and linguistical ways. The priest, Sang-hyun, is unable to fulfil his vampiric desires due to his religious and moral convictions, his lover Tae-ju is trapped in a marriage with a husband and a mother-in-law – Lady Ra – she despises, who will later be physically restrained by a stroke, and Tae-ju's Filipino friend Evelyn is trapped by her inability to speak Korean. For Park the consideration of what is 'normal' is thus vigorously debated in his films as he presents how people react in a variety of extreme situations; everyday life in South Korea can suddenly be transformed by a seemingly harmless event, and ruptures or hidden tensions can suddenly be brought into the open.

JSA critiques the division of Korea. As the soldiers meet secretly to drink, play games and swap stories, the differences as well as the similarities between the two sides are made clear. Park continually frames shots throughout the film with something crossing the centre of the screen: a tree, a flag pole or a wall. This constant dividing of the screen subtly references the national division that is propelling the narrative. The history between North and South had taken a turn for the better in 1997 with the implementation in South Korea of the so-called 'Sunshine' policy. This was one that sought to embrace North Korea rather than isolating it further. There was a surge of interest in South Korea about their northern neighbours and several high-level 'cultural exchanges' took place, as well as a tremendous increase in the number of South Korean citizens visiting North Korea (see Kim 2007: 224). In 2000 the government's 'White Paper on Unification' concluded that social and cultural exchanges between North and South Korea 'contributed to the dissolution of the cultural alienation between the people of the two Koreas due to the realities of division and restored the homogeneity of our nation' (Kim 2001: 61). This is central to the question of re-unification: the nation must overcome cultural and ideological differences to become one. In *JSA* the reunification is not shown as simply a matter of recognising the 'other' as the same as you. The ideological and cultural differences between the soldiers are continually maintained. In one striking scene South Korean soldier Li hands North Korean soldier Oh a piece of chocolate cake. When Oh marvels at the fine taste and questions why the North cannot produce cake to this standard, Li's joke that Oh could have limitless delights if he defects to the South provokes a harsh response: Oh spits the cake out and informs Li that rather than defect, his dream is to help develop the North Korean nation so that they can make a chocolate cake tastier than the South's. The ideological divisions between the two will not be so easily overcome. Oh is presented as a man who is able to transgress official lines (the soldiers meet when Oh rescues Li from a landmine that he has accidentally stepped on whilst on patrol on the DMZ) but still maintains the state ideology of the North, and refuses unification if it means the total eradication of the North Korean state that he is passionately loyal to. He wishes to become *Korean* not South Korean.

Unification can only take place with the integration of North and South into a new state of Korea. This integration is still a long way off as the scene when Li and Nam practice firing at cutout North Korean soldiers whilst whispering about their new North Korean friends illustrates. They are forced to conduct their friendship under the constant threat of violence from both sides of the barrier. It is, however, not just governmental policy that divides them. The South Korean assumption that all North Koreans would wish to join their economic prosperity is seen as arrogantly flawed, and the soldiers' rigid training in 'hatred of the enemy' eventually results in the death of all four friends. When another North Korean soldier discovers them drinking, Li and Nam automatically point their guns at him; trained from birth to fear the North Korean state they react on impulse. The resulting fight leaves all dead, except for Li who will later commit suicide due to his subsequent guilt. The soldiers had been taught to see their North Korean counterparts as nothing more than wooden targets, but in the shooting of these new friends they come to realise that the 'targets' are as human as they are, and this realisation destroys Li.

The boundaries that the soldiers have been forced to maintain for so many years have become second nature and will not be so easy to destroy. In one part of the film an American tourist's hat had blown into North Korea whilst she was on one of the official tours of the DMZ. Oh stoops to pick it up and hands it back to the South Korean border guard and then breaks into a full smile for the camera. Adrien Gombeaud argues that this smile is meant for the South Korean nation, and 'from his side of the screen, the North Korean soldier seems to tell us

"I saw you'" (2006: 239). Thus, a visual border is created between the viewer and the fiction. The viewer becomes caught up in the divisions on the screen, and, like the soldiers, cannot see past the demarcations between North and South. At the end of the film, the still of Oh handing back the cap is enlarged and we see all four soldiers entering into the frame. The camera moves around, offering images of the now-dead soldiers, each participating in military duties but aware that they have made a vital link to the other side. Although they are still divided, we are made aware that the possibility of unity had been opened up but then brutally destroyed. Its failure was a result of historical, social and military issues and the past continues to inform the present, and unless it is properly resolved the individual will continue to suffer.

The idea of borders and boundaries continues in Park's next feature, the acclaimed *Sympathy for Mr Vengeance*. After the popular success of *JSA*, many people expected a similar type of film, but they were to be disappointed. The bright visuals and action sequences of *JSA* were replaced by a dark, melancholy and disturbing image of contemporary South Korea. Park summarises the film's aesthetics thus: 'There is almost no music and little dialogue or camera movement. There is not a lot of violence but the story and atmosphere are pretty brutal' (in Park 2007: 28).The film's brutality is undeniable: rape, murder, illegal organ trafficking and torture all feature in the story of a kidnapping gone wrong. A deaf-mute factory worker, Ryu, is struggling to find the money for his sister's kidney operation. He sells a kidney to an illegal trafficker but when they double-cross him and leave him with no money and only one kidney, he and his girlfriend kidnap the young daughter of a wealthy business man. When the daughter accidentally drowns (Ryu cannot hear her screams when she falls in the river) her father, Park Dong-jin, takes terrible vengeance on the young couple.

Throughout *Sympathy for Mr Vengeance* the camera is placed in a variety of long shots that give us a birds-eye view of the action. Outside Ryu's girlfriend's apartment after she has been murdered, the camera is placed so that we can see the police going in and out, and in the corner of the frame we can just see the grieving Ryu. When Park Dong-jin is waiting to capture Ryu, the camera is positioned so that we have a CCTV-like image of the events. This use of the camera distances the audience from the characters and allows us to get an overview of the action. This is needed since we are not expected to align ourselves with any particular person. Although initially we associate ourselves with Ryu, we are then forced to experience the sorrow of the father and his search for vengeance.

There is not one character that we can empathise with. In the same way as the smile of the North Korean soldier for the camera drew the audience into *JSA*, the distancing effect of the camera in *Sympathy for Mr Vengeance* seeks to force the audience to question relationships to the images and actions being shown. We see the motives and then we witness the actions but this is not a story that will offer a narrative of redemption and the audience is left to observe the spiral of violence without any hope of intervention. Park's use of the camera as a method of distanciation forces the audience to take a critical stance to the events taking place with regard to social and cultural issues, such as class division and the use of violence as a social tool that the film acknowledges.

Many of Park's films reference economic and class divisions that are still ingrained in South Korean society. Ryu works long hours in a thankless factory job and still cannot afford medical care. He has not benefited from the economic boom of the 1980s and early 1990s, and the economic crash of 1997 has left him even more vulnerable as he is then made redundant. When he takes out a loan he is then conned by illegal organ traffickers and left with no money and only one kidney wandering naked on the street. The film takes us to slums where the poor unemployed reside. These are the victims of the economic downturn and we see one family even committing group suicide as a result of the father losing his job. Oh Dea-su in *Oldboy* is imprisoned by a very wealthy man whose money will buy him anything he wants. The killer in *Lady Vengeance* is an English teacher who preys on rich families. He kills the children and then still manages to exact a ransom from the distraught parents. His job refers to the recent trend in South Korea to see English-language competency as 'closely linked to occupational success and social mobility' (Koo 2007: 13). The presence of children at a private English class indicates the socio-economic status of the families involved, and also references the processes of globalisation that South Korean society is going though. English is seen as the main international language and Park's films feature several characters from Switzerland (Sophie-Jean, Lee Geum-ja's daughter's adopted parents come from Switzerland and it is to Switzerland that Oh Dae-su is told his daughter has moved). The use of Switzerland in his films acts as a constant presence of the Korean external 'other' but unlike in work of other directors (arguably such as Im Kwon-taek) the 'other' is not responsible for the actions of the individuals in Park's films. For Park, the presence of the 'other' is not to offer a scapegoat but rather to use the notion that the outsider can offer an insight into a collective group from an external position. Thus Sophie-Jean is the one to evaluate the real story of the shooting in *JSA*, the actions of outsider Ryu spark the narrative of *Sympathy for Mr Vengeance* and the inmates of the asylum in *I'm a Cyborg…* reveal many of the tensions in modern society. With relation to the notion of the individual's relationship to the wider group Park states that:

> People often tend to look for reasons outside of themselves when things go wrong. They blame it on society, or think God has abandoned them. And the more they think this way, their hatred expands. (Quoted in Kim 2007: 31)

This hatred is transformed into the violent actions that we see throughout Park's work as graphic violence is a common theme in his films. Even *I'm a Cyborg…* contains fantasy sequences of the nursing staff in the mental institute being brutally gunned down. Park goes on to state that:

> The moment they set their foot on the evil side, their anger aggravates, because they remind themselves why they had to become evil. I wanted to depict that pace of violence. (Ibid.).

The 'pace of violence' in Park's films goes from one extreme to the other. We experience slow torture and death alongside quick dramatic shoot-outs. For Park the concentration is on pain and fear, 'the fear just before an act of violence and the pain after, this applies to the perpetrator as well as the victim' (Park quoted in Baruma 2006). This interplay between violence and the emotional state of the individual is a constant presence in his films and is directly related to Park's own experiences.

The 1980s, the decade of Park's university education, saw many student demonstrations and extreme levels of state violence (as discussed above). Unlike many of his contemporaries however, Park, did not engage with the tumultuous and very dangerous events, something that he feels has left him with a sense of guilt. He made the comment that since the 1980s 'young people have fallen into two distinct groups. Those who participated actively are proud of their sacrifices. They changed society but they also feel deprived because they were unable to enjoy their youth. Then there are the others, who feel guilty for not having taken part. We enjoy our freedoms without having done anything to earn them. One of the worst legacies of military dictatorship is that it polarized a whole generation' (in Baruma 2006).

The legacy that violent events have on an individual would be central to the vengeance trilogy. In *Sympathy for Mr Vengeance* the poverty of one family leads to a spiral of murder and revenge. In *Oldboy* (which will be examined in greater depth in the film analysis section tht follows) a casual comment leads to a narrative trajectory that results in kidnap, murder, mutilation and incest. In *Sympathy for Lady Vengeance* Lee Geum-ja is imprisoned for the brutal murder of a child that she did not commit. On her release, together with help from her prison friends, she will track down, capture and punish the man responsible. The actual killer is found to be a serial murderer of children and in a highly disturbing scene the family of the murdered children is shown a video of the killer brutally and mercilessly dispatching their children. We are shown how the actions of this one man has affected whole families and, when Lee Geum-ja invites them to take revenge on the living body of their children's killer, we are shown how years of anger and pain are repressed and then brutally unleashed.

Children are a motif that reoccurs throughout Park's works but they are rarely symbols of joy. In *Sympathy for Mr Vengeance* the drowned daughter reappears to her distraught father but rather than comforting him this small glimpse of her makes him determined to exact his violent revenge. A child is the method through which a terrible retribution will be conducted in *Oldboy* as Oh Dae-su unknowingly commits incest with his grown-up daughter. In *Three Extremes* the film director has to murder a small boy, the kidnapper's son, in order to save his wife. Lee Geum-ja is drawn into the killer's life when she becomes pregnant as a teenager and goes to him for help. His kidnapping of her baby will lead to her dramatic confession to the murder of the boy. Children in *Lady Vengeance* are brutally murdered and their favourite small good-luck charms are found on the key ring of the man who killed them (their school teacher). These children's deaths will lead their parents to commit horrifically violent acts on the body of the man responsible, thereby opening up the question of the individual's right to pursue their own versions of justice. Lee Geum-ja gives the parents the option to take the murderer to the police or killing him himself. They choose to take justice literally into their own hands.

In *Sympathy for Mr Vengeance* Park Dong-jin refuses to rely on the police and instead hires a private investigator so that when Ryu is caught Park can gain his revenge. The interplay between justice and revenge in Park's films is complicated. The police and the law courts are presented as ineffectual and unable to protect citizens, but as the brutal death of Park Dong-jin and the despair of Oh Dae-su and Lee Geum-ja illustrate, vengeance does not offer complete satisfaction. The audience is left to draw its own conclusions about the legitimacy of the actions of these individuals. Park refuses to offer a normative 'moral' narrative but rather creates situations where the worst of humanity can be shown and we are left to deal with the consequences of violence rather than being given any possibility of redemption.

In the presentation of this violence the use of film and photography as a method of communication is something that is seen throughout Park's work. In *JSA* the film concludes on a still photograph, representing exactly the ironic and traumatic situation that the soldiers and, by extension, the states of North and South Korea have found themselves in. A photo album becomes the method through which Oh Dae-su becomes aware of his tragic actions. Lee Geum-ja becomes a notorious celebrity when, in an effort to convince a police officer it was she who killed the boy, she re-enacts the murder in front of TV crews. After showing them how she smothered the boy, she rips off the mask that has been hiding her features and stares directly at the camera. This engagement with the camera is repeated at the end of the film when, after she has committed her vengeance, the camera focuses on her smiling face and freezes as the image slowly fades. These two scenes offer the result of her narrative of revenge. From innocent victim, Lee Geum-ja has transformed herself into a woman who will stop at nothing to gain her revenge. The blood-red eyeshadow that we see her don as soon as she leaves prison comes to represent the physical manifestation of her decision to enact her vengeance. In the first scene after the death of her nemesis, she symbolically wipes away the makeup and once this is gone she is left to deal with the emotional aftermath of her actions. The film has charted her development as the angel of vengeance but at the end, as she sobbingly embraces her daughter, we are left undecided as to how Lee Geum-ja will survive now that the desire for vengeance which has kept her going for sixteen long years has been fulfilled.

Fractured and highly disturbed individuals are a constant presence in Park's work. Even in *I'm a Cyborg...* the protagonists are all mentally disturbed, harbouring violent fantasies about destroying all of mankind. In *Thirst* the kind and caring priest is transformed into a vampire and a murderer. The woman he loves (who he thinks is an abused and uncared-for wife) is a highly manipulative and amoral killer with little regard for human life, despite her innocent appearance.

Lee Geum-ja in *Lady Vengeance* is alternatively an angel and a killer. During her impassioned (and, we learn, fake) testimony in the prison church we see flashbacks of her 'good' acts. As the film will later show, these good acts were also seeped in violence: the prisoner who she is feeding in hospital is sick since Lee Geum-ja is slowly poisoning her; a session when she is seen helping a fellow prisoner to read is actually a discussion about how to commit the perfect crime; the prisoner who she comforts will become a pawn in her desire to claim her vengeance; her act of donating a kidney to another prison friend is a kind act but it also means that the recipient feels honour-bound to help Lee Geum-ja achieve her aims; and, even when she seemed to be praying we realise that she was fantasising about her vengeance. Park dong-Jin in *Sympathy for Mr Vengeance* is seen as a decent hardworking man and loving father but he is also capable of brutally electrocuting a young woman and slashing Ryu's Achilles tendons, leaving him to drown. The lead character in *I'm a Cyborg...* almost starves herself to death under the mistaken belief that she is a robot and therefore cannot digest food. Another inmate is convinced that he is a master thief and can even steal Thursday (as well as harbouring the deep fear that he is going to transform into a dot). All these figures act as a method of social critique, their extreme natures opening up debates about dominant concepts of normality and how the individual fits into wider societal structures.

Our ideas about good and evil are shattered in the presentation of characters who are both decent and diabolical, simultaneously. In *Thirst* we are shown that freedom and love can quickly lead to chaos and obsession. As the two vampires struggle with their innate differences about the value of human life, the notion of 'happily ever after' is transformed into mutual disintegration and – literally, when they go into the sun – death. Our initial impressions of the characters in Park's films are quickly shattered as we realise that nothing is what it seems. In *I'm a Cyborg...* our initial reaction to seeing the inmates as clearly 'mad' is gradually assessed throughout the film as it is made clear that, although they have some strange beliefs, they are no more 'mad' than those that society has deemed 'normal'. This is illustrated in the scene where the female protagonist is presented with a 'rice-converter' by her loving friend. He informs her that that this will help a cyborg digest food and once she has been 'fitted' with the device, we see her take her first mouthful of rice. On one level it is made quite clear that she is only a woman that is suffering from mental disturbance that makes her genuinely believe that she is a robot. In his use of narrative and images, however, such as the x-ray vision of the rice-converter working happily away inside the 'cyborg', Park manages to disrupt this belief and forces the audience to question their concept of the real.

In terms of realism it is ironic that one of the criticisms originally levelled at Park's work was his over-stylisation, since this is something that is now applauded and has become one of the most noted element of his films. One writer claims that Park's films are rooted in an East Asian tradition that includes 'Manga, Anime, and Kung-fu films but also computer games that have spread around the world from Tokyo to Seoul' (Buruma 2006). The vivid colours of Anime can be seen in the make-up that Lee Geum-ja wears on her release, the green hair of Ryu and the vivid colours in *I'm a Cyborg*....

In his section of *Three Extremes* we are shown a highly stylised set with a woman forced into position at a piano by dozens of wires that cross the entire room. The title sequences of *Lady Vengeance* are pure graphic art with patterns being drawn in red and black on a white background, and in a special edition box set released in the UK, one of the selling features was a poster image of Lee Geum-ja's highly stylised gun blueprint. Park's visuals contribute to a hyper-reality that marks his work. The narratives that he offers the audience are in themselves highly hyperbolic and the visuals serve to illustrate the stories further. The empty apartments that dominate *Sympathy for Mr Vengeance* act as a symbol of the desolation and despair that marks many of the characters lives. Lee Geum-ja's apartment is patterned by vivid red stripes and Oh Dae-su's prison cell is covered in vibrant patterned wallpaper offering a vision of the characters inner turmoil. The colour white is utilised in *Lady Vengeance* as a metaphor for purity and forgiveness. At the film's outset Lee Geum-Ja refuses the white tofu offered her but at the conclusion she accepts white icing from her small daughter, a sign of her desire to gain forgiveness for her actions. In *JSA* the soldiers' uniforms act as a constant reminder of the political situation that is controlling their actions. Even when they are all seated all together enjoying each others' company, their uniforms illustrate the divisions that lie between them.

Park is well-versed in film theory and his knowledge of a variety of genres, styles and cinematic techniques have allowed him to produce films that are remarkable in their refusal to be constrained by normative categorisation. He states that for him realism is something that he wishes to avoid and the vivid colours, costumes and narratives that he creates for the audience offer an intense world where normative narratives are rejected since, for Park, normative narratives have no part to play in the contemporary world:

> As a Korean director making a film in the early twenty-first century, it's hard to adopt the cinematic vision of classic Hollywood directors who have shown a world of perfect harmony and subtlety through their films. It seems disengaging to pursue these visions now. It doesn't suit the conditions of the world that we are living in now, or the cataclysmic events, the struggles and the anger suffered by people today. (Quoted in Kim 2007: 35)

Park therefore focuses on presenting a unique style that, for him, represents the modern South Korean age: vibrant, dynamic, aggressive, but with a visual beauty and wry dark humour. He maintains a position in the canon of alternative 'artistic' directors (seen in his presence at film festivals worldwide) with the ability to produce films that can achieve blockbuster status. His presence on the Tartan Asia Extreme film list combined with success at Cannes help promote him as a director of films which operate on both a critical and a populist level. In this way Park's films appeal to a wide range of audiences from the artistic high-brow to the conventional action or horror fan. In South Korea, Park's success at Cannes has been a matter of national celebration.

In March 2013, Park's first English-language film, the psychological thriller *Stoker*, was released internationally. Starring Nicole Kidman and Mia Wasikowska, the film received generally positive responses from audiences worldwide and clearly demonstrates that Park is becoming a truly global player who supersedes the boundaries of 'national' cinema.

The reason for his success over others is perhaps related to his ability to defy easy classification. The themes that are seen in Park Chan-wook's work are certainly similar to those seen in those of other filmmakers, but what sets him apart is the vibrant, dynamic and highly accessible style that he employs. Whilst his films have the violence of Kim Ki-duk's, the emotional sensitivity of Lee Chang-dong's and the grasp of Korean history that we can see in Im Kwon-taek's, his films are unique in their blend of popular culture, high production values and box office success.

Film Analysis

OLDBOY

올드보이
Oldeuboi

2003

Director

Park Chan-wook

Cast

Choi Min-Sik (Oh Dae-su), Kang Hye-jeong (Mido), Yu Ji-tae (Lee Woo-jin), Yun Jin-seo (Lee Soo-ah), Ji Dae-han (No Joo-Hwan [Internet Café owner]), Oh Dal-su (Prison Owner)

International Film Awards

2004 Grand Prix Jury Award, Cannes Film Festival

2004 Nominated Palme d'Or, Cannes Film Festival

2004 Grand Bell Award: Best Director

2004 Grand Bell Award: Best Actor, Choi Min-sik

2004 Grand Bell Award: Best Editor, Kim Sang-beom

2004 Grand Bell Award: Best Illumination, Park Hyun-won

2004 Grand Bell Award: Best Music, Jo Yeong-wook

2004 Best Director, Asia Pacific Film Festival

2004 Best Actor, Choi Min-sik, Asian Pacific Film Festival

2004 Maria Award (Best Film), Festival Internacional de Cinema de Catalunya

2004 José Luis Guarner Award (Critics' Best Film), Festival Internacional de Cinema de Catalunya

Plot Summary

Oh Dae-su is mysteriously kidnapped and held in isolation for fifteen years without human contact, and with no reason given for his incarceration. Via his television he discovers that his wife has been brutally murdered and the police believe that he is responsible. He is suddenly released and finds himself with money, designer clothes and a challenge to discover why he was imprisoned for so long. He is told he has five days, and a clue to the reason behind his imprisonment is that he talks too much. He meets a young woman called Mido who decides to help him and together they discover that his daughter has been adopted by a couple in Switzerland. Oh finds the building where he was imprisoned by tracking down the restaurant that provided the dumplings which he was fed each day whilst in prison. He attacks the prison, and removes all the teeth of the owner in an attempt to discover the cause of his misfortunes. After a fight with the prison owner's henchmen, Oh meets Lee Woo-jin, the man responsible for his imprisonment. Oh cannot torture Lee to find out his motivations as he has a remote control for his pacemaker that, if pressed, will kill him immediate. If Oh refuses to cooperate Lee will die and he will never know the reason behind his long imprisonment. The prison owner captures Mido and threatens to remove all of Oh's teeth but Lee intervenes and prevents this from taking place. After fleeing Mido's apartment, Oh and Mido have sex in a hotel room. Whilst they are sleeping, Lee leaves a box containing the prison owner's hand in their room. With help from his friend No Joo-hwan, who owns an internet café, and the clues left by Lee, Oh realises the reason for his imprisonment. As a teenager he saw Lee and his sister Lee Soo-ah committing incest, and started a rumour which led to her suicide. Oh convinces the prison owner to hide Mido as he is determined to enact his revenge and wants her to be safe. Oh goes to Lee's luxury apartment and is presented with a photo album which informs him that Mido is actually his daughter. To prevent Mido from being told the truth (the prison owner is secretly still working for Lee), Oh cuts out his tongue. After this Lee commits suicide. Mido is left unaware of the crime she and her father have committed. Oh goes to see the hypnotist that Lee had employed to help encourage Mido and Oh to fall in love. He convinces her to wipe his memories of the act of incest and the film ends with him and Mido embracing. The indication is that they will, however, continue their romantic relationship.

———

Laugh and the world laughs with you.
Weep and you weep alone.

Released in 2003, *Oldboy* is based on a graphic novel by Minegishi Nobuuaki and Tsuchiya Garon, and is the second film in what has come to be known as 'the vengeance trilogy' which had started with *Sympathy for Mr Vengeance*. The opening shot of *Oldboy* is of Oh Dae-sue's fist clutching a tie. As the camera pulls back we see him backlit by the sky and he informs the man, whom he is preventing from committing suicide, that he is going to tell him his story. This sudden and dramatic image sets the tone for the rest of this violent and highly transgressive film. The notion of violence and personal narrative are two of the main elements in *Oldboy* as Oh has to fight to discover the meaning behind what has happened to him.

From this dramatic opening the film then moves to a very drunk Oh sat in a police station. As we watch him fight with the police, we are introduced to a symbol that will return later in the film, a set of angel wings that he intends to give to his daughter for her birthday. Oh also presents to the police a picture of himself and his family. The image was actually taken from an earlier film staring actor Choi Min-sik, *Failen* (2002, Song Hae-song) that focused on a young woman returning to South Korea to search for her lost family after the death of her parents. This intertextual reference is a small hint at the traumas that will befall Oh. He is also going to lose his family and then find them again, but, compared to *Failen*, the situation will be very different and much more extreme.

The opening music and graphics introduce one of the key themes of the film – time. As Oh leaves the police station, the camera pans up to reveal a sign saying 'one way only'. As the film narrative unfolds we see that for Oh there is only one way; his life has been orchestrated according to the wishes of Lee Woo-jin and it is now only a matter of time before the whole truth will be revealed. As the screen fills with images of clocks, we are made aware that this film will be about time. The graphics present the title as a digital clock and throughout the film the digital image will present itself at regular intervals to notify the audience of the passing of time and the inevitable movement towards the terrible narrative conclusion.

As soon as Oh leaves the police station he is kidnapped and transported to the small room that will be his home for the next fifteen years. Park presents to us a room which is, on one level, not that unpleasant. It is warm and offers Oh a television, bed, novelty window view and regular meals and haircuts. This is not a prison cell in the 'traditional' sense but it very effectively constrains Oh. Not only does he receive no human contact but he is left to ponder all the actions that he has ever committed and wonder which one was so terrible that it deserved this extreme punishment. Throughout these many years, the passage of time is shown to us via the television which is Oh's only companion. The television shows images of the development of South Korea and the wider world; we see the rise of South Korean democracy, the death of Princess Diana, the Seoul World Cup, and also the murder of Oh's wife. He is now a wanted criminal who, ironically, is already in prison. It is after hearing of his wife's death via the television that Oh first sees the ants. The hundreds of creatures that swarm all over him present an image of horror but also one that emphasises his loneliness. Ants are a symbol of a large collective all working and living together; Oh is completely isolated from any form of human contact. This idea is emphasised later when Mido says that lonely people always see ants. The idea of a social group is denied to those that are totally on their own.

Throughout his time in the room we see Oh change from a fat drunk into a lean, fit and muscular fighter. There is an image on the wall informing him that 'laugh and the world laughs with you, weep and you weep alone', and this call for introspection and Oh gradually come to resemble each other. His wild hair and eyes – and his decision to smile in all situations, whether funny or tragic – directly reference this picture. He cannot commit suicide as he is always rescued in time and his escape attempt proves futile as he is released just before he completes it.

Oh's release sees the beginning of his quest for understanding. Released onto a rooftop he is presented with designer clothes, money, a mobile phone and a few days to discover the truth behind his imprisonment. It is here that he meets the man who is attempting suicide by jumping off the building with his small dog in his arms. We return to the opening image but this time we see a lot more of Oh's face and features. He relates his personal narrative to the man and then walks away. Oh has become the incarnation of vengeance; he is totally selfish, obsessed and uncaring to those around him. When the man commits suicide Oh does not even turn around and keeps on walking. It is shortly after his release that he meets Mido. He walks into her sushi restaurant, seemingly on a whim, although we later discover that it was all carefully orchestrated, and the first part of Lee Woo-jin's plan falls into place. Mido and Oh meet and begin to fall in love. His demand to eat something live can be see as his desire for something other than the sterile world of television. This, as yet, unresolved mystery, has consumed his life and in return his first desire seems to be to consume a life in return. The eating of a live octopus is the direct opposite to the last fifteen years of bland Chinese dumplings consumed in front of the television in that it is raw, uncooked and is devoid of links to the highly controlled environment in which he has resided over the years in captivity.

The time images and motifs continue throughout the film. The woman who informs Mido of Oh's daughter's fate works in a clock shop. She is literally surrounded by time and the irony is revealed at the end of the film when it emerges that Mido had, in essence, been enquiring about herself.

Vivaldi's *Four Seasons* is often heard playing in the background of scenes evoking the notion of time and years passing. For Lee, living in his empty penthouse surrounded by photography equipment, his life has been all about waiting. We know that he has aimed his entire life towards his long and complex revenge on Oh. For Lee the images of his sister on his wall have never dimmed and her suicide, and his perception of Oh as the cause of it, remains with him *esto perpetua*. Hints of the ending can be found throughout the film on repeat viewing.

Evergreen, Lee's internet moniker, turns out to be the English translation of the name of Oh's school where his 'offence' took place. Lee calls Oh the Count of Monte Cristo; the original emblem of vengeance, Edmond Dante was imprisoned for many years for a crime he did not commit and on release sought to punish those whom he perceived as having wronged him. Dante's vengeance becomes troubled by affairs of the heart, especially when he later encounters a son he never knew he had. Oh will later encounter a daughter who he thought was forever lost to him. Mido is called the Princess in the High Tower, evoking the fact that Lee has rigidly controlled her entire life, and that this has been in preparation for the trap in which Oh will fall. She may not have been in prison like her father but she has been similarly contained by Lee's twisted desires.

Oldboy's references to the notion of a fairytale narrative makes the ending all the more shocking. The princess has found her prince but she is now in a different type of tale – one that is in direct defiance of the incest taboo. Her prince is also simultaneously the monster who haunts this fairytale. Ergo, 'happily ever after' in *Oldboy* becomes a complex and controversial issue. Do we see their reconciliation as romantic or tragic? The ending of *Oldboy* is suitably ambivalent. The hypnotist has 'killed' the monster, the man who processes the knowledge of the act of incest, and Mido and Oh embrace. Yet questions are raised about whether Oh has really forgotten and repressed Mido's true identity. *Oldboy* cannot offer an uncomplicated happy ending in that for the romance to succeed the incest taboo will be broken. As the credits roll we see Oh and Mido standing in front of a huge snow-covered mountain. The image contains either hope for the future in the brightening horizon that is emerging from behind the mountain or, conversely, a hard rocky path. The audience is left to decipher the meaning for themselves. Their individual responses to the film are related to their own moral codes and any potential emotional investment that they have in the characters of Oh and Mido. Park does not provide a narrative conclusion that can sit comfortably with any viewer. Either one accepts an unhappy ending with Oh forever tortured and in emotional pain, or forgives the taboo of incest.

Visually the film is highly diverse. The opening scene in the police station and the flashbacks to the events that took place at the school have a realism to them that the rest of the film rejects with less stylised, more natural colours and lighting. The film is predominantly set in the urban space and we are offered a nightmarish vision of a city which is constructed to constrain and repress. Mido and Oh are always being watched and monitored by Lee. When in his prison cell Oh was monitored by video cameras, and later we realise that the photography-obsessed Lee continually captures him and Mido on film. Lee's penthouse apartment overlooks the city and provides the image of a panoptical prison. Like Michel Foucault's vision of total state power, Lee has been viewing and controlling all the actions that Oh and Mido have made for very many years. It was ironically Oh's small amount of vision that caused the events that take place. Staring through a gap in the window at Lee and his sister committing incest themselves, Oh's limited vision was the catalyst for Lee's desire to maintain total visual, and thereby physical control of Oh; and it is via the method of image he will present to Oh the 'crime' that he has committed. The photography album that presents the charting of Mido's development offers visual and irrefutable proof of the actions which have taken place.

The presentation of violence is similarly constructed around a specific point of view. When Oh breaks into the prison after his release, he proceeds to remove the prison owner's teeth. This is all shown in relatively graphic detail and the sheer brutality of the act is clearly illustrated. As the towel in the man's mouth turns from white to red and the pile of teeth on the desk grows, Oh's dream of vengeance begins to become reality. The vivid red of this torture scene changes into blacks and greys as Oh has to fight his way from the building. The corridor fighting sequence is the longest in the film as the camera situates itself at mid/long range and travels along the corridor, in time with Oh's advances. The distancing effect allows the audience to fully comprehend the violence and also the exhaustion, which is felt by all the participants by the end of the sequence; Oh and the men continue to fight with their fists, hammers, clubs and knives, and by the end they are all leaning against the wall in pain and at the point of collapse. In *Oldboy* there are no fancy weapons.; the characters use whatever is at their disposal. Oh favours a hammer, and when Lee overhears internet café owner and Oh's childhood friend Joo-hwan insulting his dead sister, he breaks a CD in half and stabs him in the throat. There is a sense of violence that pervades the whole film which relates to the continual drive for vengeance that is driving both men. All elements of the film are linked into this force and any item can be used to provide a method for obtaining revenge.

Oldboy is dominated by a variety of colours which give the film a tremendous level of intensity. Park stated that he wished the film to remind people of a thick oil painting, and the employment of bold colours such as black, red and purple serve to offer a layering affect that results in a film that is a palimpsest of colour and textures. When Mido and Oh have sex for the first time it is on vivid red sheets, clearly demonstrating passion but also, of course, danger. Their reveries will be interrupted by the arrival of the large violent purple box. The jarring nature of this deep violet against the red silk sheets and the pale bodies of Mido and Oh emphasises the vulnerability of these two in the face of the seemingly-endless power of Lee. Lee uses violet as the colour to wrap the information that he gives to Oh; these purple boxes serve as harbingers of distress since the first one contained a severed hand and the second one contains the photo album of Mido. In the end sequence when Mido sits before the box, the colour reflects on her face, evoking the fact that if this box is opened her entire life will be marked by it forever.

In terms of reception *Oldboy* succeeded on a global scale. The film performed extremely well at international film festivals, including Cannes, which is seen as the 'gold standard' for Korean cinema. Critical attention went hand in hand with financial success with the film grossing a total of US$15 million worldwide, making it one of the most profitable Korean films of the decade. In South Korea it was the fifth-highest grossing film of 2003 with over three million tickets sold, and consolidated Park Chan-wook's reputation as a serious director of note.

The Lone Woman: Kawase Naomi

> For the time being, the issue remains whether films by women actually succeed in subverting the basic model of the camera's construction of the gaze, whether the female look through the camera at the world, at men, women and objects will be essentially a different one. (Koch 1985: 144)

For many people working in visual culture the sheer lack of attention paid to Japanese women in the visual arts is astounding. Various women's groups and organisations let us know they are out there and yet very little national or international press is given to them as directors, photographers or artists. In terms of the English language (I refer here to 'non-academic' fields) the placement of East Asian women in the Western imagination is generally poor and fairly insulting with the emphasis on sex, appearances and desirability. The objectification of the female body has been a historically dominant global trend that continues to challenge women in all aspects of the visual arts.

The cultural status of women in a particular society, especially one such as Japan that prides itself on an image of homogeneity and collectivity (and this is elaborated on in more depth in the chapter on Miike Takashi), is vital in the discussion of women filmmakers. Therefore this chapter will begin with an overview of women in Japanese cinema, and since cinema cannot be seen as separate from the culture it springs from, it will also incorporate a brief overview of the social and historical status of women in Japan.

Kawase Naomi was born in Nara in 1969. Capital of the Nara prefecture in the Kansai region of Japan, Nara was briefly the capital of Japan (710–784) and the many temples there remained powerful even after the title of capital moved to Heian-kyō. These temples, of both Buddhist and Shinto persuasion, together with Nara being the site of the Heijō Imperial Palace, have meant that Nara has maintained a role as a popular tourist destination into modern times. The Nara period in history was a time that saw the increasing influence of Chinese Confucian ideals of government and the solid integration of Buddhism into Japanese daily life. Confucian teaching regarding women have had a long-standing and powerful influence on the thoughts and behaviour of those in Japan, China, Korea and many other East Asian countries. Ideals such as obedience, commitment to home and family, combined with the basic belief of the inferiority of women, were emphasised with regard to the role and placement of women in the social order. This can be seen in in Kaibara Ekken's essay *The Great Learning of Women* (*Onna Daigaku*) from 1716 where the five female infirmities were noted as 'indocility, discontent, jealousy, silliness and slander' (see Tipton 2002: 5). The legacy of this approach to gender has resulted in an endless uphill struggle for the women's movement to achieve tangible widespread recognition and positive results.

In term of literature, representations of women and 'women's culture' were found in the early Heian period in works such as *Tale of Genji/Genji Monogatari* and *The Pillow book/Makura no Sōshi*. With a few exceptions, however, the general concentration in a vast proportion of traditional Japanese literary and visual arts is on the 'private' aspects of women's lives and society rather than women as active participants in social, economic and political structures. The historical legacies of Confucianism, Shintoism, Buddhism and *samurai* traditions resulted in women's social and economic positioning in Japanese society being based on the assumption of male superiority. Prior to the modern age, the traditional emphasis on the *kōha*, or 'hard man', saw ideals of selflessness, stoical Zen-like endurance of hardship and single-minded commitment to duty become the idealised state of (male) existence. This state is personified by the *samurai* warrior or in a more modern context, the *kamikaze* pilots of World War II. The focus on the ideals of *kōha* and the various, often highly negative, religious precedents concerning the status of women in Japan meant that their social and political status in Japan was left with much to be desired (see Sievers 1983, Bernstein 1991, Liddle and Nakajima 2000, Molony and Uno 2005). Women were restricted to the domestic environment and in the face of male bravery and self-sacrifice women were left in the home and their lives were traditionally focused on the male family members, as depicted below:

> She must look to her husband as a lord, and must serve him with all reverence, not despising or thinking lightly of him ... In her dealings with her husband, both the expression of her countenance and the style of her address should be courteous, humble and conciliatory, never peevish and intractable, never rude or arrogant – that should be a woman's first and chief care. (Kaibara Ekiken [1630–1714], quoted in Lebra *et al.* 1976: 11)

It was in 1908 that arguably the first questioning of women's roles and gender politics was published. Sakai Toshiko's *Danto kankei no shinka* (*The Evolution of the Male-Female Relationship*) may have its critics but it was a beginning. The question of women's position continued with more groups demanding economic and social equality. Small successes were made; in 1922 women were allowed to participate in political meetings (revoking a law passed in 1890) and in 1930 the House of Representatives of the Diet agreed to support the suffrage bill (it was, however, later rejected at the House of Peers). There were calls for the abolition of concubinage and licensed sexual bondage and the Red Wave Society sought to provide women with a greater power and structure to their working rights and organisations (see Tipton 2002: 96).[1]

The small success of these events were, however, minor indeed when compared to the government machine that rolled into view as Japan moved towards a state of intense nationalist fervour which resulted in war. The government at this time had clear ideas about the role of women, and women as active voters and workers was not one of them. The ideal of *ryōsai kenbo* (good wife, wise mother) had long been a fixture in the construction of Japanese womanhood but it was embraced with fervour in the decades prior to, and during, World War II. The aftermath of the Sino-Japanese War (1894–95) saw this ideology being championed by the ruling elite as offering a 'proper role' for women in Imperial Japan. The growth of militarism and imperialistic ambitions that marked the post-war period saw *ryōsai kenbo* become a pervasive fixture in the mass media, the education system and other public and private institutions (see Uno 1999: 294). The focus for women became self-sacrificing wifehood and motherhood, and the mobilisation of the civilian population during wartime was based on specific gender divisions. The government's rallying call to women and women's associations was to participate in the war effort in traditional female duties such as comforting the wounded, encouraging the troops, economic efficiency, patriot savings and 'opposing the penetration of dangerous ideas' (Havens 1975: 915). Those women who resisted were seen as problematic, certainly unwomanly and potentially dangerous. A number of women's magazines and groups were banned and censors became rigid in their examination of what women were publishing. There was a constant risk of those promoting feminism being seen as aligning themselves with Western norms and ideas and therefore being unpatriotic and 'un-Japanese'. Into the 1940s the situation for the women's movement became dire. The defeat of the suffrage bill meant that women did not have the vote and they were excluded from post-elementary education, bar practical training in childrearing and 'in the heavy responsibilities of being wife, mother and daughter-in-law' (Sievers 1983: 112).

Ryōsai kenbo became an integral part of the Japanese drive for Empire; over the next few decades, especially after the beginning of the war in China, there was an institutionalisation of *ryōsai kenbo* as the governmental model of Japanese womanhood. The focus of the educational system changed from that of individual growth to that of state-approved 'moral values' such as diligence, self-denial, filial piety, intense love of country, reverence for and obedience to the Emperor and exultation of the Emperor as the 'father' of the family state (*kazoku kokka*) (see Pyle 1973: 551–60). *Ryōsai kenbo* became the main focus of citizenship requirements and aims for a woman: the 'good wife' would prudently manage the household affairs and enhance and support the success of the adult (male) family members whilst the 'wise mother' would devote herself to the growth of devoted and compliant citizens of Imperial Japan.

> The man goes outside to work to earn his living, to fulfil his duties to the State; it is the wife's part to help him, for the common interest of the house, and as her share of duty to the state … above all … bringing up the children in a fit and proper manner. (Dairoku Kikuchi, cited in Smith 1987: 2)

The 1930s saw a rapid increase in Japanese militarism and national fervour for Japan's aims to gain more 'living space' in China and other areas of East Asia. By the 1940s this focus on Japan's increasing population as the reason for Imperial expansion resulted in an intense emphasis on women as producers of children who would fight for and maintain the Imperial throne, both in Japan and on the wider world stage. In a similar fashion to Germany throughout this period pro-natalist laws and policies were passed making childbearing highly encouraged and necessarily linked to a woman's social standing and commitment to the state (see Mackie 2003: 112). Women's bodies as the site of procreation and the future of the Japanese nation were increasingly controlled and monitored as the birth control movement was repressed, abortions were banned and the National Eugenics Law (*Kokumin Yūsei Hō*, 1940) aimed to 'provide robust manpower for the Empire by preventing handicapped births' (Buckley 1999: 208). For women the focus was not on creating great works of literature or cinema but instead on breeding and supporting the male-orientated Empire.

During this period cinema in Japan flourished as a tool of communication and propaganda. The representation of women was very specific in its alignment with governmental ideas surrounding gender roles. The most terrifying figure to emerge form this cinematic period is the *gunkoku no haha* – the 'militarist mother' that bore and raised her sons with the expressed desire for them to commit to, and fight for, the Imperial throne. *Aiki Minami e Tobu* (*Our Planes Fly South*, **Sasaki Yasushi 1943**) sees the mother claim, in reference to her son, that, 'I don't care what he becomes, as long as it's of service to the nation' (see High 2003: 404). In terms of cinema, women directors were almost non-existent, with one or two notable exceptions in the pre-war period. The sadly often forgotten Atsugi Taka's documentaries bear witness to the fact that women were making films as early as 1930 and actively using them as part of a political agenda. Atsugi was a devoted communist and her work aimed to promote her political objectives. She was, of course, working outside the mainstream dominant studio system and against government ideology as the forced disbanding of the cinema group Prokino that Atsugi was a part of demonstrated. It was around this period that she was forced to change her name from her birth name Matsue Okada to Atsugi Taka to mask her identity from the Japanese police who were keen to silence her opinions. Atsugi was a passionate exponent of Western film theory (she was the first to translate Paul Rotha's *Documentary Film* into Japanese). She was also keenly interested in the questions surrounding the representation of women and female subjectivity (two topics that would become key in the Anglo-American feminist film debate fifty years later).

If I was to say that I harbored no hopes that this self-depiction that I am currently writing might be a valid attempt to 'depict a woman' it would probably be a lie. But if I am reticent about it, it is simply the fear that the gap between what one tries to depict and what one actually succeeds in depicting will be too great. (Quoted in Loftus 2002)

With this statement Atsugi articulates her desire to represent a woman's subjectivity but maintains fears about authenticity. In 1945 Atsugi made her important documentary about the everyday reality of a daycare centre, *Aru Hobo no Kiroki* (*Record of a Certain Nursery*). For this she sought to present a film that was contrary to the official nationalistic rhetoric. She stated:

I had wanted to portray the partnership manifest at these daycare centres between mothers and nurses in their desires to instill in the young lives of their charges an earnest commitment to life. If I could give expression to this unspoken feeling of solidarity, this humanistic spirit manifest in their commitment to living and life, them somehow I could function as an antidote to the emphasis on killing and dying. Looking back on it now, it may well seem like too little of an attempt at protest, but at the time, it was the most I could hope for. (Ibid.)

Here we have a clear example of the desire of a woman filmmaker to do something different with the medium. She wished to offer a new voice, one based on the feminine world of mothers, children and nurses. Atsugi noted that she not only wanted to manifest and represent the 'woman's eye' of the female director singular but also the 'multiple women's eyes' of all the women involved in the making of the documentary. Atsugi was clearly aware of the issues involved in the depiction of women as much as the constraints placed on her as a woman director. Her desire to represent women and women's lives meant that Atsugi stayed away from fictional representations, concentrating instead on documentary, but she showed a clear awareness of all the issues that would later inform international discussion on women on, and in, film. In her work *Memoirs of a Female Documentarist* (*Osei dokyumentarisuto no kaisô*, 1991) Atsugi continually questions the creation of an individual and the constitution of a 'self'. As Ronald Loftus notes this is something that revolves around the question of gender:

Atsugi clearly conceives of her identity as a process ... and she goes some length to demonstrate how the process is constantly being 'fragmented' and 'disputed' by the discourses around her ... she understands that somewhere at the core of this process is her struggle to 'depict women' accurately and sensitively. (2002)

Film as a communication tool has been central to the development of the medium and, for the marginalised in society such as women and ethnic minorities, film is a potentially powerful tool for freedom of expression.[2] A good example of this in the Japanese context is the growth in the representation of the previously ignored and marginalised *zainichi* (Japanese-Korean) experience in recent decades via film, television and print. The work of Atsugi shows an awareness of the power of the medium and she uses film to tell the stories of women and their lives, working directly against the dominant male viewpoint. As we later begin to examine in depth the work of Kawase there is a clear linkage between Kawase's styles and preoccupations and the early 'Grandmother' of Japanese film.

Atsugi was remarkable, but over the next few decades she was an exception. Japan's surrender at the end of World War II ushered in an era of military occupation (1945–52) and this period saw major changes and reforms affect all aspects of life in post-war Japan. Many of these changes were aimed at the lives of women in line with the 'democratic' ideals that America was anxious to import into Japan. In 1946 women were allowed to vote for the first time and the next year saw a very important change in terms of gender relations, and the introduction of the Japanese constitution that forbade the 'discrimination in political, economic, or social relations because of creed, race, sex, social status or family origin'. This grand statement, however, made very little real difference in the lives of women and it made no difference at all to the number of women working in the film industry.

The Japanese studio system, certainly prior to the 1960s, was based on the principle of 'learning on the job' and one of the key ways (and in reality the only way) to becomes a film director was to become an assistant or apprentice director. Kurosawa was apprenticed to Kajiro Yamamoto under the PLC (later Toho) apprenticeship programme; Shohei Imamura followed Yasijiro Ozu and Yuzo Kawashima at Shochiku and so on. The 1960s saw the peak of the Japanese film industry and yet there were few women present in directorial chairs. Two notable exceptions were Sakane Tazuko and Kinuyo Tanaka, both of whom worked with Mizoguchi Kenji. Sakana worked for Mizoguchi as his assistant director and went on to become Japan's first female feature director with *New Year's Finery* (*Hatsu Sugata*) in 1936. This was, however, her only film and it was not until 1953 that a woman once again managed to take the director's chair in the studio system, with Kinuyo's *Love Letter* (*Koibumi*, 1953). Kinuyo was already famous for her acting, primarily through the work she had done with long-time collaborator Mizoguchi Kenji and although the film achieved a modest amount of recognition it is as an actor that she is primarily remembered. It is also unfortunate that both of these women owed their chance to direct to Mizoguchi, demonstrating that there was still widespread belief in the inability of women to direct unless supported by a powerful male ally.

The 1970s and 1980s were very grim indeed for women. With the film industry beginning its decline, opportunities to direct fell drastically for anyone who was not already an established directorial (therefore male) figure. The 1989 Equal Opportunity Employment Laws lifted the barriers that had allowed studios to refuse to accept women into the directing chair but by then the Japanese film industry was in serious trouble and a vast percentage of the hiring of new staff ceased, and women's presence in the old studio system for the most part effectively ended.[3] However, the end of an era, as is often the case, opened up new doors for those seeking to enter the film industry. Major studios could no longer afford to keep on permanent directors and gradually more freelance independents were called in to fill the gap. Independent film has always been a blessing for women and, in Japan, although men continued to be dominant, a few women began to work as directors and to achieve training in filmmaking. Digital cameras and equipment became cheaper and more readily accessible, making it far easier for keen, young directors to make and produce films away from the economic and social constraints of the larger studios.

In the last few years there have been several very notable features directed by women that have entered the cinema via the film festival circuit. Hisako Matsui produced two films that examined the legacies and issues associated with Alzheimer's, (*Yuki/Solitude* [1997] and *Oriume* [2003]). Matsui was notable as she won the Japan Film Makers Association award for best new director. Miwa Nishikawa made her directorial debut in 2002 with *Hebiichigo* (*Wild Berries*), based on the breakdown of a family unit. Tadano Miako debuted in 2005 with *Sannen Migomour* (*Three-Year Delivery*), focusing on the modern anxieties of young Japanese women via a 27-month pregnancy. Kaze Shindo presented a tender lesbian drama entitled *Love/Juice* in 2000. More violent offerings came from Kei Fujiwara and Shinko Sata whose respective films, the gory *Organ* (1996) and the high-school horror *Eki Eki Azaruki Wizard of Darkness* (1995), thrilled audiences. Female directed documentaries have been strong in continuing the legacy of Atsugi. Journalist Mizue Furui focused on women in the Muslim world in *Ghada – Poem of Palestine* released in 2005. Tomoko Fujiwara achieved several domestic awards in 1997 for *Louise: Her Departure on a Journey* (*Ruizu Sono Tabidachi*). The film recounts the life of Ruizu (Louise) Ito, a social activist whose parents were killed in 1923 by the Japanese army after being charged as anarchists. Kaori Sakagami offered a documentary feature film, *Lifers* (2003) on prisoners serving life terms in the USA and questioned whether there was a need for such prison sentences in Japan. More controversially, in 2002 Hitomi Kamanaka focused on the lives of the *hibakusha* in her documentary of the same name (see the section on Fukasaku for a further discussion on *hibakusha*). *Zainichi* woman Yonghi Yang made *Dear Pyongyang* in 1995, focusing on the lives of Koreans in Japan.

Kawase Naomi is unique because she is the only female director to have emerged from Japan who has achieved sustained acclaim on the international circuit. 1997 saw *Moe no Suzaku* win the Caméra d'Or at the 50th Cannes Film Festival, making Kawase the first Japanese and youngest ever director to win this award. Kawase's visual training was at the Osaka School of Visual Arts (at the time, the School of Photography). It was during her time at Osaka that she began making short films using the 8mm format. Her early works hint at her preoccupation with documentary styles that would later be developed in her longer projects. Her first longer film in 1992, entitled *Embracing/Ni Tsutsumarete*, gained some critical attention and although initially filmed in 8mm it was converted to 16 mm for exhibition. *Embracing* was a highly personal film focusing on Kawase's relationship with her father and his abandonment of her after her parents divorced when she was formally adopted by her grandparents.

> When I made *Embracing* about my father, the main intention was not to show it to the world afterwards. It was first and foremost an exploration and a way of dealing with it for myself. It more or less just happened to develop that way and it became my way of communicating intimately and closely. (Quoted in Mes and Sharp 2005: 230)

Compare this with the opening quote from French New Wave director François Truffaut:

> I believe tomorrow's films will be even more personal than a novel, as individual

and autobiographical as a confession or a journal … Tomorrow's films will be made by artists for whom shooting is a terrific, exciting adventure. Tomorrow's films will look like those who filmed them. (1976: 218)

There is no evidence that Kawase is a firm believer in the French notion of the auteur but her work does show a highly personalised style and rhythm that is unmistakable. Her early work contains a great deal of concentration on the texture and nature of the world around her. In one scene from *Embracing* various pictures of her childhood are shown, held up against the background in which they were originally taken. Her search for her father is shown to be the tentative search for her own history and thus her own present and future. She places the younger Kawase against the backdrop of the present Kawase in an effort to try to decipher the rhythms and patterns that have formed her sense of self and place. In his review of *Embracing*, Adrian Martin makes the link between Kawase's work and Raymond Bellour's idea of the *autoportrait*:

What is an autoportrait in the cinema? It is not simply the filming of the story of your life or turning the camera upon yourself to record yourself … this autoportrait must be deciphered in motion, gleaned only through the traces it leaves: objects, rooms, scraps, things seen and heard by the filmmaking subject. Such auto-portraits are about everything that is passing, everything that is already lost. (2005)

This idea of items being deciphered in motion can be seen in many of the titles of Kawase's short films made after *Embracing*, such as *Katasumori* (1994), *See the Heavens* (*Ten, mitake*, 1995) and *Memory of the Wind* (*Kaze no Kioku*, 1995). *Katasumori* focuses on her relationship with her grandmother and once again references the impact and creation of Kawase as an individual demonstrated via the medium of film. These are not 'documentaries' in the traditional sense; rather they are a meditative view of the thoughts of an individual and the power of film to explore, capture and reveal hidden emotions and insights. There is a concentration on the images and sounds that make up film and the world that the film is endeavouring to capture and represent. These themes are clearly present in Kawase's first feature film, released in 1996. *Moe no Suzaku* was filmed in the small mountain village of Nishiyoshino-mura, in Nara, over a 45-day period and focuses on the lives of a small rural community.

The film is clearly influenced by Kawase's documentary roots as well as her background in photography. The cast was largely made up of non-professional actors, with the exception of lead actor Jun Kunimura (who plays Kozo Tahara). Kawase was well acquainted with the tensions involved in such a small community, having grown up in one herself, and she and her crew lived for a period of time in the small hamlet before picking the actors.

Moe no Suzaku is divided into two parts. The first introduces us to the family and the community. The focus is on a small family consisting of a grandmother, father, mother and their small daughter, Micheru, and the father's nephew, Eisuke, who lives with them. Kozo and the whole of the community are waiting with anticipation for the building of a railway link that they believe will bring prosperity and economic development to the poor farming region. The father, in particular, is obsessed with the railway tunnel that he sees as the future. In one scene we see him taking the children walking there and speaking of the promised benefits. The family and the community that surrounds them is in high spirits: the scenery is beautiful, the young mother and father seem in love, the children are devoted to each other and there is hope for the future. The next and longest part of the film moves to fifteen years later; the children are teenagers, the promised railway link has failed to materialise, and there are resulting economic and social problems for the few that remain in the small isolated community. The family is destitute and tensions begin to affect them, such as Eisuke's increasing attraction towards his aunt and the development of romantic feelings on Micheru's part for her older cousin. The situation is made even more traumatic by the death of Kozo and the resulting soul-searching that follows.

The film is light on dialogue and narrative is limited; the images, primarily in long-shot and in long fluid takes with little editing, create a perfect 'slice of life' approach to the topic which emphasises the natural beauty of the region as well as the frustrations and feelings of those who are trapped in the area. The use of such long, sweeping shots could alienate the viewer from feeling sympathy or empathy for the family, and yet Kawase manages to avoid that. The slightly distant approach that the camera takes allows a clear understanding and vision of the frustrations that are facing the characters. They are unable to express their emotions to each other and in the moments we see them alone we are shown how this is affecting them. A wonderful example of this is when Yasuyo gets a job at the same restaurant that is employing Eisuke. Previous to this Eisuke had always driven Micheru around on the back of his scooter – now her mother takes her place. When Yasuyo collapses at work, Micheru is left at the bus stop for several hours waiting for Eisuke until she gives up and walks the long distance home. As she miserably wanders through the fields the camera, although keeping its distance, perfectly reflects her confusion and her upset at the snub she feels her burgeoning love has suffered. When she reaches home and Eisuke comes to meet her and inform her of her mother's illness she runs towards the house, towards her mother and away from Eisuke and the emotions she feels for him. The most melancholic character is Kozo. He keenly feels the disappointment of the cancellation of the railway project and we see how the fifteen years have worn away at him. His death is never fully explained: we see him leave the house in the dark with his precious 8mm camera and move towards the railway tunnel that he imbued with such hope. The family later receive a call from the police informing them that Kozo has been found dead by the tunnel clutching this camera. Whether this is suicide or an accidental death we are not sure but his demise results in Yasuyo's decision to return to her family leaving the grandmother and Eisuke behind.

Moe no Suzaku was the first 35mm film by Kawase but she does not forget her 8mm roots. At the end of the film the family sit down to watch Kozo's footage that contains similar images to those seen in Kawase's own short film. Images of plants, birds, landscapes, people and spaces all combine to create a simultaneous remembrance of Kozo and the small dying community.

Although *Moe no Suzaku* was very well received internationally and was the first film to establish some recogniton in her home country, Kawase expressed clear dissatisfaction with it, believing she had not portrayed the harshness of the family's existence in its entirety. As a result she returned to the region to shoot a 'true' documentary short film (she reverted to the 8mm format) about the same village's inhabitants, entitled *The Weald* (*Somaudo monogatari*). *The Weald* presents a world that is alien to most urban-dwelling Japanese. It tells the stories of six groups of elderly people living in the mountains of Yoshino, Nara Prefecture. In her writing on the film Kawase, states that the film focused on how

The accumulation of their lived days has taken root in the earth and returned to nature. Just as massive trees withstand the wind and the rain, the cold and the heat, these people endure the twists and turns of life by simply existing, developing deep wrinkles. Replacing the 'facts' of the life they have spun with my own 'truth', I spin a tale in cinema, so that this may become a film that continues from the past to the present, the present to the future. (2003)

For Kawase, the focus returns again to the mixture of past, present and future that the camera can capture and present. During this period her personal life was gaining the attention of the Japanese press when she married *Moe no Suzaku*'s producer Sentō Takenori and changed her name to Sentō Naomi, an action that provoked criticism from various feminist groups (that Kawase chose to ignore). The marriage ended two years later but during this period she made two documentaries under her married name. The first (*Wandering at Home: The Third Fall Since Starting to Live Alone/Tayutafu ni Kokyo – Hitorigurashi o Hajimete, Sannenme no Aki ni*, 1998) was made for television and focused on the legacy of a father's suicide from the viewpoint of the dead man's adult children. *Kaleidoscope* (1999) saw Kawase engaging in power conflicts with the Japanese photographer Shinya Arioso. The premise of *Kaleidoscope* is Kawase filming Arioso photographing a series of portraits of two young actresses: Machiko Ono (Micheru in *Moe no Suzaku*) and Mifune Mika (granddaughter of Toshiro Mifune). This documentary demonstrates how Kawase gained power as a director as well as her command of the medium as a form of communication, as she clashes with Arioso about the nature of the piece.

> This relates to that kind of use of the camera, but establishing relationships with people through the camera, while it can be a form of communication, also raises the issue of the relations of power there. In particular, when I saw *Manguekyo* [1999], I felt one had to think of the power relationships there. The set-up is that you are supposed to compete with the photographer Arioso in shooting these two young women, but when you look at it in the end, you can't help but think that you are the most powerful one in the film, that you hold the reins. And perhaps that is because you hold the film camera... (2003)

Kawase's confidence saw her once again tackle a feature film, working for the production company her ex-husband had set up called J-Works.[4] In an interview in *Japan Vogue*, Kawase described *Hoteru* as her attempt to 'make a film like *Betty Blue* or *Empire of the Senses*, that had an acute pain of love'. The story focuses on the relationship between a stripper and a potter and is once again set in Nara, as opposed to the bustling lights and action of Tokyo or Osaka. At the Locarno Film Festival in 2000 *Hoteru* won the FIPRESCI prise 'for the intensity and originality of its personal and universal approach towards the conflict between tradition and modernity' (FIPRESCI 2000). *Hoteru* was a far bigger-budget event than *Moe no Suzaku*, and served to cement Kawase as one of the leading Japanese female directors (even if she was not hitting the big cinema screen or film magazine popularity lists).

Her reputation resulted in the French/German television channel Arte offering Kawase the funding to make a further addition to *Embracing* (her estranged father had recently died). *Sky, Wind, Fire, Water, Earth* (*Kya Ka Ra Ba A*, 2001) allowed Kawase to blend together the documentary-style approach of *Embracing* and her other short films with more narrative fictional sequences. The themes of rites of passage become key as she questions whether to get the same tattoo as her father had in this moving film. Her body becomes the method through which she debates the relationship between her past, present and future. We see her pain as the tattoo is etched in and this is followed by a shot of the naked Kawase running off into the distance. Her back a mass of colour – a redux of her father's tattoo – and this is inter-cut with the images of her absent father. Her body has become a literal embodiment of her art via the use of her own skin as a key prop in her filmic exploration, and, at the same time, her art is a highly intimate testament of her attempts to construct a personal connection to her now deceased father. Her work is part of the generation that was designated as coming 'after Kitano' and this usage of the body as a means of communication is perhaps one link that can be made between the two filmmakers. Unlike Kitano, however, Kawase's works maintain a sense of hope and beauty. Her vision of society, although often imbued with sadness, is never the continual wish for death that marks Kitano's work.

The idea of beauty and hope even in death would be seen in her next film. In *Letters from Yellow Cherry Blossom* (*Tsuioku No Dance*, 2003) Kawase films the dying critic and photographer Nishii Kazuo. Although the film is unfliching in its presention of the terrible death that he is undergoing there is a love and humanism that inundates the work. Nishii's hard and bloody cough is terrible to hear but Kawase's hand-held intimate aesthetics present a loving portrait of a dying man. Nishii was famous for his continual desire to question the role of the visual in contemporary Japanese society and in his decision to have his final days filmed (as he, in turn, photographs Kawase) results in *Letters from Yellow Cherry Blossom* being a remarkable examination of the dialogue that takes place between filmmakers and their subjects.

This dialogue is especially interesting when it concerns a female filmmaker since, as already stated, female directors are few and far between in Japanese (and indeed world) cinematic history. For those of us who have been educated in Anglo-American mainstream film theory, the role of women in and on film has been clearly laid out. From its beginnings in the 1970s, feminist film theory was focused on questions of image, representation and spectatorship. This question of spectatorship was developed alongside a call for the rediscovery of often-forgotten female directors to be included as part of the cinematic canon, and a search through their work and the work of other remembered female directors for 'feminist' messages and statements. In male-directed mainstream cinema the roles and presentation of women was closely examined and then later re-examined with new results (Tania Modleski's [2005] work on Alfred Hitchcock is a case in point), what was neglected at this time was a focus on women working outside Anglo-American dominance. Writers such as bell hooks (1992) have sought to reposition the role of black female spectatorship and Trin Ti Min-ha (1991) has been vocal on the need for Asian women to claim the cinematic space (it is also interesting that Min-ha has made a documentary about the arts of Japan [*The Fourth Dimension* 2004]). Yet the works of these women have not been readily translated or discussed in the work of Japanese cinema theorists. Japanese cinematic theory has had nowhere near the exhaustive debate that has taken place in the academic circles of the West on the role of woman in, and on, film. Kawase's active engagement with her own artistic processes naturally relates to her positioning as a woman and although Japanese feminist theory may not be in abundance, the historical legacy of the questions surrounding gender roles and development that started in earnest in Japan in around the early 1900's can be seen to influence and mark her work. *Seitō's* (*Bluestocking*) inaugural issue published in 1911 announced that

> In the beginning the woman was the sun. An authentic person. Today she is the moon. Living through others. Reflecting the brilliance of others. And now, *Bluestocking*, a journal created for the first time with the brains and hands of to-day's Japanese women raises its voice. (Cited in Tipton 2002: 94)

Compare this with a comment made by Kawase in the 1990s:

> The age I came into contact with film was a time when I didn't really have a way to talk about intimate things with the people around me, because there weren't any people around to share them with. I also discovered that when I used film as a

medium, people were ready to listen to what I have to say very carefully, more than when I didn't use film. So I found that it functioned for me as a tool of communication at the time. (Quoted in Mes and Sharp 2005: 229)

For Kawase as a woman living in a culture that is not the most woman-friendly in terms of employment or social and economic standing the question of gender is related to her ability to communicate her feelings and opinions. The role of director gives her a power, influence and confidence to express herself and her narratives. In 2008 an exhibition of photographs by Kawase highlighted her physical and emotional reactions to her son's birth. This undoubtedly gender-specific narrative of birth and motherhood illustrates the ability of Kawase to articulate her personal experiences and feelings via a variety of artistic mediums.

Kawase's touching film *The Mourning Forest* (*Mogari no Mori*, 2007) follows the relationship between a young nurse grieving after the death of a child and an elderly man suffering from dementia. Like many of her films *The Mourning Forest* is set in Nara and the sweeping woods, fields and mountains, so the region once again acts as a central part of the film as the unlikely pair forges a firm and loving bond. The opening shots of trees blowing softly in the wind pull back to offer a vivid lush panorama of green fields as a funeral procession slowly makes its way across them. From this sad procession Kawase takes us to the heart of the forest and minutely observes the nature that can be found there, linking immediately in the audience's mind the forest and the passing of life. This idea develops as it becomes clear that the old man, Mr Shigeki, is convinced that there is a link between the forest and his dead wife. Unable to form coherent thoughts for more than a few sentences at a time and unable to remember and convey all his ideas and beliefs, he clings to his feelings and the vague and illogical memories and thoughts that he experiences. Shigeki is not presented as a victim of an illness. Although he, like many of the other patients, can no longer live independently, the nursing home run by kind caring staff is seen as a positive and pleasant place to reside.

The Mourning Forest is not a film about dementia; rather it is a film about how humanity can survive even if the mind no longer functions. It bears comparison with other films that present an image of the decaying mind such as *Iris* (Richard Eyre, 2001) or *Away From Her* (Sarah Polley, 2006) which focus on the trauma of the loved ones' inability to think or remember. In *The Mourning Forest* the focus is on a more positive image of a man and a woman who manage to share a common feeling of warmth and care despite their personal difficulties. In one of the early scenes a Buddhist monk comes to talk at the nursing home and in his answer to the question that Shigeki puts to him he offers the heart of the film's narrative. Shigeki asks him 'am I alive?' and the monk offers a two-fold answer. He states that there are two meanings to the word 'alive'; one is the simple distinction that if you eat then you are alive. Your body still functions since you continue to feed it. However, he goes on to elaborate that being alive is not enough, you must also *feel* alive: 'if your heart is empty then life in its true meaning will escape you'. He goes on to prove his point when he asks Machiko to hold Shigeki's hand. This human contact provides Shigeki with a sense of well-being that the monk tells him is vital to experiencing life. Without human contact life is left unfilled and empty. This is a theme that is seen in all of Kawase's work, whether it is trying to forge a link with her dead father or taking care of an elderly relative: for Kawase the need for human contact and care is a key focus. The following question posed to the monk is 'how can I live alone?' The priest pronounces that being alone is a product of contemporary society. In *The Mourning Forest* Kawase focuses on what she feels has been lost in Japanese contemporary society – genuine contact between people. For Machiko the young nurse, the old man's ruminations on life and death are of vital importance to her since she is still grieving for the loss of her son. Through the angry words her husband directs at her we are led to believe that she was indirectly responsible for his death since she 'let go of his hand'. The assumption would seem to lie in that the son was killed in a road accident or another similar tragedy as a result of his mother's inability to keep hold of him. Machiko fails to maintain physical contact and as a result she loses her son.

The boundaries between living and dead, human and nature, old and young are clearly blurred throughout this film, making a haunting film seeks to maintain at all times the humanity and dignity of the two characters. Shigeki may be suffering from dementia but in focusing on his abilities such as his continuing sense of fun (demonstrated by his and Machiko's games in the fields), and his careful and thoughtful questioning of the visiting Buddhist priest about the meaning of life, means that his humanity still shines through despite the limitations which the disease causes him. In one of the more unusual scenes in the film the nurse strips off her clothes and embraces the elderly man in an effort to prevent him from succumbing to hypothermia. There is no sexuality involved in the act, just common humanity and care. For Machiko the contact she has with Shigeki and her increasing understanding of his never-ending love for his long-dead wife allows her to reconnect with her own feelings and begin to let go of the trauma of her son's death. At the end, with Shigeki dying with a happy smile on his face, Machiko sits alone in the wood and raises to the sky the music box that belonged to Shigeki's wife. Her sorrow at Shigeki's passing is combined with her new-found belief in humanity and the benefits of human contact. *The Mourning Forest* won Kawase the Grand Prix at the 2007 Cannes Film Festival and helped develop her international reputation as well as her popularity and status in Japan.

In 2009 Kawase joined with Korean director Hong Sang-soo and Filipino director Liv Diaz to create *Visitors* (2009), a three-part film funded by the South Korean Jeonju Digital Project. In her segment, *Koma*, Kawase deals with the strained and difficult relationship between Japan and Korea when the grandson of a Korean migrant worker from the colonial period returns to Japan to present a scroll to a Japanese family. The film offers an image of the two nations combining as a relationship begins between the Korean man and the Japanese daughter of the family. *Koma* contains many aspects which have come to be familiar in Kawase's work; the focus on a small village (*The Weld*, *Moe no Suzaku*), an unarticulated history (*Shara*, *The Mourning Forest*, *Embracing*, *Katsumori*) and the slow development of a relationship (*Shara*, *The Mourning Forest*). The camera drifts above the small town to show us the tiles of the houses and engages with the natural world that surrounds the village. She creates and intimacy between the natural and the urban environment and, as in *The Mourning Forest*, spirituality and the power of the natural environment is constantly hinted at. Rather than dealing with the conflicts that have marked the history of Japan and Korea, Kawase gives hope for the future via her meditative and though provoking images.

In 2011 Kawase directed *Hanezu no tsuki*. Premiering at the 2012 Cannes Film Festival, this film is set in the Asuka region of Japan and is once again a meditative focus on the interconnectedness of people and the natural environment that surrounds them. *Hanezu* is an ancient word used to refer to a shade of red (found in the eighth-century poetry collection, the *Manyoshu*, that the film links into) and Kawase comments that

> By resurrecting an ancient word in the present, I wanted Japanese – who aren't familiar with this word – to savour its meaning. No one can know the reality that

lies in the ground, but my role as one who lives in the present is perhaps to turn an ear to the voices of the dead and to weave a tale. What does it mean to live as a person within the unavoidable transience of life – the flux of the waxing and waning moon, people's hearts, the era, time? I believe there is a deeper truth in the tales of nameless people who are hidden in the shadows of major events and neglected by the trivial riches of the daily media. (2012)

Thus, the aim of the film, similar to *The Mourning Forest*, *Moe no Suzaku* and *Shara*, is to explore how the cycles of life and death are present in all aspects of existence, and how an exploration of these cycles can reveal 'deeper truths' and understanding of the modern world. In *Hanezu no tsuki*, therefore, Kawase's highly personal, reflective and innovative approach to film is once again demonstrated.

In terms of international profile, her regular appearances at Cannes and other film festivals, the release of a large box-set of her earliest works in 2007, as well as the fact that several of her feature films are available throughout America and Europe (although some only have French subtitles) is making her work more internationally available and recognised. Although this chapter is entitled 'The Lone Woman', I want to stress that Kawase is not actually alone; there is an increasing number of female directors that are beginning to make their voices heard and achieve recognition; not simply as 'women directors' but as representatives of the Japanese movie industry. This recognition is slow in coming, however, and it may be many years before Japanese women directors are as acclaimed and successful in gaining funding, promotion and popularity as their male counterparts. A good example is that fact that of 581 members of the Directors Guild of Japan only eight per cent (at the time of writing) are women.

This is not an unusual situation as the global positioning of women in film goes: UK, USA, China and South Korea all suffer from a lack of women in the cinema industry and even in France, where women have historically been consistently represented inside the cinema industry, only 13.7 per cent of films released in the 1990s were made by women. This rather depressing situation is improving, however, and in Japan more women than ever are entering the film industry. The Japan School of Moving Images has seen the proportion of women admitted rise from ten per cent to around forty per cent, and a film festival held in 1997 had around thirty per cent of the 730 entries submitted by women directors (see Anon. 2007). Of the three hundred or so films released in Japan in 2007, over twenty were made by women; significantly more than the four out of 180 made in 1997 or indeed the paltry five made in 2005. These women are entering the cinematic world, not by the traditional route of studio training as an assistant director, but rather they have been aided by the arrival of cheap and available digital equipment that is making it easier for more directors, including women, to make films. In the last couple of years the rise in numbers has gone hand in hand with an arguable rise in quality and indeed popularity of independent cinema and this bodes well for the future of women and film in Japan. The work of Kawase Naomi demonstrates that women can perform on both a national and international level and hopefully she will soon be joined by others.

NOTES

1 Under the gender blindness of Marxism, however, many of the movements that were aligned with socialism ended up neglecting the specific issues of women and gradually during the 1930s and 1940s women were sidelined from the agendas of the male leaders.

2 For more information and debate on the political and cultural impact of film see Shohat and Stam 1994, Martin 1995, Chanan 1997, Guneratne and Dissanayake 2003, and Christensen and Haas 2005.

3 Interestingly however there were some women in less 'formal' film genres. Key examples are Yumi Yoshiyuki and Sachi Hamano who contributed dozens of titles to the soft porn *Pinku* catalogue.

4 J-Works produced films such as Ayoyama Shinji 's *Eureka* (2000), Suwa Nobuhiro's *H-story* (2001) and Ishiis Sogo's *Gojoe* (2001) which was later blamed for bankrupting the company and the result is that many of J-Works films are not available to view. Kawase's film *Hotaru* (*Firefly*, 2000) is unfortunately one of the works.

Film Analysis

SHARA

沙羅双樹
Sharasojyu

2003

Director

Kawase Naomi

Cast

Kohei Fukungaga (Shun), Yuka Hyyoudo (Yu), Naomi Kawase (Reiko), Katsuhisa Namase (Taku), Kanako Higuchi (Shouko)

International Film Awards

2003 Nominated Palme d'Or Cannes Film Festival

Plot Summary

Whilst out playing with his brother in the town of Nara, a young boy, Kei, disappears without a trace. Five years later, Kei's family are still struggling to cope with his disappearance. It is especially hard for his brother, Shun. Kei's mother, Reiko, is heavily pregnant with another child and his father, Taku, is involved in organising an important local festival and parade. Shun is good friends with his neighbour, Yu, who lives with her aunt. Her aunt finally tells Yu the truth about her parents which is that after her father left the family, Yu's biological mother could no longer cope so she was adopted by her aunt. Shun discovers that his brother is definitely dead. The festival goes ahead despite a heavy downpour of rain and the new baby is born. This new arrival allows Shun and Yu to come to terms with the past and look towards the future.

———

People calculate what you can watch with your eyes and touch with your hands, and seek after progress for bigger, higher and faster, an existence that people have lost sight of; in reality this existence is alive within daily life of Japan, this movie lets us know that. (Kawase 2005)

Shara not only offers an examination of Kawase Naomi as a director but also Kawase as an actor since she took on the role of the pregnant mother when the original actor Reiko Karaoka dropped out. The narrative of *Shara* is the simple tale of a family struggling to put their lives back together after the disappearance of their son. Kawase has stated in interviews that she had been considering focusing on a tale of murder for her first film after *Moe no Suzaku* but decided instead to focus on an ordinary family that experiences a tragic event.

The film's opening is reminiscent of *Moe no Suzaku* and Kawase's 8mm shorts. The camera slowly pans around a naturally-lit store-room focusing on the traditional blocks used in the production of Indian ink. Leaving the room, the camera then focuses on small twin boys playing in the garden. We follow the twins as they run around the neighborhood touching the Buddhist wall hangings, running around trees; until suddenly one boy (Kei), disappears without a sound or trace leaving his brother (Shun), standing bewildered and unable to answer his parents' demands to know where his brother has gone.

The opening sequence is striking in its resistance to melodrama. The narrative of the lost child is one we are all familiar with in terms of contemporary television and film but Kawase takes this narrative and transforms it. The aesthetics of the opening scenes lack the menace we associate with the disappearance of a child; the soft light, slowed-down shots, beautiful trees, neat houses, all are the antithesis of the action that occurs. The film then returns to the family five years later. Kawase does not concentrate on the immediate aftermath of the disappearance, such as the police searches, the emotional distress and the questioning that would have followed Kei's vanishing; instead we return to a family that have tentatively, at least on the surface, got their lives back together again. Shun is in school, a budding artist with romantic interests in his friend and next-door neighbour, Yu: Reiko is pregnant again and Taku is passionately involved in the planning of a local festival.

We quickly see, however that the legacy of Kei's disappearance is still very present in the family. Shun struggles to cope without his brother and is continually fixated on his fate (which his parents have tried to keep from him). The preoccupation with his brother's disappearance results in Shun been unable to achieve any form of genuine connection with another person; when Yu calls for him he pretends not to be there; later, when her mother arrives in the shoe repair shop where they are both standing, he leaves without reason. For Shun the question that opened the film, 'where is your brother?', haunts him throughout. As Yu's aunt tells her in a story about a set of classical twins, the bond between brothers is very close and the missing twin means that perhaps Shun will never be able to form another functioning relationship. He is preoccupied with the exact time that his brother disappeared and he wanders the streets of Nara searching for his brother, remembering fragments such as his mother crying and the endless questions about Kei's whereabouts. We see his tear-stained face looking towards the sky in an effort to find a trace of his missing sibling. His parents struggle to cope with their own grief and their desire to move forward for Shun and their unborn baby's sake. They are presented as a loving couple who are faced with a parent's worst nightmare, the disappearance and then death of a child.

Like many of Kawase's films there is little dialogue. We are fully aware of the family's emotional state but Kawase does not indulge in dramatics; instead, the film offers a meditative vision of a normal family that must come to terms with a tragic event. The long takes which Kawase employs gives the audience a tremendous sense of connection to the events taking place. The camera follows many of the characters around the city in one long continuous take and this evokes the image of a narrative that is interconnected. The movement of the characters is reflected in the movement of the camera as is the slow rhythm of their existence.

It is in the story of Yu that Kawase's own life is perhaps referenced. Kawase herself was abandoned by her parents and then adopted by a relative. Rather than a dramatic display of emotion, Yu's aunt calmly tells her as they walk along the street about her father's abandonment of Yu as a baby and her mother's sad inability to care for herself and her daughter. In Kawase's early work, such as *Embracing* and *Katasumori*, her relationships with her adopted parent is closely referenced and Yu's reaction to her aunt's story is a telling reflection of Kawase's own experiences of this situation. Rather than responding with the emotional outpouring that would be expected, Yu just re-establishes the bond with her aunt by referring to her as 'mum'. Her aunt shows her the shoes that once belonged to her father and this small item is all the contact that Yu will have with her missing parent. Yu, however, is aware that emotionally her aunt has been her key carer and as such, she accepts the story of her parents and takes time to digest it. Her burgeoning love for Shun is seen as an important part of Yu's development; her focus on making a connection with him allows her to transfer her confused and pained feelings over her parent's story into a new and future part of her life. It is she that is the most active in pursuing the relationship; she kisses him first and gives him a small token of her affection, claiming it means that they will always be linked. This is vital for Shun as it is a sense of a missing connection to another person that most haunts him with regards to Kei's disappearance.

It is through his relationship with Yu and the birth of a new brother that Shun is finally able to let go of Kei. He paints a life-size picture of his brother, his mirror image, and as he and Yu stand next to it she takes hold of his hand. It is this gesture that is the beginning of Shun's decision to let his brother go. The new baby brother is not a replacement for Kei but we become aware that the baby represents a new beginning for the whole family. As Taku, Shun, Yu and her aunt all assist in the delivery of the baby they all gain a new sense of connection to each other and an idea of the ever-present ebb and flow of life. The ending of the film mirrors the opening; the camera moves slowly away from the happy family admiring the new addition and goes out in the streets. The voice-over states, 'time to leave now', and we are left to consider that this is Kei, letting go of his family, and as the camera moves upwards to focus on the houses and the rooftops we are left with the feeling of Kei's sprit moving into a new space.

The blending of old and new is very predominant in *Shara*. The new modern houses are set up alongside more traditional structures, such as the temples and older houses. The *basara* (fire) festival which takes place amidst the modern shop fronts is an interesting item to include since it is a modern festival which aims to combine dance and performance forms, both old and new. As Yu, Taku and Shun take part in the energetic dances, they are contributing to a new tradition in a city that is so imbued with older rituals and processions. At the opening we see Yu and Shun cycling home with Yu balanced on the back of Shun's bike. As they cycle through the narrow streets and over railway bridges we are given a distinct sense of place. As in all Kawase's films this urban environment is intercut with segments of film devoted to close-ups of plants, flowers and insects, and continual interplay between the living natural environment and the physical non-living space. In the dramatic dance sequences of the *basara* parade the streets are transformed into a long line of dancing and celebrating people, bringing energy and a remarkable sense of life to the film. Although it is about loss, we are made aware that loss is part of a much wider narrative of life and death; for example, the wooded area where Shun first loses Kei becomes the site where he first kisses Yu. The film is imbued with religious imagery that relates to the spiritual history of Nara, as well as providing a vision of the new and modern *basara* dance festival. There are small shrines on the street corners and the dominant sound throughout the film is a temple bell. In one scene people sit in a temple passing round the circular prayer beads, an ideal image of the notion of the circular continuance of life. The presence of the old and the new references the passing of time and the constant development that is endlessly taking place, not only in the urban and natural environment but also within the main characters.

Shara was not as successful as Kawase's previous feature *Moe no Suzaku* or indeed her later film *Mogari no Mori* but it presents many of the themes that are present in both of these more successful films. The importance of human connection and humanity is emphasised and the documentary feel allows the audience an intimacy that is often denied in modern cinema. *Shara*'s gentle but emotional resonance offers a sense of the narrative of life as the traumatic tale of a missing child blends into a narrative of hope for the future.

As of the writing of this chapter *Shara* is available in Europe but only with French subtitles. The continuing critical popularity of Kawase's work hopefully means that her films will soon be more widely available on the international market.

Bad Guy: Kim Ki-duk

A young Korean man removes the head of a public statue in Paris to give to the women he loves.

Faced with her incredible paranoid jealousy, a young woman undergoes intensive plastic surgery to discover whether her boyfriend really loves her.

An elderly priest paints symbols on a wooden deck using the tail of a white cat he has dipped in ink.

An American-Korean boy attacks his mother with a knife and forcibly cuts away a tattoo bearing his father's name from her breast.

The above scenarios are just a small selection of the remarkable images and narratives that can be seen in the work of Kim Ki-duk. In his films Kim offers a bizarre and often surreal world where gender, race, nationality, globalisation and art come together to produce films that often disturb, sometimes offend, but always challenge. *Spring, Summer, Autumn, Winter... and Spring* (*Bom, yeoreum, gaeul, gyeoul, geurigo... bom*, 2000) became the highest-grossing Korean film at the US box office with takings of over $23 million. This tale of a priest situated on a remote floating temple captured the attention of the worldwide audience and saw Kim nominated for a variety of international awards and winning at the Locarno, San Sebastian and the Blue Dragon film festivals. On its home territory, however, *Spring, Summer, Autumn, Winter... and Spring* made less than US$300,000 (see Russell 2005). This difference is representative of directors like Kim (other arguable examples could be Kawase Naomi and Thai director Apichatpong Weersethakul) who have built their reputations and drawn their fans from a broad international spectrum rather than from a purely domestic base. Unlike other directors such as Im Kwon-taek and Lee Chang-dong, Kim's rise to recognition inside South Korea itself has been slow, despite the fact that he is one of the better-known South Korean directors on the international stage.

Kim was born in 1960 in a small mountain village in Kyungsang Province, eastern South Korea. He was nine when his family, like many during this period of economic turmoil, moved to the outskirts of Seoul. He attended an agricultural college until he was forced to quit, aged 17, when his older brother was expelled. He then went to work in a series of factory jobs and later, like many Korean men, enrolled in the Army and served in the Marines as a non-commissioned officer from the ages of 20 to 25. Whilst working as a church volunteer with the visually impaired he contemplated becoming a priest but instead chose to focus on becoming a painter. In 1990, using all the money he had to buy a ticket, he flew to Paris and studied art, travelling to other regions, including Germany, whilst earning enough to survive by selling paintings on the street.

Returning to South Korea three years later, he focused on becoming a scriptwriter and his first two scripts, *Painter and Prisoner* and *Illegal Crossing*, won several competitions (although neither ever made it to production). Despite no official training or experience Kim wrote and directed his first feature film, *Crocodile* (*Ag-o*), in 1996.

Kim's background is very different from many directors working in South Korea today. He did not attend film school, he has never worked as a director's assistant and he maintains that his love of film and individual style come from his background in painting and his keen interest in contemporary culture rather than from a passionate love of film:

> I find ideas for my films not in films, but in social news items. Western cinema critics notice the influence of great Western directors on Asian directors, but that's not my case. I often watch people; that helps me a lot to find cinematographic ideas. (Quoted in Gombeaud *et al.* 2006: 114)

Kim's interest in the work around him directly relates to his own life experiences. He is fascinated by the interplay between East and West and the legacy of the Korean War. Many of his films offer a presentation of those who are marginalised by Korean society and suffer as a result of their socio-economic and cultural background. In short, his characters 'often constitute the lowest possible social status of hoodlums, pimps, beggars and petty thieves' (Kim 2004: 8).

Whilst his narratives are often hard and troubling, what sets Kim apart is *how* he presents his stories. The most striking elements of his films are, without doubt, their aesthetics. Whilst he may disown a specific influence in terms of film, European painting and art has played a crucial role in Kim's unique construction and presenting of individuals and narratives. Adrian Gombeaud quips that his films are 'an unreasoned catalogue of twentieth century art' and he goes on to summarise that 'in frameworks with a sometime Impressionist flavour, human beings anchored in their realism fight against their own demons with Expressionism, and most often tip over into Fauvism' (2006: 39). Many of his films are marked by haunting landscapes that are worthy of Claude Monet or Pierre-Auguste Renoir. *Spring, Summer, Autumn, Winter… and Spring* is a good example of this, as we see the seasons change around the small floating monastery. When a young murderer, hotly pursued by the police, flees to the monastery the priest paints Buddhist sutras all over the wooded deck of the temple which the man carves and paints as a meditative response to his inner tensions. Despite themselves, the police officers that have come to arrest him also choose to partake in the process before removing him to the mainland. From the side of the ship in *The Bow* (*Hwal*, 2005), the young girl watches the moving expanse of seawater lit by the sun. In *The Isle* (*Seom*, 2000), the small fishing huts float on a wide expanse of river and are framed by rolling hills and mists in the background. At the end of the film, as the woman pulls up the anchor of one of the small huts to escape from the police after murdering a prostitute and her pimp, we are granted a wide sweeping vista of the surrounding river area with the small yellow house floating towards the sea.

The landscapes in Kim's films can be soothing (*The Isle* or *Spring, Summer, Autumn, Winter… and Spring*) or they can be harsh and terrible such as the barbed-wire beach front in *The Coast Guard* (*Haeanseon*, 2002), the empty countryside of *Address Unknown* (*Suchwiin bulmyeong*, 2001) or the urban cityscape of *Real Fiction* (*Shilje sanghwang*, 2002). These landscapes serve as the backdrop to Kim's narratives of the obsessed, deranged and isolated characters, and his use of wide-sweeping panoramas is an ideal method to convey the isolation of the individuals inside this world.

Austrian artist Egon Schiele is a particular influence, and his paintings feature in several of Kim's works. In *Birdcage Inn* (*Paran daemun*, 1998), the young prostitute arrives at the hotel with a large reproduction of an Schiele's painting *Schwarzhaariges Mädchen* (1911) that focuses on the naked figure of a young girl. In *Bad Guy* (*Nabbeun namja*, 2001), student Sun-hwa is flipping though a book of Shiele's images when she commits the act that will result in her becoming a prostitute. Schiele was most famous for nudes of prostitutes and the image of the prostitute is returned to again and again in Kim's work, and Schiele's paintings are a mixture of beauty and ugliness that again can be seen in Kim's work. In *Birdcage Inn* the owner and the prostitute who works from his motel paint pictures together on the side of the motel wall; straight after this touching moment of emotional bonding he rapes her. In *Real Fiction* we see a couple make illicit and adulterous love on a bed of roses. This striking image of them entwined on the bright red flowers is later evoked when the cheating woman is then brutally murdered and decorated with the same blossoms that she has earlier enjoyed. Here, in the mixture of sex and death, Kim references two of the key themes that exist in both his, and the long-dead Shiele's, work. In *The Coast Guard* a young couple's lovemaking on a forbidden beach is interrupted when the young man is shot thought the buttocks by an overzealous guard. He is then destroyed by a grenade and in a disturbing image his girlfriend kisses and caresses his blown-off hand. Later in the film the same woman (now mad) sinks into a fish tank to recover from the forced and amateur abortion that the local soldiers enforced on her to hide their sexual abuse of her. In *Spring, Summer, Autumn, Winter... and Spring* the young women delivers her new born baby to the temple only to fall through the ice and drown. Here, illicit sex leads to a child and this child leads directly to his mother's death in the frozen lake. *Breath* (*Soon*, 2007) focuses on the relationship between a young mother and a convicted murderer. As their relationship intensifies we become aware that through the act of sex with the man she is embracing death itself. As a convicted murderer awaiting the death sentence, he is literally a 'dead man walking'. The woman herself is highly troubled and seems to be contemplating suicide, and her relationship with the man is the method through which she seems to embrace death, but turns back at the last moment to capture life. Visiting him in his prison cell she transforms the cell on each visit into images of the various seasons; she pastes panoramas of respectively, spring mountains, summer beaches and autumn woods onto the wall of the cell, dresses in the appropriate clothing and sings to him songs related to the season that she is trying to evoke. At the end of each session the couple try to grasp a few moments of sexual pleasure but are always thwarted. The women's desire to move the seasons on each time refers to the accelerated passing of time and the knowledge that death will all too soon arrive for the condemned man and that sex is just one method through which they will try to reassert life. The French euphemism for orgasm is *la petite mort* which literally translates as 'the little death', and in the work of Kim we are aware that sex and death are never far apart. He states that 'the world is born and dies in their conflict. So we must live in balance between black and white which are in us. This is what I try to express in my cinema. I don't speak as a philosopher or theologian, but from what I draw from my experience of life' (Kim 2005: 113).

His focus on art as part of real life is something that is echoed in Kim's desire to offer social reality and events via the medium of film; this is not in terms of documentary but rather in using art/film as a method to present 'Life' in all its forms. This often involves the use of extended metaphors: thus we have narratives such as the young woman offering herself to men for free (*Samaritan Girl* [*Samaria*, 2004]), a frog tied to a stone tries to escape until it dies (*Spring, Summer, Autumn, Winter… and Spring*) and an endless cycle of plastic surgery (*Time* [*Shi gan*, 2006]) all acting as reflectors of issues that face contemporary South Korea. Kim comments: 'I use film as a medium to illustrate the metaphors that are important to me. Many people may not see my metaphors because of the harsh realities I have portrayed (2001).

A wonderful example of this mixture of harsh reality and metaphor can be found in *Address Unknown*. After losing her eye several years earlier when her brother fires a toy gun at her, the teenage Eun-ok finds an American GI called James to be her boyfriend in order to get her eye fixed. In one of their meetings he papers over her ruined eye with the eye of a woman from a magazine. Eun-ok stares at the camera, a mixture of East and West, one Korean eye and one Western. This image works on a variety of levels. Eun-ok has become the body that represents Korea and the Korean past. Her eye was lost as a result of her brother wanting to participate in 'war games' and shooting her with his homemade gun. Her white and unseeing cataract-covered eye becomes a living reminder of the past and in her interactions with James she becomes the living body of American neo-colonisation. She, in essence, sells her body to the man with economic and social power. When James places the magazine image over her ruined eye it symbolises not only the new life and prosperity that Eun-ok sees America offering to her but also reinforces James's desire to see her as a passive object, a disposable body to comfort him during his time away from home. He literally pastes the Western image onto her face symbolising his perceived power to control, and therefore own, her body. His providing of an eye operation results in his belief that Eun-ok's body belongs to him. Later in the film he will literally attempt to carve his name into her chest as a mark of his ownership.

The position of the female body as the site of tension is common in Kim's films. The legacy of the Japanese colonisation and the enslavement of hundreds of Korean women as 'comfort women' and the sex workers for the military sex-workers has resulted in women maintaining a highly ambivalent placement in the construction of modern South Korean identity. As Kim Myung-Ja notes:

> In a patriarchal culture that strictly controls women's sexuality under an ideology of chastity and allows women's position and existence only within a space related to men, the colonised Korean female body is taken as a sign of shame and humiliation that damages the self-image and masculinity of the Korean male. (2007: 249)

With reference to the work of Kim, Kim Kyung-hyun states that 'women function as masochistic and passive objects predicated on the patented image of mother and whore' (2004: 9). This reading is one that is hard to refute. Women in the work of Kim Ki-duk are often rendered helpless in the face of male aggression and rarely deviate from the two poles of saint or sinner. Kim's first film *Crocodile* features a violent loner (who goes by the title name) who resides under a bridge on the Han River in Seoul. He saves a young woman from committing suicide but then proceeds to imprison, rape and beat her. In *Real Fiction* the maladjusted young artist viciously murders women for real or imagined insults and *Bad Guy* sees a young college girl forced into prostitution by an abusive pimp. The men, from the disturbed solider in *The Coast Guard*, the incest-driven 'grandfather' in *The Bow*, the violent 'Crocodile' and the husband in *3-Iron* (*Bin-jip*, 2004) are all shown as unable to conduct relationships with women, except by using a dialogue of abuse. Love is often conveyed through violence since the men are seen as having no other method with which to communicate their feelings. This inability to communicate except via violence is most often seen in the literal inability to talk that emerges in several of Kim's films. In *The Isle* the male protagonist swallows fish hooks and then proceeds to pull them out, rendering himself mute. *Breath* sees the imprisoned murderer (played by Chinese actor Chen Chang) stab himself in the throat several times. He will also spend the film silent, only able to communicate via his physical actions. Tae-suk in *3-Iron* remains silent for the entire film, leaving us to ponder his actions. Even the men who have no physical reason for their lack of speech are highly uncommunicative leaving us unable to understand fully their motives. The grandfather in *The Bow*, the eponymous *Crocodile*, the father in *Birdcage Inn*, Kang in *The Coast Guard* and Chang-guk in *Address Unknown* all refuse to verbalise their feelings, and their primary means of communication is through their bodies and their physical actions. In *Birdcage Inn* the father articulates his feelings of desire in forcing the young prostitute to have sex with him. Tae-suk (*3-iron*) breaks into people's homes whilst they are away. He takes photographs of himself, fixes any broken electrical goods, cleans and tidies. Whilst his actions are never actually violent he has little consideration for the legal and emotional ramifications of what he is doing. In *Address Unknown* we only see Chang-guk speak for any length of time when he is rebuking the bullies who are targeting his friend. Rather than speaking in Korean, however, he demonstrates his skills in English, his knowledge of which is the bitter legacy of his African-American father and his mother's desire to see him 'Americanised'. We are aware that he despises this element of himself since his mixed-race parentage is the reason for his isolation. Language in this case, rather than allowing him to participate in social communication, only further highlights his positioning as 'other' from the society which surrounds him. Although Ji-woo, the young man in *Time* is highly educated and articulate, in the end, words and vocalisation fail him too and he resorts to his own body to make his message heard. When his insecure girlfriend Seh-hee vanishes, he is left to try to rebuild his life and he gradually meets another and falls in love again. He eventually discovers, howeve,r that Seh-hee has had radical plastic surgery. Faced with such a betrayal he results to plastic surgery himself, seeking to transform his body and face in order to find some form of understanding and revenge against Seh-hee. Ji-woo's body becomes the only method through which he can communicate his feelings. He will eventually die under the wheels of a car, his face and neck smashed and bloody, symbolising the physical rendering of his pain. In *The Bow* we rarely see 'the grandfather' speak. Instead, he makes marks on a calendar leading up to his adopted 'granddaughter's' sixteenth birthday, the day he has decided that they will marry. Living isolated on a ship in the middle of the sea he has had the girl with him since she was a toddler and she has never seen land. He quietly stockpiles clothes and ornaments for this wedding on his trips to the mainland and when asked to explain his motives refuses to elaborate. When the young woman attempts to escape with her boyfriend, he tries to hang himself with a rope connected to the small fishing vessel she is leaving on. This rope, tightly wound around his throat, literally cuts off his voice. Kim's films never expose or elaborate the motives of his characters, and there are no clear narrative conclusions that provide convenient and easy endings for the audience.

These silent violent men relate to one of the predominant models of masculinity that has dominated recent South Korean cinema. The troubled, alienated, aggressive and highly dysfunctional 'angry young man' figure, as mentioned in the chapter on Lee Chang-dong, has become a prominent figure in modern South Korean cinema. They are fractured individuals in search of a consolidated identity. The notion of *han* is strong throughout Kim's films but the causes for this sorrow are related to modern society rather than the historical problems that infuse the films of Im Kwon-taek. The characters struggle with their intense feelings of this 'Korean' deep sadness. Kim himself speaks of his father and those of his father's generation as being infused with the *han* of the Korean war (logically the *han* of the previous generation will be the Japanese occupation) but for Kim his *han* comes from a different source. He states: 'My *han* stems from my belief that I am not able to fit into mainstream society or even its fringes. Other Koreans who are in the same situation have inferiority complexes' (2001).

All of these men are unable to function in the acceptable fashion that society demands from them. The older men are marked by a violent national history and the younger men by their perceived feelings of inferiority. The husband in *3-Iron*, despite being financially successful, beats his wife for not giving him enough affection and thus adds to his *han* of inadequacy. This, of course, becomes a vicious circle: he beats her so she withdraws further from him and as a result he feels even more insecure and beats her even more, and so on. In *The Coast Guard* Private Kang is so obsessed with killing a spy that he shoots a young couple having sex on a beach. Kang's *han* stems from his desire to participate in a war that is long over.[1] The film reveals the pure idiocy of the military lifestyle as soldiers spend their time fighting each other and abusing the civilian population rather than fighting an enemy. When Kang is expelled from the army on the grounds of mental instability he decides to attack his former platoon and all the army's training and weapons are rendered useless when under attack from one of their own (he even steals a gun from a fellow soldier which he proceeds to use to shoot his former colleagues). Kim has spoken about the film's focus on the division of North and South Korea, and even when the young men are engaged in leisure activities they play their game of volleyball on a court with the outline of the Korean peninsula marked out. The net offers a strange version of the 38th Parallel and is a continual reminder of the trauma of Korean history that continues to have such a negative influence on the present and future.

As discussed in the chapter on Park Chan-wook, the division between North and South continues to affect the Korean construction of self-identity and nationhood. In *The Coast Guard* this division, and the militarism that has resulted from it, is seen as the original reason for the death and destruction that follows. In *Real Fiction* the legacy of the events of the 1980s is seen in the murderous behaviour of a street artist that we learn was tortured by the police in the 1980s. The film itself is a masterpiece of alternative filmmaking since it was shot in very few hours, using static and handheld cameras positioned around the streets of Seoul. Each scene is one continuous shot and as we follow the psychotic protagonist around the city, he enacts revenge on all those he perceives as having harmed him; the relationship between reality and fiction, history and future, is thus impossibly blurred. In *The Coast Guard* Kang is seen in the end performing military manoeuvres on the streets of Seoul to the incredulity of the bystanders. They think he is performing but when he stabs a young man they realise that the violence that was so deeply ingrained in the social structure and history has come life in the figure of the disturbed soldier.

Although the traumatised male figure features in many of Kim's films, also evident is a sustained presentation of women, and specifically the figure of the prostitute. *Wild Animals* (1996) Kim's second film, features Laura, a young Korean woman, who is persuaded by her French boyfriend, Emil, to work in his club as a peepshow dancer. In *Birdcage Inn* we follow the story of a young prostitute, Jin-a, who works in a small seaside inn. Working at night we see her deal with a variety of unpleasant customers, many of whom attempt and often succeed in raping her after the 'official' transaction has taken place. *Bad Guy* sees the female lead forced to work as a prostitute by a man she has spurned. In *Samaritan Girl* two schoolgirls become involved in prostitution initially to fund a trip to Europe and as a result one of the girls dies as she leaps from a hotel window to escape the police.

Prostitution in South Korean society can be seen as an integral part of the social structure. Although illegal, in 2007 the sex trade in South Korea was estimated to amount to approximately 1.6 per cent of the nation's GDP. Despite government campaigns, which include offering male office workers money to try and curb the 'normal' evening structure of heavy drinking and buying sex, there are estimated to be over one million people involved in the South Korean sex industry. *Birdcage Inn* clearly offers a critique of this as the young woman working out of the motel is not lacking in clients. A whole economic system has been set up based upon the use of Jin-a's body. She pays 'rent' to the family for the use of the room and it is made clear that the family's success is dependent on her. Despite their need for her economic input, the family treat her terribly. The father rapes her, the son spies on her and eventually sells nude pictures of her to a porn magazine, and the daughter, Hye-mi, openly insults her and makes it clear that she sees her as nothing more than 'worthless trash'. Although *Birdcage Inn* is one of the few Kim Ki-duk films with a 'happy ending' (they eventually all realise the innate value in each other and co-exist happily in familial harmony), Jin-a is still working as a sex worker and the location of woman as the site of economic exchange is never denied. Hye-mi is determined to remain a virgin until she marries since she believes that her economic and social worth will be diminished by the act of sex. Throughout the film the relationship between the two young women is key and in one scene they take turns to follow each other around a market place, each copying exactly the actions of the other. This linkage between the two women offers a narrative that constantly seeks to align female sexual activities with economic structures. Listening to and watching the activities that Jin-a performs in her daily sex work awakens Hye-mi's sexual desire and it is telling that it is in a shopping precinct that they first start to bond. Towards the end of the film after Jin-a has attempted suicide, Hye-mi comforts her and eventually takes Jin-a's place with a client to spare the sick Jin-a.

This film thus offers a real notion of a world of female solidarity as Hye-mi and Jin-a bond, and the film ends on an image of the two women smiling down at a fish in the ocean below them. Filmed from below we see the two girls bonded together and, for Hye Seung Chung, the final shot links to the water functioning as 'a regenerative space, a pulsating space of a semiotic *chora* wherein the two female subjects are in the process of becoming one, unfettered by language and largely outside the symbolic order' (2012: 93). Utilising Kristeva's construction of the *chora* as a 'representation of the subject in process' (1998: 134), the *chora* functions as 'a space of perpetual motion and infinite renewal' (Chung 2012: 93) and in this way the final shot of the two women can be seen as a positive move towards the renegotiation of a female subjectivity outside the dominant mode of masculine discourse.

Many feminist groups have seen Kim's works as highly misogynistic in their presentation of women as the site of sexual and economic objectification. In the same way, however, that Kim's representations of men reveal specific tensions and concerns with relation to their alienation from the social space, can his films about women be seen to challenge dominant ideology with regards to women? Do they offer a notion of a space where women can engage and challenge the dominant structures via their own embodied interactions? This can arguably be seen in *Birdcage Inn* when Hye-mi rejects her previously held 'socially correct' notions on the importance and value of her own virginity in order to help and support her injured friend. This sexual act, however, also helps sustain the family unit which we see happy and content after this exchange has taken place. Has Hye-mi therefore fallen into the role of sacrificial female rather than offering a serious narrative of female deliverance and empowerment?

In many ways this dual narrative of female solidarity simultaneous to the sacrifice of the female body can also be seen in *Samaritan Girl*. The two teenagers throughout the film are seen as holding an irreversible and powerful bond that cannot be disrupted, even by death. In order to save for a tip to Europe the two girls engage in prostitution; one, Yeo-jin, acting as booking agent and organiser, and the other, Jae-yeong, actually performing the sexual acts. The film opens with Jae-yeong telling the tale of the prostitute Vasumitra, whose clients apparently became devout Buddhists after sexual encounters with her. After Jae-yeong's death in order to assuage her guilt at her friend's death Yeo-jin makes contact and sleeps with all of Jae-yeong's clients, and at the end of the sexual act she repays the men the money that they had previously paid Ja-yeong. In line with the Vasumitra story some of the men do indeed repent of their actions following their encounter with Yeo-jin. Is Kim therefore presenting a transformative and empowering female sexuality that can transform and affect the world around them or are we actually seeing a young and naïve girl being sacrificed to assist ageing paedophiles for cinematic visual pleasure? In the figure of the prostitute that he presents, is he articulating a figure that can move beyond and challenge the dominant hierarchy or simply presenting a vision of woman as whore? The answer to this question is perhaps related to personal opinion. If one reads the women as sacrificial victims to dominant masculinity, is Kim simply articulating an opinion regarding women that dominant society holds but refuses to articulate? By presenting the extreme logic of this approach (women as object that cannot be articulated beyond the virgin/whore binary) is Kim aggrandising the dominant structures in an effort to challenge and critique them?

This idea can be seen in Kim's films that engage not only with prostitution in contemporary Korea but also where the historical legacy of prostitution is clearly referenced. Prostitution began on a large scale with the arrival of the American military bases after the Korean War; Japanese tourism in the 1970s and 1980s continued the demand and the South Korean male ritual of going *en mass* to establishments that sell beer and sex all under the same roof has kept the industry growing. As Kathleen Berry notes:

> The demand for sexual service is most significant where men congregate in large groups separate from home and family. The sexual demands of military men, travelling business men or sailors or immigrant labourers create a demand for women's bodies. (Berry 1979: 59)

The legacy of this usage of the female body is most clearly referenced in *Address Unknown*. Chang-guk's mother is ostracised and rejected by society as a result of her affair and subsequent illegitimate child by an African-American Marine who had been stationed in South Korea during the war. This negative legacy of the Korean War is most clearly shown in the social reaction to the children that were born as a result of relationships between US soldiers and Korean women. Chang-guk's mother is seen as a warning to young girls against fraternisation with the GIs (Eun-ok is cautioned that she could end up like her). Women who had relations with soldiers are often referred to as *Yanggongju* and Hyun Sook Kim notes that

> Used derogatorily it means 'Yankee whore', 'Yankee wife', 'UN Lady' and/or 'Western Princess'. This epitaph 'Yanggongju' relegates Korean women working in militarised prostitution with foreign men to the lowest status within the hierarchy of prostitution … In post-war Korea, the epitaph 'Yonggongju' has become synonymous with 'GI Brides' so that Korean women in interracial marriages can also be viewed as 'Yonggongju.' (1998: 178)

The link here is made between prostitution and any woman who becomes involved in an inter-racial relationship. The status of the *Yonggongju* is one that refers back to the *han* of the (male) Korean population. The Japanese 'comfort' women and *Yonggongju* are related in that both are constructed as a mark of shame on the national collective psyche. In her work on military comfort women, Yang Hyunah quotes from a letter that was sent to a prominent newspaper around the time that the debates surrounding the Japanese lack of apology for the events that took place during the occupation of Korea:

> 'This [Military Comfort Women] issue will not end with the apology of the Japanese Prime Minister. Nor will the issue be settled by compensation only to the old women victims. The event amounts to an act in which the Japanese have thrown their dirty sperm bucket into our Korean people's faces. (1998: 130)

The linguistic coding of this letter is telling. The usage of 'sperm bucket' clearly invokes the image of Japanese men defiling Korean women. The notion of 'our Korean people' offers an image of a homogenous and unified society (*minjok*, as discussed with reference to Im Kwon-taek). The focus of the comment is related to the idea that when a crime is committed against one 'member' the whole group suffers. The underlying premise is that the humiliation and abuse of Korean women is the humiliation and abuse of the whole nation, therefore directly contributing to the *han* of the Korean people. The easy dismissal, however, of the 'old women victims' implies that there is a basic fault in the underlying assumption of collectivism. The group still maintains a hierarchy and as Yang points out, 'as implied by this "mans" talk', those who are able to invade women's sexuality, and those who are obliged to protect it, are males, and 'this exemplifies how males become the only subjects involved in the questioning of nation and sexuality' (ibid.). Women in this way become the site and object of confusion and distress: in short, they themselves become *han* for the male counterparts. The women in Kim's films are often the main focus of the male's aggression, fear and antagonism. Even the least violent of Kim's films, *Time*, sees the male protagonist's life ruined due to the insecurity of his girlfriend. She becomes the reason for, and the living embodiment of, his own personal *han*. Is this anti-women or does it represent a lack/problem in the *male* character? Seh-hee in *Time* is obsessed with her looks because dominant structures constantly emphasise the need for women to be beautiful and rate their value according to their physical appearance. Is Seh-hee Ji-woo's *han* or is it the social and cultural structures that make her so insecure that cause him to suffer? It is not implied that Chang-guk's mother was actually a prostitute but her mixed-race child has relegated her to this level in the eyes of her neighbours and, as such, Chang-guk must live with the legacy of this. The question is raised, however, of whether it his status as a mixed-race son of a *Yonggongju* the source of Chang-guk's *han* or is it the way the wider social society treats him that causes his actions? Kim's presentation of Chang-guk, and, indeed, Eun-ok's relationship with James, raises the spectre of issues that wider South Korean society does not wish to deal with, and therefore Kim's films directly challenge a dominant ideology that consigns such events to the uncomfortable past. Women, like men, are used as a method for Kim to question social constraints and dominant ideology. As the close examination of *Bad Guy* in the next section will show, Kim's films, although highly problematic, seek to challenge and question rather than to provide simple explanations for his characters' behaviour. For Kim, the inability to fit into social structures is his *han* and in his films, although his characters often act in fairly incomprehensible ways, the blame lies in the fact that dominant society will not offer any alternative other than their own bodies and the bodies of others, to articulate their pain. Their pain causes their actions and their inability to link into any social system only intensifies their isolation. This isolation can be clearly seen it *The Isle* where a young women manages a series of small fishing huts. She will eventually bond with a man hiding after murdering his wife and her lover, and together they will find solace from their troubles. It is via their infliction of mirror injuries on themselves that they will eventually be united. The man's suicide attempt by swallowing fishhooks and then ripping them out will be the impetus for the women to care for and fall in love with him. When the man eventually leaves her she places fishhooks in her vagina and it is her screams of pain as they are pulled out that cause him to return to her. His film *Dream* (*Bimong*, 2009) features a man and a women intimately connected via their dreams. Complete strangers, they discover that whilst one dreams the other acts out their often-violent actions in a somnambulant state. Both the main characters are highly troubled individuals and it is via the bodies of *each other* that they will enact their unconscious rage and fears.

Outside of the narrative content of his films Kim Ki-duk is the ideal representative of the interplay between the national and global. His reputation and popularity developed from his international festival success rather than initial domestic acknowledgement. Inside Korea his films have generally performed poorly at the box office and South Korean critics have lampooned his films for

185

the levels of violence and aggressive sexuality. In terms of financing only one of Kim's films have been financed by a large production company (*The Isle*); the rest have been financially pieced together from smaller more obscure film finance units. A large proportion of his recent films have been financed by companies from outside Korea (see Davis and Yeh 2008: 162) and he continues to struggle to get films made. As already mentioned, even though *Spring, Summer, Autumn, Winter... and Spring* did very well in foreign markets, its domestic performance was less than sterling. In 2004 he won both Best Director in Berlin for *Samaritan Girl* as well as Best Director for *3-Iron* in Venice, but despite this the film that followed, *The Bow*, was only screened in one theatre in Seoul and only recorded 1,400 ticket sales (see Park 2007). Kim's relationship with Cineclick Asia, a major distributor of Korean film worldwide, has resulted in international success but domestic audience acclaim still continues to elude him.

Despite the continuing problems he has in financing his own productions in the last few years Kim has also produced the films of up-and-coming young Korean directors. Lee Seung Young's *Nowhere to Turn* (*Yeogiboda eodingae*, 2007, Jeon Jae Hong's *Beautiful* (*Areumdabda*, 2008) and his recent release *Rough Cut* (*Yeong-hwa-neun yeong-hwa-da*, 2008) were produced by Kim. Jeon Jea-hong in particular is following in his mentor's footsteps and has even earned the moniker 'little Kim'. His continuing support of young filmmakers is a highly positive step in promoting cutting-edge and often challenging South Korean film that, like his own work, does not conform to dominant expectations.

In 2011 Kim completed two films entitled *Arirang* and *Amen* respectively. *Arirang*, produced entirely by Kim alone, delves into the personal crisis he experienced after actress Lee Na-young nearly died when a hanging sequence went wrong on *Dream* in 2007. Recorded with a camcorder in his mountain home, *Arirang* focuses on Kim discussing his filmmaking career, his opinions on the Korean film industry and his emotional engagement with his art, and the impact that the incident in *Dream* left on him. *Arirang* and *Amen* mark a return to filmmaking from Kim after a three-year gap and both films premiered in Europe (*Arirang* at Cannes and *Amen* at the San Sebastián International Film Festival). International response to both has been highly mixed and it is clear that those who dislike Kim's work remain unconvinced; however, his deeply personal and emotive films continue to be admired by many and his place on the international film circuit continues to be maintained.

NOTE

1   Although at the time of publication, July 2013, new tensions in the region means that this situation is currently been revisited with the North reasserting the lack of an armistice treaty to confirm that they still see themselves at war with the South.

Film Analysis

BAD GUY

나쁜 남자
Na-bun-Nam-Ja

2001

Director

Kim Ki-duk

Cast

Cho Jae-hyeon (Han-gi), Seo Won (Sun-hwa), Kim Yun-tae (Yun-tae), Choi Duk-moon (Myung-soo), Choi Yung-young (Hyun-ja), Shin Yoo-jin (Min-jung), Kim Jung-young (Eun-hye)

International Film Awards

2002 Orient Express Awards, Catalonia International Film Festival

2002 Grand Bell Award, Grand Bell Awards

2002 Winner Best New Actress: Seo Won

2002 Nominated Golden Bear, Berlin International Film Festival

Plot Summary

Whilst walking in Seoul, pimp and gangster Hang-gi sees Sun-hwa, a young college student, sitting on a park bench and forces her to kiss him. After she publicly rejects him he engineers a situation where she is framed for theft and as a result forced into becoming a bonded-sex-worker. She will have to work as a prostitute until she has paid her debt. She is taken to the red light district and installed in a room with a two-way mirror. She asks to lose her virginity to her college boyfriend rather than a client but, although she is allowed to meet with him, Hang-gi sends his helpers to beat him up before they can have sex. Instead she is forced to have sex with a client whilst Han-gi observes her through the mirror. Although at first she protests and is horrified by the work, she gradually begins to adapt to the lifestyle and actively solicits clients. She and Hang-gi begin a strange courtship based on her gradual awareness of his voyeurism. When she manages to escape by seducing Myung-soo, an employee of the brothel, Hang-gi recaptures her and takes her to a beach where they see a woman walk into the sea. Sun-hwa picks up some photos which the woman had buried but the faces are missing. When his friend and employee Hyun-ja murders a rival mob boss who had tried to kill Hang-gi, Hang-gi allows himself to be charged with the crime to save his friend's life. When she discovers that he is facing a death sentence Sun-hwa is devastated and realises that she loves him. She returns to the beach when she finds the missing parts of the photos and realises they are of her and Hang-gi. Hang-gi escapes with help from Hyun-ja who is struggling with the guilt of allowing Hang-gi to take the blame for her actions. He returns to Sun-hwa and leaves her by the park bench where they first met. Hang-gi gets in a fight with Myung-soo and is stabbed. Sun-hwa goes to the beach and contemplates the photo of her and Hang-gi. He arrives and they embrace. They choose to travel together with Sun-hwa working as a mobile prostitute from the back of a van.

If one condenses the storyline of *Bad Guy* down to its bare essentials, it is a tale of a man who forces the women he loves into prostitution. She gradually accepts working in the brothel and falls in love with the man that has orchestrated her fall into the sex trade. Unsurprisingly *Bad Guy* received a stern amount of criticism from viewers for its representation of violence towards women and the female response towards this aggression. An initial reading is that the film is nothing more that a male masochistic fantasy conforming to the old adage that all women are potential prostitutes. With regard to this approach, several Korean critics saw the film as an insight into Kim's own beliefs concerning women; one critic going as far to say that it reflected that fact that the 'director's mother must not have loved him' (Choe 2007: 68). Comments such as these, which Kim actively refuted, resulted in him making the statement that he would no longer be conducting any interviews with Korean journalists (a vow he has generally kept to).

The wider issues of the film's reception will be discussed shortly but the narrative and visual construction of the film is such that, on initial reading, it is sometimes hard to refute the claim that it is highly negative in its portrayal of women. As with many of Kim's works, however, *Bad Guy* cannot easily be dismissed as offering a simplistic patriarchal rendering of gender and society.

The film opens with the main protagonist Hang-gi walking through the streets of Seoul. As the camera picks him out from the crowd in the popular student area of Daehak-Ro, it is clear that he is not part of 'respectable' society. His clothes, attitude and the visible scar across his throat all alienate him from the surrounding crowds of students, workers and businessmen. His meeting with college student Sun-hwa further illustrates his social position. When he sits next to her she quickly shows her distaste and moves away to another bench and proceeds to complain loudly about him to her boyfriend. Her boyfriend's retort of 'don't worry about him' is a dismissive and patronising rejection of someone who clearly does not 'belong' in their construction of the social world. Hang-gi is rejected by Sun-hwa and dismissed by her boyfriend for superficial reasons, and the film will see him demonstrate his anger at this situation. Their out-of-hand dismissal of Hang-gi relates to Kim's fascination with those that make-up the Korean underclass. He will assert his potential power on the body of the middle-class Sun-haw. He forces Sun-hwa to kiss him and refuses to offer an apology when she arrogantly demands one. Kim has made the statement that for him 'no one deserves to be treated that way because of the way they look'

(2001). In this middle-class district the student's reaction to Hang-gi is a telling reflection of a society which does not wish to be confronted by the realities of a class system that controls people's social status. In an interview Kim offers an insight into this situation:

> The question I was trying to ask is, why is it that though everyone is born the same, with equal rights and equal qualities, we are divided and categorised as we grow older. Why are we judged according to our looks and appearances? According to these standards, which are imposed after we are born and grown up, we become divided into ranks and social classes that don't go along with each other. (Quoted in Hummel 2002)

The divisions in society will be brought to the for when Sun-hwa is later transported to the brothel. Here in this liminal space, the class system is rendered physical as we see a series of middle-class businessmen utilise the bodies of the underclass for their own enjoyment.

The process of Sun-hwa's fall into prostitution begins with Hang-gi returning to the park the next day and following Sun-hwa as she and her boyfriend wander around Seoul. In a very telling precursor of what will later take place, he watches Sun-hwa through a shop window trying on a dress; it is through a shop window that Sun-hwa and the other women will later be forced to sell themselves. The image of a woman for sale is further enhanced when we see Sun-hwa flipping though a book of images by Egon Schiele. Schiele's images of prostitutes, as mentioned in the previous section, are present in many of Kim's films, most notably *Birdcage Inn*. Poised between the end of the art-nouveau movement and the beginning of Expressionism, Schiele was himself arrested for pornography and obscenity, two charges that have been levelled at Kim's treatment of women in his films, especially *Bad Guy*. It is during the examination of the book that Sun-hwa commits the two crimes which lead to her falling into Hang-gi's orbit. Whilst she is busy tearing out an image from the book, Hang-gi's accomplice plants a wallet next to her; when she sees the wallet she immediately pockets it. It is this act that will lead to her falling into the arms of Hang-gi when the 'owner' of the wallet confronts her and claims there is a vast amount of money missing. She is faced with the option of social disgrace (being labelled a thief) or signing an illegal loan document which places her body as collateral. The literal terms laid down is that she 'will give up the rights to her face and body' until the money is paid back. What the audience is aware of, and Sun-hwa is not, is that the whole situation is being orchestrated by Hang-gi. In the signing of the loan agreement Sun-hwa has, in essence, sold herself to Hang-gi. Her body now carries monetary value in the same manner as any other commodity.

An interesting point to note, however, is that although Hang-gi sets up the situation, it is through a process of *choice* that Sun-hwa falls into it. She chooses to steal the wallet and then she chooses to sign the loan agreement rather than face the police and her family. If one sees *Bad Guy* as a negative comment on a social situation then Sun-hwa's almost apathetic agreement to the bond document can be related to the established social positioning of women in South Korean society. We know from a scene where she refused to allow her boy-friend to enter her apartment that society has constructed Sun-hwa as a 'good' woman. She is not sexually active and generally conducts herself according to the dominant gender values that surround her. As Vincent Brandt notes regarding women in Korea:

> The Confucian tradition in Korea has a puritanical aspect that emphasises structures of physical modesty and reticence regarding sexual matters. Such values are linked to the subordinate role of women and the emphasis on deference and obligation rather than emotion in personal relations. (1971: 133)

This emphasis on obligation is perhaps the reason why Sun-hwa behaves in the manner which she does. Just as society has constructed an ideal image of a woman, Sun-hwa has also absorbed these values and self-constructs her identity according to the dominant ideology. When she is confronted by the deviation from these values (in the theft of the wallet), she reverts to her idealised image based on obedience and deference. Most viewers, given the situation, would rather face the police than an illegal loan shark but Sun-hwa is anxious to 'mend' her deviation from her vision of herself and so goes along with the commands of others. She has internalised the idea of the subordinate nature of women to such a degree that she can almost be accused of acquiescence in her fate. This is not a criticism of Sun-hwa; rather Kim is highlighting the basic issues at play in a system that preaches the role of women as being passive objects.

The notion of women as passive objects with an innate monetary value can be seen to have a physical face in the rows of women being forced to sell themselves from shop windows. Bonded prostitution has been a problem in modern

South Korean for some time. The real-life practices of women being forced into the sex trade to repay loans gained attention in the press in recent years when the Korean Bar Association sought to take brothel owners to court over the violation of the women's human rights. For Sun-hwa there is no escape or help offered; the man whose wallet she stole tries to rape her and when she is 'rescued' by Hang-gi's associates they just transfer her to the brothel. The notion of women as commodities is quickly established when Sun-hwa arrives at the red light district. It is lined with women selling themselves through the glass windows as male customers stroll the streets 'choosing' the women. Installed in a dim and badly decorated room Sun-hwa becomes quickly aware of the realities of her situation. The brothel is run by an ex-prostitute who we late find out has been badly scarred on the chest by the gangsters for seeking to run away. She quickly shows her dislike for Sun-hwa and her middle-class background stating that 'she needs to learn she is only worth 70,000 KRW' (about US$45). The location of the female body at the centre of economic exchange is one that again relates to the social critique that is being offered. The fact that bodies have on them a registered rate of monetary exchange clearly opens up the narrative of slavery and oppression. The women are modern-day slaves but in the presentation of this state, Kim is referencing a real-life situation that the wider society generally chooses to ignore. As he states:

> If you think of my film as Kim Ki-duk *creating* the misfortune of the woman it depicts, than that's very dangerous, But if you think of it as the depiction of a problem that already exists in society than you cannot really hate *Bad Guy*.' (Quoted in Hummel 2002; emphasis added)

Kim presents the female characters as doubly marginalised; first in the physical treatment of them and then in a more insidious way by a society that so strenuously constructs their social and cultural boundaries. They become victims to a system that seems to endlessly repeat itself. The police are seen to be avid brothel visitors and refuse to help the women that are captive in the establishments.

Just as the women are caught in this matrix of violence and oppression, so to are the men. Like many of Kim's male characters, Hang-gi is silent throughout the film. His slashed throat indicates that his body is one which has been formed by violence and it is through bodily violence that he will conduct his relationships. His rebuked attraction for Sun-hwa will be shown in his desire to physically punish and contain her. When he takes her to the beach for the first time they sit in silence together; when Sun-hwa tries to walk away he catches hold of her and forces her back into the car. His love for her means that he does not want her to leave him but, rather than traditional methods, he can only convey this by once again containing her in the space of the brothel. It is after their trip to the beach that Hang-gi first goes into Sun-hwa's room but rather than having sex he embraces her with such a pathetic devotion that it is hard to conflate him with a vicious abuser. He cannot vocalise his feelings so he find other methods of communication. When Hyun-ja's father is diagnosed with cancer Hang-gi beats Hyun-ja for his drinking but then later pays for his father's operation. Hang-gi does not offer any condolences or comfort but he responds to Hyun-ja's pain in one of the few ways he understands; hard currency. When Hyun-ja murders a rival gang member Hang-gi shows his fear, care and concern for his friend by attacking him and nearly strangling him. Straight afterwards we are made aware than Hang-gi has confessed to the crime. He cannot convey his love or care except via physical means. In this case he offers his body for punishment in place of Hyun-ja's and later on he will convey his pain at Sun-hwa's leaving by viciously attacking Myung-ja. Kim states that:

> The reason that in my movies there are people who do not talk is because something wounded them. They had their trust in other human beings destroyed because of promises that were not kept ... the violence that they turn to, I prefer to call a kind of body language. I would like to thing of it more of a physical expression rather than just negative violence. (Quoted Hummel 2002)

For Kim, Hang-gi's lack of a literal voice can be a metaphor for his lack of voice in wider society. For Kim he is the original victim and it is only through placing Sun-hwa in the role of victim that he begins to rebuild himself by associating with her pain. His body is marked by violence and this separates him from the wider social group and in return he marks Sun-hwa; she then acts for Hang-gi as the ultimate living embodiment of what he can never be. In his entrapment of her he comes to exercise his pain but simultaneously learns how to escape his existence and transcend his nature. We see his body undertake punishment which should have killed him. He is hit on the head with a brick, stabbed twice and brutally beaten, and yet he survives. When we see him at the end of the film there are no marks on him; the indication is that in his abandonment of this previous lifestyle and his embrace of a future with Sun-hwa allows him to be re-born. In this way, rather than a narrative of degradation, the film becomes a narrative of redemption. Kim offers the idea that this film is an appeal to the audience to 'reflect on their past and plan a better, more beautiful life in the future' (2001). For him the union of Sun-hwa and Hang-gi is the triumph of love and forgiveness over the harsh demands of societal convention.

The conclusion of *Bad Guy* is the one that is hardest for viewers to reconcile themselves with. Why does Sun-hwa continue to work as a prostitute and why does Hang-gi wish the woman he loves to continue in such activities? The answer perhaps lies in seeing their actions as a final refusal to conform to dominant expectations. Sun-hwa no longer sees the need to conform to the dominant standard of exultation of chastity so she feels content to earn her money via any means at her disposal. The empowerment model of prostitution is one that has been sustained by some feminist writers on the subject[1] and in her choice to use her own body to earn income Sun-hwa can be seen as confirming her desire to continue to live her life by an alternative method that allows her freedom from social constraint. In her embrace of the rough and ready lifestyle of living and working out of a van, Sun-hwa has moved a long way from the young college girl that rejected Hang-gi for his lowly status and appearance.

The previous photos of the couple, as well as the mysterious woman who walks into the sea and who appears to drape a coat over Sun-hwa's shoulders as she wanders the streets of Seoul, all seem to point to a relationship that is predestined. The images that Sun-hwa finds on the beach point to the notion that she and Hang-gi are destined to meet and fall in love and that their respective fates are eternally intertwined. She does not find the faces of the couple until she has fallen in love with Hang-gi, and the final complete photo acts as the visual proof of their love. Once Sun-hwa finds the photos she tapes them together and places them on the mirror. Throughout the film we see her and Hang-gi's faces reflected on these images via the mirror on the wall but it is only at the end that there is a perfect fit. The mirror was the dividing line between them and once that has gone they are able to fulfil their destiny and be together without boundaries.

The image that was used to sell the film was of a naked Sun-hwa seated at a table holding up a mirror in which Hang-gi's face is reflected. The indication seems to be that she and Hang-gi are the mirror-images of each other. This is upheld throughout the film as they lie looking at each other, but with the mirror inbetween them so they are simultaneously staring at their own reflections. At first Sun-hwa is unaware of Hang-gi's presence behind the mirror but as the film progresses she becomes more aware of his presence and gradually the barrier between them is brought down. The literal barrier is the mirror but the wider constraints are presented as their social differences. The ending sees them brought together and the dominant class boundaries that were presented so clearly at the opening are destroyed. *Bad Guy* is a film that is undoubtedly hard to watch but like many of Kim's films there is a hidden message and social critique if viewers can look beyond the controversial presentation of the topic.

Bad Guy was at the time of its release the most successful of Kim's films in his home country, grossing US$3.5 million. This is due in no small part to the presence of actor Cho Jae-Hyun (playing Hang-gi) who had, concurrent with the release of *Bad Guy*, achieved popularity with his role in the South Korean television drama *Snowman* (Lee Chang-soon, 2001). This controversial series, which featured the story of an affair between a teenager and her brother-in-law, furthered Cho's star persona as an actor who was not afraid to take risks. He also starred in Kim's *The Isle* and *Address Unknown* and his increasingly popularity as an actor inside South Korea has helped to bring Kim Ki-duk's work to a wider audience in its home country. This brief flutter of popular domestic success, however, would not help his next few features that continued to perform poorly at the domestic box office.

NOTE

1   For more details on such debates see Ryan and Hall 2001, Brooks-Gordan 2006 and Jeffreys 2009.

Miike Takashi:
Welcome to the Dark Side

There has been no lack of causative factors proposed to account for this crisis, including materialism, consumerism, the collapse of the economic bubble, economic
restructuring, the influence of Western 'individualism', a stressful and competitive
education system, nuclear families, the decline of extended families, smothering
mothers, absentee working parents, decline of parental and other authority; not
transmission of normative values, lack of socialization, lack of outdoor activity, ur-
banization, spatial isolation, media prurience, or solitary absorption in electronic
media, particularly electronic games or the internet. (Taylor 2006)

For many in the West the work of Miike Takashi is well-known. Benefiting in
the UK from the introduction of the Tartan Asia Extreme label, a relatively large
percentage of Miike's feature-length films have made it to the UK and USA DVD
market and, as such, his work for many personifies what they consider to be
Japanese contemporary cinema: very violent, stylistic and highly transgressive.
Although Miike is primarily known for either violent high-action gangster thrill-
ers such as *Dead or Alive* (*DOA Deddo Oa Araibu – Hanzaisha*, 1999) and *Ichi
the Killer* (*Koroshiya 1*, 2001) or the disturbingly deranged *Audition* (*Ôdishon*,
2000) in fact his dramatic take on the *samurai* narrative in *13 Assassins* (*Jūsannin
no Shikaku*, 2010) and the charming *Bird People in China* (*Chūgoku no Chōjim*,
1998) illustrate how wide-ranging his work actually is. Films such as *Ichi the Killer*,

Audition and *Agitator* (*Araburu Tamashii Tachi*, 2002) have given Miike serious cult appeal and yet few are aware of the wider aspects of his work, choosing instead to concentrate on the famous scenes such as the removal of the feet in *Audition* and the eyeball killer in *MD Psycho*.

Miike Takashi was born in August 1960 in a working-class neighborhood in one of the towns surrounding the large and vibrant city of Osaka. His family had originally come from Kyushu Island but his grandparents had lived in occupied Korea and China prior to returning to Japan at the end of World War II. This family relationship to the geographical boundaries of Japan is something that can be seen through Miike's work in his frequent presentation of those from non-Japanese backgrounds. This link was also enhanced by the fact that a large immigrant community populated the region in which Miike resided. His mother was a seamstress and his father was a welder who offered a vision of masculinity that drank and gambled heavily. The socio-political circumstances that surrounded Miike growing up were a fertile area for organised crime, and becoming a *yakuza* gang member was a real career option for the teenage boy. Later in his career Miike made many references to those that he knew who had taken this option, and for many in his neighborhood the *yakuza* were a part of everyday life. His knowledge of this lifestyle would come to be reflected in films such as *Shinjuku Triad Society* (*Shinjuku Kuroshanki*, 1992), *Lay Lines* (*Nihon Kuroshanai*, 1995), *Rainy Dog* (*Gokudō Kuroshankai*, 1997) and *Dead or Alive*.

Rejecting the option of a life in crime, Miike enrolled at the Yokohama School of Broadcasting and Film, which had been founded by the legendary director Imamura Shohei. Although his attendance record at Yokohama left much to be desired Miike began to work frequently as a freelance crewmember on a variety of television dramas. He worked in television for nearly ten years until he decided to make the change to feature-film production and succeeded in working as one of Imamura's assistant on both *Zagen* (1987) and the acclaimed *Kuroi Ame* (*Black Rain*, 1989), which focused on the fallout of the Hiroshima atomic bomb. After his training process, Miike and many other directors like him, benefited from the biggest economic boom in Japan's history. The late 1980s and early 1990s saw the peak of post-war economic growth and many investors that had benefited from this growth sought new industries to invest in (this was also the time where US$1 million golf club memberships were genuinely offered).

The straight-to-video market was seen as a growing area and it was into this aspect of filmmaking that the investment money poured. Tōei studios quickly realised the lucrative opportunities and started producing what became known as V-Cinema. These straight-to-video productions provided a platform for younger and less established directors to take the directorial reins and, although often highly formulaic, V-Cinema saw less stringent censorship and therefore offered a chance for riskier content than theatrical cinematic releases. Unlike in the UK or USA where the made-for-video market is largely for poor quality and relatively ignored films, Japanese V-Cinema has a far higher level of public appreciation and audience interest. The basic rule was that as long as a director produced a film within budget and to the set timescale and roughly within the proscribed genre (comedy, gangster and erotica are popular V-Cinema staples) then the director was free to play with narrative and style. Miike is a prolific contributor to the V-Cinema industry; directing up to a remarkable six films per year, a vast percentage of Miike's output has been straight-to-video or DVD productions. In 1997 for example he produced four films: two for video and two for the cinema. Similarly in 2001 when alongside his theatrically released films (*Dead or Alive: Final*, *The Happiness of the Katakuris* [*Katakurike no Kofuku*], *Agitator*, *Graveyard of Honor*) he also directed a television show (*Sabu*) and a music video (*Go! Go! Fushimi Jet*).

His first feature-film made for theatrical release was *Shinjuku Triad Society*. This violent high-octane gangster film was produced and distributed by Daiei Studios and this collaboration would continue for several of Miike's other gangster films, from *Ley Lines* to *Dead or Alive*. *Shinjuku Triad Society* focuses on a corrupt policeman struggling to deal with Chinese organised crime. The sex, violence and vivid, exaggerated colours would come to represent key elements of Miike's work. Many of his films focus on *yakuza* society, and in 1996 he directed *Ambition Without Honor* (*Jingi Naki Yabō*), a direct reference to Fukasaku's *Battles without Honor or Humanity*. The films shared the same composer (Toshiaki Tsushima) and several actors, but the films' themes are radically different. Whilst Fukasaku was making comment on the nature of post-war Japan, Miike is offering an image of disaffected youth. His tale of a son rebelling against his father had little political aim but sought to offer a dramatic and violent vision of the generation gap that had developed in contemporary Japan. This generation gap and its violent consequences would be something that Miike would return to often. In 1996 he also directed *Fudoh: The Next Generation* (*Gokudō Sengokushi Fudō*) that would again deal with a father/son relationship. Unlike *Ambition without Honor*, *Fudoh*, although initially a V-Cinema production, gained a theatrical release. The bloody story of the Fudoh family begins when, to settle a debt, the father decapitates his eldest son as a peace offering to a rival gang. The youngest son, Riki, who was a small child when the murder took place, swears retribution against the father and the film follows the bloody and brutal path of his revenge. *Fudoh*, which played at festivals in Belgium and Canada, would spark an interest in Miike's work from an international audience and would begin the global narrative that focused on him as a representative of the new lurid, violent Asian film industry.

After the success of *Fudoh*, rather than another theatrical production, Miike instead directed several other V-Cinema gangster films. His next cinematic release would see him shift from his previously-set precedents and, rather than another violent action film, he directed *Bird People in China*, a gentle and uplifting tale of two Japanese men who travel to a remote Chinese valley. The same year he offered the Japanese teen and pre-teen market *Andromedia*, featuring two teenage popular bands, Speed and Da Pump. *Andromedia* held mass-market popular appeal containing humour, romance, action and special effects, and was one of the most financially successful of all of Miike's films. Never a director to be constrained, Miike was here demonstrating a willingness and ability to work in a variety of genres and styles.

It would, however, be his next cinematic release that would gain him the most critical and popular attention. In 2000 Miike made one of his most internationally famous films, *Audition*. This tale of disturbed and obsessive love would feature at several international film festivals, and was critically acclaimed as well as being the first of his films to be theatrically released outside of Japan. Furthermore, *Audition* would place Miike in the minds of many non-Japanese viewers as the key filmmaker of the Asia Extreme label. Tartan Asia Extreme was for many years the main distributor of alternative East Asian cinema in Europe and the US. It was Tartan that released many of Miike's works, as well as the films of other directors such as Park Chan-wook, Nakata Hideo and Tsukamoto Shinya, to an international audience. The brand, however, was also responsible for the general misconception in the West that East Asian cinema is always extremely violent (there was never a 'Asian Non-Extreme' list, for example), and in the case of Miike, films such as *Bird People in China* or *The Kumamoto Tales* (*Kumamoto Monogatari* (2002); a series focusing on the folk traditions of Kyushu), were ignored in favour of his works that are undoubtedly 'extreme' in their presentation of sex and violence.

Despite this, Miike's next few notable films most certainly lived up to his reputation as a director that focused on violence. *Visitor Q*, which will be examined in more detail in the next section, was released in 2001, the same year that Miike released *Ichi the Killer*. That film, based on a Manga by Yamamoto Hideo, directly challenges the audience's relationship to the violent images that are shown. The film served to enhance Miike's reputation as a director who provoked strong feelings, and it was heavily cut by the British Board of Film Classification before its release in the UK.

Rather than just presenting a lurid exploitation film, however, the violent images that Miike portrays force viewers to question their own relationship to such images. As Tom Mes notes, Miike's use of *suggested* violence in *Ichi the Killer* calls into question what the audience's own input into the narrative is:

> The violence the viewer purports to have seen took place not on the screen but in his or her own head. The viewer creates and then decides for himself the intensity of the violence in these scenes. If it shocks the viewer, then to all intents and purposes the viewer is shocked by his own imagination. (2003: 237)

Miike is, therefore, asking the viewer to evaluate their own critical positioning to the images that they see onscreen. This can be seen in *The Happiness of the Katakuris*, Miike's 'zombie musical', where terrible acts such as suicide and murder take place at a family hotel but, as they are presented using the genre conventions of a musical, the viewer is left to interpret their own subject positioning to the tale. *Visitor Q*, with its series of questions posed to the audience, would even more clearly emphasise issues of point of view and cognitive input into the events being portrayed.

Miike's exploration of filmic conventions does not only apply to his presentation of sex and violence. Throughout his career Miike has denied any allegiance to any genre or visual conventions: *Visitor Q* was filmed entirely on digital camera, his *yakuza* films offered unconventional characters and plots, *One Missed Call* (*Chahushun Ari*, 2004) offered a self-aware parody of the popular J-horror products, and *The Happiness of the Katakuris* blends music, horror, family melodrama, animation and zombies. This blending of genres can be seen in the opening sequence where a creature crawls out of a plate of soup and rips out the throat of the disturbed diner before flying off. *The Happiness of the Katakuris* focuses on the apparently conventional tale of a family that is seeking to start a new peaceful life by opening a guesthouse in the countryside. We see the tense dynamics that exist inside the family unit but when a guest dramatically commits suicide the film suddenly transforms into a musical. The film's allegiance to black comedy is clearly seen in the deaths of the next guests: a Sumo wrestler suffers a heart attack and dies crushing his schoolgirl lover beneath him, and later in the film all the dead transform into zombies and the hotel is destroyed by a volcano.

The Happiness of the Katakuri's bright, lurid visual style refers back to his earlier works such as *Shinjuku Triad Society* and *Dead or Alive* but all his films retain a unique approach to film aesthetics. His segment of the *Three Extremes* film (together with Fruit Chan and Park Chan-wook) is a surreal tale of a contortionist and her memories of a twin sister who she accidentally killed in a fire. Miike's segment is hauntingly still, muted in colour with none of the dramatic action sequences that have come to mark his other works. Rather than the frenetic costumes and colours of *Ichi the Killer, Audition* presents simple and bold block colours., and *13 Assassins* offers dramatic sweeping panoramas of the lush green countryside where the battle will take place. *Bird People in China* lovingly presents the isolated valley with its unique mountains, rivers and fields where the two lead characters will find themselves. In short, as *Film Comment* puts it, Miike is 'ultra prolific and stylistically unpredictable' (Anon. 2000: 3).

Miike's violent and often bizarre work frequently focuses on those who are in some way marginalised from mainstream culture, such as those from different ethnic backgrounds, in the face of the primarily homogenous Japanese nation. Indeed, one of the most striking elements of Miike's oeuvre is his use of non-Japanese characters. *Blues Harp* (*Burūsu Hapu*, 1998) focuses on a mixed-parentage teenager Chuji whose father is African-American and mother Japanese. Chuji is marginalised both by his looks and by his criminal and alternative actions. He deals drugs and plays a harmonica in a blues club owned by an openly gay American played by Mickey Curtis. *Dead or Alive* and *Shinjuku Triad Society* both feature main characters who are *zanryu koji*, a term which literally translates as 'orphans who have remained behind', referring to the children of Japanese parents that were left behind in China after Japan's defeat in World War II. These individuals struggle to find a place for themselves inside the space of Japan; as one character states they 'feel like Japanese but not Japanese, like Chinese but not Chinese'. This lack of connection or feeling of social obligation to Japanese society that surrounds them is seen as the impetus for Ryuichi and his small group of friends to try and make their own place by trying to take over the Shinjuku underworld and the drug trade from Taiwan. *The City of Lost Souls* (*Hyôryû-gai*, 2000) is especially notable because throughout the film the Japanese characters are sidelined in order to concentrate on the central figures of Japanese-Brazilian Mario and his Chinese girlfriend Kei. Here Japan is seen as rigidly controlling its border but with little effect. When the authorities try to deport Kei, Mario rescues her (in a dramatic helicopter chase scene) and in the process releases dozens of other illegal immigrants. Chinese gangster Ko controls the city and the racist Japanese police are seen as unconcerned by the death toll amongst the foreign inhabitants.

The presence of non-Japanese characters raises specific questions about Japanese society. Historically there has been a trend to see Japan as a nation that is distinctly unique. This ideal of an ethnically and culturally homogenous national group is also still widely believed inside Japan; the narrative of unified nationhood was heavily emphasised in post-war Japan where the 'otherness' not only of Westerners but also of those who were Chinese or Korean was dominant. This ideology of *kokutai* is based on the notion of the Japanese nation as a racially homogenous entity linked by blood to a single Imperial family. Although the term has now fallen into disuse due to its links to a period Japan would rather forget, *kokutai*'s conception of Japan as a bounded unit results in clear narratives of inclusion and exclusion. The legacies of these concepts live on in contemporary Japanese society and discrimination against foreigners is considered to be rife, with non-Japanese people suffering in all areas, from housing availability to permanent job contracts (see Yates 1990). In Miike's films the constant presence of non-Japanese characters forces the Japanese audience to consider their notion of national identity, not only as it relates to the West but also the rest of Asia. Although many of Miike's films feature a violent and destructive society in a state of crisis, this crisis is not blamed on the presence of foreigners. Japanese and non-Japanese alike each behave as atrociously as each other. The police discrimination that the non-Japanese characters suffer from in films such as *The City of Lost Souls* is seen as a negative statement on the nature of a system that sees some lives as less valuable than others. This is also present in *Shinjuku Triad Society* where the lead character is confronted with the illegal organ donation market that exists in Taiwan and is informed that most of the purchasers of these organs are Japanese. When asked what the police are doing to stop the illegal trade he is informed that as far as the police are concerned it is a financial transaction based on market forces, therefore they do nothing.

The new globalised state that Japan now is is clearly referenced here. The cross-cultural ability to buy an organ in one place and import it to another is a grisly rendition of international economic structures.

This notion of a global Japan is also shown in Miike's continual blending of a myriad of Asian and Western languages in his films. Rather than an insular state, Japan now has to engage with ideas and people from around Asia and the wider world. The positives and negatives of this presentation are, however, open to debate. Tony Rayns states that

> Miike's films not only take as given that Japan is as 'Asian' as any of its neighbours, but also implicitly argues that a bit of cross cultural fertilisation does Japan's uptight mainstream culture a power of good. (2000: 31)

Whilst it is undoubtedly true that Miike's films do seek to disrupt the normative trends and to offer an image of a Japan that is cosmopolitan in its outlook, 'deconstruction', according to Mika Ko, does not involve a 're-construction'; here Ko is expounding her theory that Miike's films do not 'involve the radical project of a reconstruction of a new "Japan", rather, as the apocalyptic ending of *Dead or Alive* suggests, the break-up of the national body leads to the obliteration of Japan' (2004: 36). In short, Ko sees it as a non-constructive deconstruction. An examination of Miike's films reveals that this argument could perhaps hold true for a large percentage of his work; his films are marked by a chaotic, apocalyptic approach and his deconstructions and rupturing of dominant values rarely offer any alternative to what they have destroyed. Despite been trained by Imamura, a director who belonged to the politically motivated Japanese New Wave, who as David Desser notes 'have been concerned with creating a film content and form capable of revealing the contradictions within Japanese society' (1988: 4), Miike appears to reject any notion of providing social critique. In this sense he relates to Japanese writer Murakami Ryu whose books, such as *Almost Transparent Blue/Kagirinaku tōmei ni chikai burū* (2002) and *Coin Locker Babies/Koinrokkā Beibīzu* (2002), focus on a disaffected Japanese youth culture. Murakami's novels continue many of the violent and disturbing images and situations that would not look out of place in Miike's films, indeed *Audition* was an adaption from Murakami's work. The question that drives Murakami is 'what would happen at the collapse of the social system?' In *Almost Transparent Blue* the lead character's continual drug-taking removes him further and further from society, and

Piercing/Piasshingu (2007) focuses on two people whose past experiences of child abuse prevents them from functioning according to normative standards. In *Coin Locker Babies* the two main protagonists, who were both abandoned as babies in coin lockers (based on several real-life cases of this in Tokyo), decide to gas the whole of Tokyo in an effort to find out what would indeed happen with the collapose of the social system. This narrative was also an uneasy reminder of the Aum Sarin subway gas attacks in 1995 when a group of religious fanatics attempted to do just that. For many Japanese people, the Aum subway attacks, babies left in lockers and other recent cultural phenomenon such as children committing murder and rape, personified a society that was spiraling into decline. As David Leheny states, 'anyone wishing to make a case that the country was on a downward spiral would find ready emblems for disaster' (2006: 3). With this in mind, the films of Miike seem to offer a vision of a post-modern social state that was destroying itself. Isolde Standish comments that 'in Miike's films there is no redemptive humanism because his films form part of a postmodern sensibility [that] portrays a world in which there is indeed no salvation, but on the other hand nothing to be saved' (2006: 228).

Murakami and Miike are not, however, nihilists searching for death, as in the case of Kitano; instead, their project is to explore the social, sexual and emotional taboos of contemporary post-modern society. To this end, Miike's films have an energy and vibrancy that defies a reading of them as purely intent on deconstruction without aim. What his films seek to do is to interrogate the boundaries of social normative behaviour and scenarios. Miike manages this via a process of drawing the audiences into the films' narratives and events and forcing them to confront their own relationship to the images being shown.

Bodies in Miike's films are often the site of this transgression of social and behavioral boundaries. In *Ichi the Killer* Kakihara's mouth is slashed as a form of body art, clearly marking his desire to have pain inflicted upon his own body. *Yakuza* tattoos to mark criminal activities are well recognised cultural signs but in *Fudoh*, Riki's tattoo is actually etched with the blood of his dead brother. Riki therefore becomes both the method for his brother's revenge and also a living testimony to this death. In one sequence of *The Happiness of the Katakuris* the bodies of the zombies, which have long been seen as the disturbing link between the living and the dead (see, for example, Creed 1996), get up and dance in a grotesquely funny sequence. In *13 Assassins* the brutal and sexually deviant behaviour of the soon-to-be assassinated Lord Naritsugu is embodied in the figure of the peasant girl whose arms, legs and tongue were removed by him, and once her role as a sexual plaything has been fulfilled she is thrown into the street to die. Her traumatised and highly disturbing figure will be the impetus for the lead assassin Shinzaemon to agree to kill Naritsugu. In *Ichi the Killer* we see the results of Ichi's masturbatory actions in a pool of semen outside a door. Semen is rarely seen on cinema screen outside of the porn industry and in presenting the audience with this very physical and visceral reminder of Ichi's sexual deviancies, Miike opens up questions of how the audience will react to seeing such sights. There are several characters in his films that demonstrate 'alternative' and transgressive sexualities such as the obsession with sadism and masochism that is seen in *Ichi the Killer*. *Fudoh* also features a transsexual character who continually seeks to subvert the normative gender categories by alternating his/her gender alignment. S/he engages in sex with both male and female partners and, sporting both male and female sexual organs s/he is able to succeed as both male and female, transgressing commonly held gender, and indeed bodily, barriers. The use of gender as a method to challenge expectations can be clearly seen in *Audition* as we follow the narrative of the middle-aged businessman Aoyama's search for a young girlfriend. The most remarked-upon scene is when Asami, the woman that Aoyama has begun a relationship with, sticks needles in his face and chest and removes his foot with piano wire. *Audition* is perhaps a film that can claim to be both an alternative feminist film and an excellent example of dominant misogyny. Aoyama meets Asami when he and his friend set up fake auditions for a fictional film with the idea that Aoyama will be able to pick the one he likes best. In this way women are reduced to objects notable only for their looks and their ability to attract men. The situation is reversed, however, by the end of the film as Asami overpowers and tortures Aoyama. His inability to treat women as equals has been transformed into a murderous woman who shows no pity for his pain or pleas for mercy. The dominant expectation of women as victim is reversed to make Asami the ultimate predator. Asami has been treated badly before and the film is littered with references and images of her previous acts of revenge against several individuals; for example, we are told that when the police discovered the body of her old manager they also found an extra tongue, ear and three fingers. Yet despite the fact that her actions are undoubtedly shocking and she is clearly a highly unstable character, in her attempt to make Aoyama promise to love only her, we realise that her violent actions are as a result of her desire to find another individual who she can totally trust. As Tom Mes suggests

'*Audition* is about two people who misunderstand each other, and this (often unconscious) treatment, works in both ways' (2003: 203). Therefore Asami and Aoyama are victims of their inability to communicate with each other and are unable to fully integrate in a relationship.

Miike's constant use of an individual that is unable to ever fully belong to a society or wider social grouping refers to his own conception of selfhood. As he states in interview:

> The Japanese, even if we live in Japan, we are all drifting. Especially me. My family is originally from Kumamoto in South Kyushu. When Japan was defeated in World War II, my grandmother was in Korea. When she came back, she went to live in another town in Japan. So since my grandmother, my family hasn't lived in Kumamoto. I grew up in Osaka, but for this reason I don't think Osaka is my home town. I've always felt that I'm drifting, that I don't have a home town that I can go back to. Portraying such people in my films is very natural for me, even in the *yakuza* stories. (Miike 2001)

This notion of drifting can be seen not only in his usage of non-Japanese characters but also by the fact that several of his films focus on Japanese people abroad. In *Rainy Dog* the lead character is a *yakuza* who resides in exile in Taipei. Although he speaks the language, he refuses to attempt to communicate with those around him, choosing instead to live in isolation. He has lost his passport and now resides in a rootless no-man's-land where he cannot return to Japan and yet seems unwilling to make Taiwan his permanent home. In *The Guys from Paradise* (*Tengoku kara kita otoko-tachi*, 2000), a young businessman is arrested in the Philippines for drug possession and ends up in a Filipino jail, removed from his comfortable and familiar surroundings. *Bird People in China* follows two Japanese men (one a *yakuza*, the other a hard-working salaryman) as they visit a remote region of China. This film is interesting because at the same time as it reflects a notion of static place, in this case a remote untouched valley, it also offers the notion of continual movement via the legend of the flying man. There is no indication that either man will find an essential mode of being; rather their embrace of the rootless and drifting state allows them a new freedom that was previously denied. Wada, the obedient office employee, has gained a new sense of freedom as the opening scene of him standing on the roof of an office building wearing a giant pair of wings illustrates. Uijie, the violent *yakuza*, will reject his gangster lifestyle, and Japan, and instead he chooses to remain in the valley and continue to try and learn to fly. His desire to learn to fly indicates that he is not staying in the valley because he decides that it is 'home' but rather because the valley offers a space of freedom from dominating structures of place and space.

Several characters in Miike's work will, like Uiiji, reject a given identity. The *Zanryu Koji* gangsters openly defy any notion of belonging, and in *Fudoh* the son rejects any familial links in his decision to kill his father. *Audition*, *Dead or Alive 2*, *Rainy Dog* and *Ichi the Killer* all feature orphans who struggle to define their identities in the face of their alienation from those around them. This alienation can take the form of an inability to communicate, as in *Audition*, or psychotic behaviour, as in *Ichi the Killer*. The latter presents a series of individuals who are 'othered' by mainstream society in a variety of ways. Ichi is a deeply disturbed young man who has been hypnotised to become the definitive killing machine; he faces Kakihara (Tadanobu Asano), the ultimate masochist-turned-sadist. The fim personifies precisely Miike's rejection of 'heroic fantasies of moral endings, depicting instead the social outcasts' and the delinquents' delight in violence; no one is saved and no apparent heroes exist, 'all are damaged individuals existing as global drifters lacking any geographical or emotional sense of connectedness' (Standish 2005: 330).

For the protagonists of *Ichi the Killer*, the search for sex and death are the primary motivators for their actions. Kakihara is suffering after Ichi has killed his boss Anjo, not because he feels the honorable commitment to his master that was seen in older narratives, but rather because Anjo was the perfect sadist to Kakihara's masochist. Ichi, despite his childlike behaviour is seen as a perfect sadist since he is motivated by the deep desire to cause pain. When he defends a prostitute from being beaten and raped by her pimp, he is only aiding her in order to take the pimp's place; for Ichi love and care can only be displayed via violence. When he fails to find a sadist to hurt him Kakihara hurts himself, first by cutting off his tongue and then by rupturing his ear drums. He welcomes the arrival of Ichi since he sees him as the perfect means to achieve the orgasmic painful death that he so desires. The film's ending offers no form of redemption or narrative conclusion, and we are left uncertain as to the fate of both Ichi and Kakihara.

One interesting element of these narratives is the fact that, like Asami and Aoyama in *Audition*, Ichi and Kakihara are both looking for their ideal partner. Their failure would seem to confirm the statement by Ko that Miike is seeking to offer a deconstructed view of Japan without offering any structural alternative. The presence of social groups in Miike's work, however, raises new questions. From *Fudoh* to *One Missed Call*, Miike offers the possibility of people uniting as a method of overcoming the harsh world around them. Although these groups, such as the gangs in *The City of Lost Souls* may well fail, there is still the possibility that they may succeed. In *The Happiness of the Katakuris* and *Visitor Q*, the previously fractured family groups are, by the end of the film, united. These family units are highly dysfunctional but they do offer a sense of belonging to their members. At the end of *Audition*, although they are both crippled it is implied that it is the first and only time Aoyama and Asami achieve total connection. In *Bird People in China*, Uiiji finds happiness and contentment in his role as teacher and playmate to the valley's children. He may have embraced an alternative lifestyle but it appears to be one that fulfills and satisfies him. In *13 Assassins*, although, all bar one of the assassins are dead; so is Naritsugu and his forces, and it is made clear that out of this carnage a new and bright future can appear.

These sudden examples of hope and happiness, compared to the notion of his work as focusing on destruction and nihilism, prove how the work of Miike Takashi is almost impossible to categorise. His ability to apply himself to both small screen and larger production makes him a highly versatile director, and the multitude of genres that he works inside is equally dazzling. Like Kim Ki-duk, his films seek to challenge and subvert without recourse to dominant morality but, unlike Kim, Miike has managed to be recognised in his home country. His films have not been met with the critical acclaim that has greeted Kitano's work but he continues to appeal to an international audience. He works in a wide range of media platforms from V-Cinema DVD releases, to big-budget film productions that travel worldwide, and as such can be seen as a figure that represents modern East Asian media structures.

His works and his status as a lead East Asian director has led to a level of intertextuality to his works that extend beyond the film themselves. In the Thai film *Last Life in the Universe* (Pen-ek Ratanaruang, 2003) Miike takes on a cameo role as a brutal gangster. Starring Asano Tadanobu, the film continues includes references to *Ichi the Killer* and Miike's *yakuza* films. In this way the works of Miike can be seen to have permeated into popular Asian culture, and have come to represent a brand of modern Asian film that operates globally. Although many have seen him as a figure representing a new cultural emptiness (see Ko 2004, Standish 2005), Miike's works offer innovative challenges to dominant structures.

209

He may not have the political agenda or gravitas of a director such as Fukasaku but his films are far from trite. There is a visual and narrative depth to his works that force the audience to question their own relationships to the images on screen. In short, as Tony Rayns (2000: 30) concludes, Miike refuses to bend to accepted norms of narrative, film style or film grammar.

Film Analysis

VISITOR Q

ビジターＱ
Bijitā Kyū

2001

Director

Miike Takashi

Cast

Kenichi Endo (Kiyoshi Yamazaki / Father), Shungiku Uchida (Keiko Yamazaki / Mother), Kazushi Watanabe (The visitor), Jun Mutô (Takuya Yamazaki / Son), Fujiko (Miki Yamazaki / Daughter)

Plot Summary

After having had sex with his under-aged, runaway daughter, an unemployed television reporter Kiyoshi brings home a man who has hit him on the head with a rock. His wife Keiko is beaten by their son Takuya, and she becomes a prostitute to pay for her heroin habit. Their son is being badly bullied by a group of boys from his school and as a result he beats his mother. Kiyoshi has been unemployed since a group of students attacked him whilst he was attempting to make a documentary, but he has not informed his family. The 'visitor' never speaks but he exerts a powerful influence on the reporter and his entire family. He gives Keiko back her self-esteem by showing her how to lactate from her breasts. She is ecstatic about this achievement and begins to defend herself against Takuya's attacks. When Kiyoshi rapes and murders a colleague he and Keiko are reconciled when she helps him after he has become stuck inside the dead woman (rigor-mortis sets in during an act of necrophilia). Together they kill the schoolboys who are bullying their son and, after lying face down in his mother milk, Takuya tells the visitor that he is going to concentrate on his school work. The visitor leaves, but then encounters the daughter who propositions him. We next see the daughter enter her parent's home with a bloody and bruised face. She goes to the garden where she finds her father suckling from her mother's breast and she starts to feed from the other. The film ends with the family unit together at last.

––––––

Filmed using digital video technology *Visitor Q* was one of the cheapest films that Miike has ever produced. It was filmed as the sixth and final part of the *Love Cinema* series that consisted of V-Cinema productions that were given theatrical releases via a brief but exclusive run at the Shimokitazawa cinema in Tokyo. The six films, all by independent filmmakers, were conceived as a low-budget exercise to explore the benefits afforded by the low-cost digital video medium. Shot for the equivalent of US$55,000 *Visitor Q* relishes its digital format, and the handheld camera acts as a key method of drawing the audience into this surreal (and potentially highly offensive) tale of a dysfunctional family unit.

For the viewer well acquainted with the classics of European film, *Visitor Q* has parallels with Pier Paolo Pasolini's neo-realist film *Teorema* (1968). In this masterpiece of Italian cinema a handsome stranger, played by British actor Terence Stamp, arrives at a family's home and gradually seduces every family member. He then departs leaving them all emotionally destroyed. *Visitor Q* sees another stranger integrate himself into a family's life but this time, rather than divide the family, the stranger acts as a surreal catalyst to bring the family back together.

The family in this case is the Yamakazis. We are introduced to them one by one and we see their myriad individual problems. The overwhelming image is how dysfunctional this family unit really is. The son, Takuya, is moody, withdrawn and dreadfully bullied by his school peers. He responds to this by viciously beating his mother, who in return, has developed a heroin habit to mask her pain and pays for the drug via prostitution. Her daughter, Keiko, is also working as a prostitute in the city and in the opening scene of the film, one of her customers turns out to be her father, Kiyoshi. The incest taboo is almost forgotten in light of Kiyoshi's poor sexual performance and the pathetic fact that he cannot even afford to pay the full amount. Kiyoshi is on leave from his job ever since a group of teenagers he was trying to interview for a documentary he was trying to film on 'youth today' attacked him and sodomised him with his own microphone.

The visitor of the title is introduced to the family when he bashes Kiyoshi on the head with a rock and then proceeds to integrate himself into the family unit. The family and their problems are in themselves extreme examples and metaphors for real issues facing Japanese society. Questions of bullying, teenage prostitution, crises in masculinity and the collapse of the family unit are all referenced, but in true Miike style there is no condemnation of the family, nor of the often appalling actions and events that we see take place. Rather there is a concentration on the development of the family as individual people and their eventual attainment of happiness. Tom Mes states that 'the film cannot properly be deemed social critique since the element of condemnation is missing' (2003: 210). However, as Adrienne Rich points out, social critique, in its basic form, is the process that 'in order to change what is, we need to give speech to what has been, to imagine what might be' (1979). The base line for social critique is the interrogation of existing structures and a proposal for the future. In this sense *Visitor Q*, although in a highly unique and controversial fashion, succeeds.

213

The initial element which links the family is the fact that they are all victims of an existence which renders them vulnerable and disenfranchised inside their respective spaces. Takuya should be safe from the boys who bully him at school but they come to his home and taunt him, and hurl fireworks at his bedroom window. *Ijime*, a form of extreme bullying, has been an established problem in the Japanese school system for many years. There have been cases of children committing suicide over such bullying and even being murdered by their peers (see Werly 2001). It is not just students that have been the instigators; teachers have frequently been accused of bullying students in order to punish those that are seen as 'different'. As referenced in the previous chapter on Miike, the notion of the homogenous Japanese nation is something that continues to resonate in the discourse of Japanese nationhood. In her article charting this rise, and the public debates that have been going on inside Japan concerning them, Marie Thorsten-Morimoto (1996) focuses on the continuing emphasis in Japanese schools of the maintenance of a vision of homogeneity.

In Takuya's case, we are shown a vicious cycle that results in the entire family being victims of bullying. His father is shown as being a failure as a father, worker and husband. Kiyoshi is bullied and horrifically humiliated by the teenagers who he tries to interview, by his work colleagues and, when he fails to perform sexually with Miki, his daughter, she ridicules him (she comments on his small penis and nicknames him 'early bird' for his premature ejaculation). To add insult to injury, he cannot even afford the cost of the dismal (and of course illegal) sex. after the dismal (and of course illegal) sex. Kiyoshi is unable to defend himself from any of the attacks and is seen to mutely accept the treatment which is handed out to him. He is seen as an abject and apathetic figure of fun who is failing both himself and his family.

In the same way as his father refuses to defend himself, Takuya does not fight against the bullies but chooses instead to transfer his feelings and aggressive tendencies onto the body of his mother. He is the very figure of impotent teenage rage. At the films beginning he beats Keiko for buying the wrong toothbrush claiming that she does not care if his teeth bleed. His violence is unpredictable but the message is clear; as far as he is concerned his parents' lack of support and protection is the reason for the terrible aggression he suffers at school. His mother is the major target of this aggression since she offers little defence. Keiko fills the perfunctory role of mother; she feeds the family and cleans the house but she fails to protect and defend her son and as a result she becomes the focus of his teenage rage. Kiyoshi, in similar fashion, fails to fulfil his role as father and husband and as a result he is unable to support his son and does nothing to protect his wife from his son's violence. He even compounds his daughter's situation by becoming a customer rather than attempting to remove her from the sex industry. His focus is on his working life but he is as much a failure at work as he is at home. To add to all this he also plans to actually use his children to aid his career. After the failed first attempt to make the 'youth today' documentary he decides to follow his own children and film their lives. When Takuya's bullies attack the house, rather than face them and defend his son, Kiyoshi responds with 'I don't know how I should feel; what should we do with this wonderful gift of bullying?' For Kiyoshi, witnessing first-hand *Ijime* delights him as he sees it as a chance to aid his career but he does not act in an appropriate fashion as an adult and a father.

This is further personified by his sleeping with his daughter. Miki working as a prostitute is again a reflection of a concern existing inside Japanese society with reference to teenage girls. *Enjo kosai* is one of the most insidious and troubling developments that has occurred with the development of Japan's economic bubble economy. It literally means subsidised or compensatory dating and involves school girls prostituting themselves to older men either for cash or material goods. For many it reflects the Japanese obsession with materialism and a decline in traditional values of hard work. Some feminists have suggested that the movement should be seen in a more positive light since the women are bucking cultural stereotypes and using men's desire to gain profit (see Leheny 2006: 71–81). This argument, however, is one that seems to ignore the fact that compensatory dating is little more than prostitution. Although Miki seems to be fairly well established as a prostitute, her youth and her attitude (at one point we see her in a school uniform) make direct links to *enjo kosai*. Her childish looks are a boon in this industry and she is clearly charging a relatively large sum of ¥50–100,000 (US$500–800) when compared to her mother who is also engaged in prostitution for a far more paltry sum. We see her servicing a man in his hotel room by beating him with a belt in a vision of tawdry and decidedly un-erotic sadomasochism. She then proceeds to spend her money on the heroin which she buys from a man in a school playground.

The figure of the mother is the person that most changes throughout the film. When we are first introduced to her we see an abused, drug-addicted woman who is unable to relate to her husband, son or daughter on any meaningful level.

She fulfils the mechanical duties of wife and mother but it is clear that she takes no pleasure in this function and refuses to defend herself against her sons' violent rages. Her only concern is that he does not hit her face as she still wishes to maintain the outside appearance of a 'normal' family unit. This desire to provide a façade of normality can also be seen in Kiyoshi who has not informed his family of his compulsory leave of absence. He maintains the image that he is going to the office every day when in fact he is secretly following and filming his children. The stranger changes all this. He shows Keiko how to massage her breasts until they lactate and she immediately starts to gain tremendous sexual pleasure from the experience, and from this we see her take the first steps towards empowerment. The key indication that she is beginning to change is when Takuya attacks her and she responds by throwing a kitchen cleaver at him (which only narrowly misses his head). Her happiness in her newfound lactating becomes incredible as when the visitor next sees her she shows him how she can now manage to produce milk from her breasts in prolific quantity. The kitchen is now flooded with milk, evidence of her sexual excitement at the act. The boundaries between fiction and reality which are so often explored in Miike's films are here enhanced by the fact that the actress (and famous *manga* artist) Shungicu Uchida was actually breast-feeding at the time and the close-up's of her breasts leaking and squirting milk over some distance are in fact real.

As Keiko gains satisfaction from her own body Kiyoshi still manages to emerge himself in an even greater state of abjection. His obsession with filming his son's bullying sees him following Takuya with a camera, accompanied by his co-worker and occasional lover, Asoko. When Asoko rejects Kiyoshi's documentary idea and attempts to walk away from him, he attacks her, sexually assaults and inadvertently murders her. Asoko's death and Kiyoshi's lack of control is all filmed by the visitor using Kiyoshi's digital camera. The visitor makes no attempt to intervene and just allows the camera to keep rolling. Still being tapped by the visitor Kiyoshi takes the body back to the house and plans to dismember and bury her. Whilst the visitor goes inside to get plastic bags (at this point we cut to him entering the kitchen to be confronted by an ecstatic and lactating Keiko), Kiyoshi sinks to further deprivation. Whilst drawing on Asoko with a pen in order to decide the easier way to cut her up, he become sexually excited and proceeds to have sex with the corpse. In his excitement he begins to believe that Asoko is responding to his sexual skill by 'getting wet'; however, when he puts his hand down to investigate, he is greeted with the fact that it is only her dead body voiding itself of faeces. To make matters worse, rigor-mortis has set in and he is now stuck inside the dead woman. This revolting and blackly humorous situation then becomes the bonding narrative that Kiyoshi and Keiko need. Seeing her husband's distress, Keiko quickly moves into action with a passion and enthusiasm that she had never illustrated in her chores before. As the distressed Kiyoshi looks on with amazement she applies herself to sorting out the situation. She goes to the grocery store to buy vinegar and oil and when that refuses to work she utilises her heroin. Once a symbol of her escapism from her life, the heroin shrinks Kiyoshi's member and with a superimposed 'pop' sound for emphasis, he is released and passionately embraces his wife with a newfound love and respect. The use of the heroin is once again a reversal of usual family tales: in true Miike fashion rather than driving them apart, destructive drugs bring the estranged husband and wife together. Rape, murder, necrophilia and heroin are all parts of a 'positive' narrative of family reconciliation. As the old horror film *American Gothic*'s (John Hough, 1988) tagline goes, 'the family that slays together stays together', and we see Keiko and Kiyoshi unite to murder Takuya's bullies when they break into the garden to chase him.

In response to his parent's sudden and drastic protection of him Takuya is found in the kitchen face down in Keiko's milk. He thanks the visitor for coming and resolves to work harder at school. It appears that the visible demonstration of his parents' defence of him, in their murdering of his bullies, gives him the manifestation of care that he truly desires. As he lies face down in his mother's milk he has in a peculiar way returned to his mother's breast and, now nourished with the display of his parents' care and physical interaction with his mothers' love (for what better way, Miike seems to argue, does the mother show her love than by breastfeeding?), he seems ready to embark on the adulthood that had previously escaped him. Leaving the house the visitor encounters Miki and, after agreeing to pay for her services, the film cuts to Miki entering her parents' house bruised and battered. Going to the greenhouse she takes her place beside Kiyoshi suckling on Keiko's breasts. The wounds that had been seen on Keiko from Takuya's beatings and the damage on Miki's face disappear and, after the frenetic violence, the film ends on a peaceful and still image of a smiling Keiko nurturing her husband and daughter.

Visitor Q disturbs on a number of levels. First, the content systematically breaks many culturally-held boundaries that exist worldwide. Incest, necrophilia, parental abuse, prostitution, rape and murder are all presented as an almost natural part of this dysfunctional family narrative. The film avoids any form of moralising and, indeed, the lack of a moral and ethical code together with the actions that take place in the film present the narrative as part of an almost natural tale of family reunion. What is even more disturbing is how the hand-held digital camera brings the viewer closer to the action and makes them intimate witnesses and participants in the acts committed. One of the most disturbing scenes is Kiyoshi's rape and murder of his co-worker and ex-mistress. Whilst waiting in the car, watching Takuya being beaten, Asoko finally has enough of Kiyoshi's ridiculous pretensions for television fame and storms off. Kiyoshi had instructed the visitor to film what he was doing and the visitor does just that. As Kiyoshi attacks Asoko the visitor films in close-up with no form of emotion and the viewer watches the attack from the same dispassionate position. The visitor's refusal to intervene or show any concern for the acts taking place becomes the only position for the viewer to take in order to maintain alignment with the plot. If the audience loses interest in the family as a result of the violent and sexual acts committed then the heart-warming message of a family reconciled will be lost. The use of inter-titles enhances this. The audience is asked various questions such as 'have you slept with your dad?', 'have you ever been hit on the head?', 'have you ever beaten your mom?' The subjectivity of the audience is thus called into question as the film seems to speak directly to us. The framing of the shots occasionally place us in the position of 'spying' on the family. We take on the position of voyeurs in this troubled narrative rather than being distanced by traditional filmic techniques.

There are a series of handheld cameras used in the film and the inter-cutting between them raises questions as to which viewpoint is supposed to be the 'subjective' gaze of the camera. This is particularly clear in the opening scene where we alternate between Kiyoshi's camera and the camera that the audience will try to align themselves with. The notion of audience subjectivity is ruptured as the film attempts to consistently engage them in the narrative by forcing the audience to take an active role in the film. We look at the murder of Asoko from the same viewpoint of the visitor and as such we must disown the characters' guilt in the act, otherwise we incriminate ourselves for watching without comment.

Miike's film contains a series of references to well-known social problems which are facing modern Japanese society. His film seeks to present and allow the audience to make their own considerations about these social structures.

Placing us in the position of voyeurs Miike calls into light the whole cinematic process. Hollywood will often present sex and violence and allow the audience to maintain a safe distance from the acts so they are not forced to consider them as related to their own lives. In *Visitor Q* the audience is forced to confront their own culpability in the actions and their continuing desire to watch.

Although it only had a limited cinematic release *Visitor Q* has done well in terms of worldwide DVD sales gaining distribution in the UK (Tartan which became Palisades Tartan in 2008), Europe (Rapid Eye Video), and the USA (Tokyo Shock/Media Blasters). It's subject matter has meant that television channels have shown an understandable reluctance to buy the rights for braodcast but it was heavily advertised by Tartan as part of their 'extreme' range and as a result has become a cult classic among those who are fans of this brand of anarchic cinema. The performance of the film in Japan was modest but given its small budget the film is a relatively profitable production.

Miike Takashi's skill as a director lies in his ability to surprise and challenge and *Visitor Q* certainly succeeds in this aim. With reference to Miike's wider work, there are direct parallels with many of his others films: impotent and ineffective men, repressed rage, casual murder, a family in crisis and a high level of sex and violence. These themes are combined with a unique and controversial filming style that brings a level of (sur)realism to the tale which draws the audience attention despite the tremendously taboo material.

Conclusion

A nation's interest in its national cinema, while often absent in small-nation contexts, nonetheless has something unsurprising about it. At an intuitive and pre-theoretical level, the absence of domestic appeal registers as a sure sign of inferior quality, but its presence is easily equated with the quasi-natural state of affairs in any well-functioning sphere of national cultural production. Transnational, inter-national, or global awareness of a small state-supported cinema's offerings is, on the other hand, far more striking, for the obstacles to wider circulation – linguistic, cultural, and other – are more readily apparent. (Hjort 2005: 2)

In the conclusion to her recent book reflecting on the state of the South Korean film industry, Jinhee Choi makes the comment that 'the continuing prosperity of the South Korean Film industry is uncertain' (2010: 193). This uncertainty is not only present in South Korea but is shared by almost all film industries outside of the dominant global player, Hollywood. The global financial crisis that has taken place in the last few years will doubtless have severe and long-lasting affects on the cinematic industries of all nations, including Japan and South Korean.

There have been several key trends that have had a huge impact on the Asian cinematic industry and many of the directors that this book has exam-ined engage directly with the developments that have been taking place around them. The rise and popularity of Japanese and Korean films at international film festivals has seen global awareness of selected directors from these regions remain relatively constant in the film festival circuit. This has led to a continuing division between those films that prove popular with general audiences and those that appeal to the art/film festival circuit. All the directors featured in this book have engaged with this debate in various ways and in their recent and current works they continue to negotiate an often difficult balance between the international art scene and commercial success.

The continual development of a specifically East Asian film festival circuit has also been an important factor in the last decade. Not only is Asian cinema looking inward for recognition but this has also proved to be an important site for 'opportunities for exchange' which are 'important as a key transnational and infrastructural node that make new networks and alliances possible' (Iordanova 2010: 17). This process of change, as well as governmental moves towards the development and support of co-productions and international cooperation (see Davis and Yeh 2008, Choi 2010), is leading to new connections and developments in the Asian film industry.

One important development is a constant focus on co-productions and partnerships has helped sustain the cinema industries of the Asian nations. The practice of a pan-Asian cinema is growing with companies such as Applause Pictures, Sidus, CJ Entertaiment and Raintree Media Corp. specifically developing pan-Asian funding and film development. Films such as *Jan Dara* (Thailand/ Hong Kong, 2001), *Perhaps Love* (Hong Kong/China, 2006), *The Eye* (Hong Kong/ Singapore, 2002), *One Fine Spring Day* (Korea, 2001), and *Three* (South Korea/ Thailand/Hong Kong, 2002) have gone on to break box-office records across Asia. After a long hiatus and despite some residual bad relations between the two nations Japanese/Korean co-productions have been seen with films such as *One Missed Call Final* (*Chakushin ari final*, Manabu Asô, 2006), *Virgin Snow* (*Hatsuyuki no koi*, Han Sang-hee, 2007), *Black House* (*Geomeun jip*, Terra Shin, 2007), *Don't Look Back* (*Nae cheongchun-ege goham*, Kim Young-nam, 2006), *Boat* (Kim Young-nam, 2009) and *Higanjima* (Kim Tae-gyun, 2011). Miike Takashi and Kim Ki-duk have been engaged with the move towards Japanese/ Korean co-productions with *Like a Dragon* (*Ryû ga gotoku: gekijô-ban*, 2007) and *Dream* (2008) respectively. Co-productions with European agencies have also risen considerably in the last few decades with companies such as Fortissimo, Celluloid Dreams and Paradis all producing films with East Asia. In line with this trend, Kawase Naomi has worked several times with Arte, the Franco-German

TV Network, and Miike Takashi's *13 Assassins* was a Japanese/British production. The drive for co-productions in Asian Cinema is, as Davis and Yeh summarise:

> A push towards market consolidation, creating an enlarged, unified film market that sustains investment in medium-to-large scale movies and marketing. Nevertheless, it aids cultural diversity by ensuring local tastes and expectations are served. (2008: 110)

Whilst pan-Asian cinema is not a new invention (see Yau 2009, Taylor 2013) the drive towards this mode of production will clearly have an affect on the whole cinema industry. The balancing act between the local and the pan-Asian is a difficult line to tred and whilst some films have been very successful (*13 Assassins* is a case in point) many other have failed to impress either target market.

The presence of Hollywood is a constant element in any national cinema and it continues to be a factor in Japanese and South Korean film markets. South Korean and Japanese films still struggle to compete with the Hollywood machine but the recent moves towards higher production values, more dynamic narratives and multi-platform engagement with a film product (such as fan-sites, fan-titles, blogs, comics, TV shows and merchandising) has meant that Asian cinema as a wider unit has continued to sustain itself and do well. The constant threat of cultural appropriation is ever present, however, as Park Chan-wook's move to Hollywood and the continual round of remakes of Asian films demonstrate. Possibly the greatest threat to Japanese and South Korean cinema will be closer to home from the Chinese territories, as the ever-growing vast linguistically, cultural and economic rise of the China and pan-Chinese cinemas will see the region's cinematic landscape transformed again. This new landscape will also need to consider and include the growing markets of South East Asia. This developing region is not only a huge market for East Asian cultural products as the success of Korean television drams in Malaysia and Indonesia demonstrate but is also a new and potentially powerful collaboration and production space.

The directors who have featured in this book are all examples of how the cinemas of Japan and South Korea have developed since the 1950s. Representation of the complex narratives of gender, politics, war, race and ethnicity and socio-economics are contained within their respective works and this is placed together with a sustained questioning and exploration on the meaning and aesthetics of cinema. What the future holds for those directors still working will remain to be seen but one thing is certain: their fates will go hand-in-hand with the cinematic environments in which they work. What the future holds for the Japanese and South Korean film industries is unclear, but for the moment the future still looks bright.

Bibliography

Abe, Casio (2004) *Beat Takeshi Vs. Takeshi Kitano*. New York: Kaya Press.

Abelmann, Nancy and Kathleen McHugh (eds) (2005) *South Korean Golden Age Melodrama: Gender, Genre, and National Cinema*. Detroit: Wayne State University Press.

Aldrich, Daniel P. and Martin Dusinberre (2011) 'Hatoko Comes Home: Civil Society and Nuclear Power in Japan', *Journal of Asian Studies*, 70, 3, 1–23.

Anderson, Benedict (2006) *Imagined Communities: Reflections on the Origin and Spread of Nationalism*. New Edition. London: Verso.

Anderson, Joseph and Donald Richie (1983) *The Japanese Film: Art and Industry*. 2nd ed. Princeton, NJ: Princeton University Press.

Anon. (2007) *On the Megaphone: Female Directors Enter the Movie Scene* Available at: http://web-japan.org/trends98/honbun/ntj981006.html (accessed 21 July 2008).

Antoniou, Anthony (2004) '*Bataru Rowairu/Battle Royale*', in Justin Bower (eds) *The Cinema of Japan and Korea*. London and New York: Wallflower Press, 225–34.

Arai, Andrea (2000) 'The "Wild Child" of 1990s Japan', *The South Atlantic Quarterly*, 99, 841-863.

Aristotle (1999) *Physics*. Oxford: Oxford University Press.

Atsugi, Taka (1991) *Josei dokyumentarisuto no kaisô/Memoirs of a Female Documentarist*. Tokyo: Domesu shuppan.

Bakhtin, Mikhail (1982) *Dialogic Imagination: Four Essays*. Austin: University of Texas Press.

Baruma, Ian (1984) *A Japanese Mirror: Heroes and Villains of Japanese Culture*. London: Jonathan Cape.

____ (2006) 'Mr Vengeance'. Available at: http://www.nytimes.com/2006/04/09/magazine/09park.html (accessed April 11 2008).

Baskett, Micheal (2009) *The Attractive Empire: Transnational Film Culture in Imperial Japan*.

Honolulu: University of Hawai'i Press.

Benedict, Ruth (2005 [1946]) *The Chrysanthemum and the Sword: Patterns of Japanese Culture*. Boston: Mariner Books.

Bernardi, Joanne (2001) *Writing in the Light: The Silent Scenario and the Japanese Pure Film Movement*. Detroit: Wayne State University Press.

Bernstein, Gail (1991) *Recreating Japanese Women, 1600–1945*. Berkeley, CA: University of California Press.

Berry, Chris (2003) *Chinese Films in Focus: 25 New Takes*. London: British Film Institute.

Bitō, Takeshi (1984) *Takeshi-kun, Hai!*. Tokyo: Shinchōsha.

____ (1999) *Watachi wa sekai de kirawareru*. Tokyo: Shinchōsha.

Bock, Audie (1985) *Japanese Film Directors*. New York: Kodansha America.

Bordwell, David (1988) *Ozu and the Poetics of Cinema*. Princeton, NJ: Princeton University Press.

Bowyer, Justin (ed.) (2004) *The Cinema of Japan and Korea*. London and New York: Wallflower Press.

Brandt, Vincent (1971) *Korean Village*. Cambridge, MA: Harvard University Press.

Brooks-Gordan, Belinda (2006) *The Price of Sex: Prostitution, Policy and Society*. London: Willan Press.

Bruno, Guliana (1987) 'Ramble City: postmodernism and *Blade Runner*', *October*, 41, 61–74.

Buckley, Rodger (1999) *Japan Today*. Third ed. Cambridge: Cambridge University Press.

Buehrer, Beverley Bare (1990) *Japanese Films: A Filmography and Commentary, 1921–1989*. Jefferson, NC: McFarland.

Burch, Noel (1979) *To the Distant Observer: Form and Meaning in the Japanese Cinema*. Berkeley, CA: University of California Press.

Buzo, Adrian (2002) *The Making of Modern Korea*. London and New York: Routledge.

Cazdyn, Eric (2003) *The Flash of Capital: Film and Geopolitics in Japan*. Durham, NC: Duke University Press.

Chanan, Michael (1997) 'The Changing Geography of Third Cinema', *Screen*, 38, 4, 372–88.

Ching, Leo (2000) 'Give Me Japan and Nothing Else!: Postcoloniality, Identity, and the Traces of Colonialism', *The South Atlantic Quarterly*, 99, 763-788.

Cho, Eunsun (2002) 'The Female Body and Enunciation in Adada and Surrogate Mother', David. E. James and Kyung Hyun Kim (eds.) *Im Kwon-Taek: The making of a Korean National Cinema*. Detroit: Wayne State University Press.

Choe, Steve (2007) 'Kim Ki-duk's Cinema of Cruelty: Ethics and Spectatorship in the Global Economy', *Positions: East Asia Cultures Critique*, 15, 1, 65–90.

Choi, Chungmoo (2002) 'The Politics of Gender, Aestheticism, and Cultural Nationalism in Sopyonje and The Genealogy', David. E. James and Kyung Hyun Kim (eds.) *Im Kwon-Taek: The making of a Korean National Cinema*. Detroit: Wayne State University Press.

Choi, Chungmoo, and Elaine Kim (1998) *Dangerous Women: Gender and Korean Nationalism*, London: Routledge.

Choi, Jinhee (2010) *The South Korean Film Renaissance: Local Hitmakers/Global Provocateurs*. Middletown, CT: Wesleyan University Press.

Chua, Beng-huat, Kōichi Iwabuchi and Chris Berry (2008) *East Asian Pop Culture: Analysing the Korean Wave*. Hong Kong: Hong Kong University Press.

Chung, Hye Seung (2005) 'Toward a Strategic Korean Cinephilia: A Transnational Détourent of Hollywood Melodrama', in Nancy Abelmann and Kathleen McHugh (eds) *South Korean Golden Age Melodrama: Gender, Genre, and National Cinema*. Detroit: Wayne State University Press, 117–28.

___ (2012) *Kim Ki-duk*. Urbana, IL: University of Illinois Press.

Chung, Hye Seung and David Scott Diffrient (2007) 'Forgetting to Remember, Remembering to Forget: The Politics of Memory and Modernity in the Fractured Films of Lee Chang-dong and Hong Sang-soo', in Francis Gatewood (ed.) *Seoul Searching: Culture and Identity in Contemporary Korean Cinema*. New York: State University of New York Press.

Chung, Sung-ill (2006) *Im Kwon-taek*. Seoul: Korean Film Council.

Christensen, Terry and Peter T. Haas (2005) *Projecting Politics: Political Messages in American Film*. London: M. E. Sharp Press.

Ciment, Michel (2003) 'Créer un tempo', *Positif*, 513, November, 10–15.

Cummings, Bruce (1997) *Korea's Place in the Sun*. New York: W. W. Norton.

Dairoku Kikuchi cited in Robert J Smith (1987) 'Gender Inequality in Contemporary Japan', *Journal of Japanese Studies*, 13, 1, Winter, 1-25.

Davis, Darrell William (2001) 'Reigniting Japanese tradition with *Hana-bi*', *Cinema Journal*, 40, 4, 55–88.

Davis, Darrell William and Emily Yueh-yu Yeh (2008) *East Asian Screen Industries*. London: British Film Institute.

Desser, David (1988) *Eros Plus Massacre: Introduction to Japanese New Wave Cinema*. Bloomington, IN: Indiana University Press.

Dissanayake, Wimal (1994) *Colonialism and Nationalism in Asian Cinemas*. Bloomington, IN: Indiana University Press.

___ (1996) *Narratives of Agency: Self-making in China, India and Japan*. Minneapolis: University of Minnesota Press.

Eagleton, Terry (1997) *The Illusions of Postmodernism*. Oxford: Blackwell.

___ (2003) *After Theory*. London: Allen Lane.

Friedländer, Saul (1992) 'Trauma, Transference and Working-Through', *History and Memory*, 4, 39–55.

Friedman, Jonathan (1990) 'Being in the World: Globalisation and Localisation', *Theory, Culture and Society*, 7, 311-28.

FRIPRESCI Award http://www.fipresci.org/awards/awards/awards_2000.htm (accessed 30 June 2006).

Fukasaku, Kinji (2001) 'Interview' http://www.midnighteye.com/interviews/kinji_fukasaku.shtml (accessed 31 August 2002).

Gatewood, Francis (2007) *Seoul Searching: Culture and Identity in Contemporary Korean Cinema*. New York: State University of New York Press.

Geok-lin Lim, Shirley, Larry. E .Smith and Wimal Dissanayake (1999) *Transnational Asia Pacific: Gender, Culture and the Public Sphere*. Illinois: University of Illinois Press.

Gerow, Aaron (2002) 'Recognizing "Others" in a New Japanese Cinema', *Japan Foundation Newsletter*, 29, 2, January, 2–3.

___ (2003) Interview with Naomi Kawase, http://www.yidff.jp/docbox/16/box16-1e.html (Accessed 13th Dec 2007)

___ (2007) *Kitano Takeshi*. London: British Film Institute.

___ (2010) *Visions of Japanese Modernity: Articulations of Cinema, Nation, and Spectatorship, 1895-1925*. Berkely, CA: University of California Press.

Girard, Rene (2005 [1977]) *Violence and the Sacred*. London: Continuum.

Gombeaud, Adrien, Anaid Demir, Cédric Lagandré, Catherine Capdeville-Zeng and Danièle Rivière (2006) *Kim Ki Duk*. Paris: Dis voir.

Gu, Jeong-a (1997) '*Threesome*: Impossible Dream of a Cinephile', *Cinema Forever*, 2, 134, 1.

Guneratne, Anthony and Wimal Dissanayake (2003) *Rethinking Third Cinema*. New York and London: Routledge.

Han Cinema Available http://www.hancinema.net (Accessed 13th June 2008).

Hastings, Adrian (1997) *The Construction of Nationhood: Ethnicity, Religion and Nationalism*. Cambridge: Cambridge University Press.

Harootunian, Harry (2000) 'Japan's Long Postwar: The Trick of Memory and the Ruse of History', *The South Atlantic Quarterly*, 99, 715–39.

Havens, Thomas R. H. (1975) 'Women and War in Japan, 1937–45', *American Historical Review*, 80, 4, 913–34.

Hayward, Susan (2000) *Cinema Studies: The Key Concepts*. 2nd ed. London: Routledge.

High, Peter B. (2003) *The Imperial Screen: Japanese Film Culture in the Fifteen Years' War, 1931–1945*. Madison: University of Wisconsin Press.

Higson, Andrew.(1989) 'The concept of National cinema' *Screen*, 30.4, 36-46.

Hirano, Kyōko (1992) *Mr Smith Goes to Tokyo: The Japanese Cinema under the American Occupation, 1945–1952*. Madison: University of Wisconsin Press.

Hjort, Mette (2005) *Small Nation, Global Cinema: The New Danish Cinema*. Minnesota: University of Minnesota Press.

Hjort, Mette and Scott Mackenzie (2000) *Cinema and Nation*. London: Routledge.

Hoare, James and Susan Pares (1988) *Korea: An Introduction*. London and New York: Routledge.

hooks, bell (1992) *Black Looks: Race and Representation*. Boston: South End Press.

Hummell, Volker (2002) 'Interview with Kim Ki-duk', *Senses of Cinema*, March-April.

Hunt, Leon and Wing-Fai Leung (2008) *East Asian Cinemas: Exploring Transnational Connections on Film*. London: IB Tauris.

Ichiki, Masashi (2011) 'De-Mystifying a post-war myth: Reading Fukusaku's *Jinginaki Tatakai*', in Kate. E. Taylor (ed.) *Dekalog 4: On East Asian Filmmakers*. London and New York:

Wallflower Press, 107–21.

Igarashi, Yoshikuni (2000) *Bodies of Memory: Narratives of War in Post-war Japanese Culture 1945–1970*. Princeton, NJ: Princeton University Press.

Iles, Timothy.(2008) *The Crisis of Identity in Contemporary Japanese Film: Personal, Cultural, National*. Boston: Brill Academic Publishers.

Im Kwon-taek (ed) (2003) *Sopyonje: Movie Book*. Seoul: Hanul Press.

Iordanova, Dina and Ruby Cheung (2011) *Film Festival Yearbook 3: Film Festivals and East Asia*. St Andrews: St Andrews Film Studies.

Ivy, Marilyn (2000) 'Revenge and Recapitation in Recessionary Japan', *The South Atlantic Quarterly*, 99, 819-840.

Iwabuchi, Koichi (2003) *Recentering Globalization: Popular Culture and Japanese Trans-nationalism*. Durham, NC: Duke University Press.

___ (2004a) 'Complicit Exoticism: Japan and its Other', *Continuum*, 8, 2, 49–82.

___ (2004b) *Feeling Asian Modernities: Transnational Consumption of Japanese TV Dramas*. Hong Kong: Hong Kong University Press.

James, David E. and Kyung Hyun Kim (2001) *Im Kwon-Taek: The Making of a Korean National Cinema*. Detroit: Wayne State University Press.

Japanese Constitution of 1947, http://history.hanover.edu/texts/1947con.html? (Accessed 8th Dec 2001)

Jeffreys, Shelia (2009) *The Industrial Vagina: The Political Economy of the Global Sex Trade*. London: Routledge.

Joang, Cho-hae (2002) 'Sopyonje: It's Cultural and Historical Meaning', in David E. James and Kyung Hyun Kim (eds) *Im Kwon Taek: The Making of a Korean National Cinema*. Detroit: Wayne State University Press, 134–57.

Johnston, Kenneth (1993) 'The point of view of the Wondering Camera', *Cinema Journal*, 32:2, Winter, 49-56.

Katzenstein, Peter and Takashi Shiraishi (2006) *Beyond Japan: The Dynamics of East Asian Regionalism*. Ithaca, NY: Cornell University Press.

Kawase, Naomi (1997) 'Interview' http://www.yidff.jp/97/cat009/97c036.html (accessed 13 December 2007).

___ (2003) 'Spiritual director depicts family trauma and recovery' http://www.japan-101.com/forums/showthread.php?t=310 (accessed on 13 December 2007).

___ (2005) '*Shara*' http://www.kawasenaomi.com/en/information/ (accessed 31 July 2005).

___ (2012) 'Cannes Film Festival Hanazu no Tsuki press kit' http://www.festival-cannes.fr/assets/Image/Direct/040259.pdf (accessed 31 May 2012).

Kehr, David (1998) 'Equinox Flower', *Film Comment*, March/April, 31–2.

Kim, Andrew (2000) 'Korean Religious Culture and its Affinity to Christianity: The Rise of Protestant Christianity in South Korea', *Sociology of Religion*, 61, 2, 117–33.

Kim, Hyun Sook (1998) 'Yanggonju as an allegory of the nation: images of working-class women in popular and radical texts', in Chungmoo Choi and Elaine Kim (eds) *Dangerous Women: Gender and Korean Nationalism*. London: Routledge.

Kim, Ki-Duk (2001) 'Interview' Available http://www.badguythemovie.net/splash.html (accessed 19 February 2002).

___ (2002) 'Interview with Jung Seong-il' *Cine21* Issue 339, Feb. 5-19.

___ (2006) 'Interview with Daniele Riviere' in Gombeaud, A., A. Demir, C. Lagandré, C. Capdeville-Zeng, and D. Rivière (eds.) *Kim Ki Duk*. France: Dis voir.

Kim, Kyung-hyun (2002a) 'Korean Cinema and Im Kwon-Taek: An Overview', David. E. James and Kyung-hyun Kim (eds) *Im Kwon-Taek: The Making of a Korean National Cinema*. Detroit: Wayne State University Press, 19–47.

___ (2002b) 'Is This How the War is Remembered?: Deceptive Sex and the Remasculinzed Nation in *The Taeback Mountains*', in David. E. James and Kyung-hyun Kim (eds) *Im Kwon-Taek: The Making of a Korean National Cinema*. Detroit: Wayne State University Press, 197–223.

___ (2004) *The Remasculization of Korean Cinema*. Durham, NC: Duke University Press.

___ (2011) *Virtual Hallyu: Korean Cinema of the Global Era*. Durham, NC: Duke University Press.

Kim, Myung-Ja (2007) 'Race, Gender, and Postcolonial Identity in Kim Ki-duk's *Address Unknown*', in Francis Gatewood (ed.) *Seoul Searching: Culture and Identity in Contemporary Korean Cinema*, New York: State University of New York Press, 243–64.

Kim, So-young (2000) 'Korean Film History and Chihwaseon', Korean Film Council http://www.koreanfilm.or.kr/attach/1KoreanFilmHistoryandChihwaseon.pdf (accessed 31 January 2002).

Kim, Suk-Young (2007) 'Crossing the Border to the 'Other' Side: Dynamics of Interaction Between North and South Korean in *Spy Li Cheol-jin* and *Joint Security Area*', in Francis Gatewood (ed.) *Seoul Searching: Culture and Identity in Contemporary Korean Cinema*. New York: State University of New York Press, 219–42.

Kim, Sun-Hwan (2001) 'The Achievements and Problems of Social and Cultural Exchange Between South and North Koreans', *North Korean Journal*, April, 61–9.

Kim, Young-jin (2007) *Park Chan-wook*. Soeul: Seoul Selection.

Kirihara, Donald (1992) *Patterns of Time: Mizoguchi and the 1930s*. Madison: University of Wisconsin Press.

___ (1996) 'Reconstructing Japanese Film', in David Bordwell and Noël Caroll (eds.) *Post-Theory: Reconstructing Film Studies*. Madison: University of Wisconsin Press.

Kitano, Takeshi (1995) 'Fukkatsu Takeshi "motto nebaru'. *Asashi Shinbun*, 2 February, 27.

___ (1998) 'Mizuumi mitaina umi ga ii', *Cahiers du cinema Japan*, 23, March, 70–3.

Ko, Mika (2004) 'The Break-up of the National Body: Cosmetic Multiculturalism and films of Miike Takashi, *New Cinemas*, 2, 1, 29–39.

Koch, Gertrude (1985) 'Ex-changing the gaze: Re-visioning Feminist Film theory', *New German Critique*, 34, 140–2.

Koo, Hagen (2007) 'The changing faces of inequality in South Korean in the age of globalisation', *Korean Studies*, 31, 1–18.

Kristava, Julia (1998) 'The Subject in Process', in Patrick French and Roland-Francis Lark (eds) *The Tel Quel Reader*. New York: Routledge.

Kwak, Han-ju (2002) 'In Defence of Continuity: Discourses on the Traditional and the Mother in Festival' in David. E. James and Kyung Hyun Kim (eds) *Im Kwon-Taek: The Making of a Korean National Cinema*. Detroit: Wayne State University Press.

___ (2004) '*Seopyeonje/Sopyonge*', Justin Bower (ed.) *The Cinema of Japan and Korea*. London and New York: Wallflower Press, 151–60.

Kwon, Youngmin (2005) *Modern Korean Fiction: An Anthology*. New York: Columbia University Press.

Lau, Jenny Kwok Wah (2003) *Multiple Modernitites: Cinemas and Popular Media in Transcultural East Asia*. Philadelphia: Temple University Press.

Lebra, Joyce C., Joy Paulson and Elizabeth Powers (1976) *Women in Changing Japan*. Boulder, CO: Westview Press.

Lee, Chang-dong (1998) 'Dirt in the Seoul in World socialist' http://wsws.org/arts/1998/may1998/fish-m19.shtml (Accessed 3 August 2002).

___ (1992) *There's a Lot of Shit in Nokcheon*. Seoul: Moonji.

___ (2005) *Nokcheon: Suivi de nn éclat dans le ciel*. Paris: Cadre Vert.

Lee, Hyangin (2000) *Contemporary Korean Cinema: Identity, Culture, Politics*. Manchester: Manchester University Press.

___ (2005) '*Chunhyang*: Marketing an Old Tradition in New Korean Cinema', in Chi-Yun Shin and Julian Strginer (eds) *New Korean Cinema*. Edinburgh: Edinburgh University Press, 63–78.

Leheny, David (2006) *Think Global, Fear Local: Sex, Violence and Anxiety in Contemporary Japan*. Ithaca, NY: Cornell University Press.

Lent, John (1995) 'Lousy Films Had to Come First: Interview with Im Kwon-Taek', *Asian Cinema*, 7, 2, 86–92.

Leong, Anthony (2003) *Korean Cinema: The New Hong Kong*. Bloomington, IN: Trafford Publishing.

Liddle, Joanna, and Sachiko Nakajima (2000) *Rising Suns, Rising Daughters: Gender, Class and Power in Japan*. London: Zed Books.

Lifton, Robert .J. (1991) *Death in Life: Survivors of Hiroshima*. Chapel Hill, NC: University of North Carolina Press.

Loftus, Ronald (2002) *Depicting Women: The Memoires and Documentary Film of Atsugi Taka*, Available http://intersections.anu.edu.au/issue7/loftus.html (accessed 13 December 2007).

Lu, Sheldon Hsiao-Peng (1997) *Transnational Chinese Cinemas: Identity, Nationhood, Gender*. Honolulu: University of Hawai'i Press.

Mackie, Vera (2003) *Feminism in Modern Japan: Citizenship, Embodiment and Sexuality*. Cambridge: Cambridge University Press.

Marchetti, Gina and Tan See Kam (2007) *Hong Kong Film, Hollywood and New Global Cinema: No Film is an Island*. London and New York: Routledge.

Martin, Alexander (2005) 'Shara' http://www.trendesombras.com/num3/esp_shara3ing.

asp, (Accessed 11th June 2006)

Martin, Michael. T. (1995) *Cinemas in the Black Diaspora: Diversity, Dependence and Oppositionality*. Detroit: Wayne State University Press.

McClintock, Anne (1995) *Imperial Leather: Race, Gender and Sexuality in the Colonial Contest*. New York: Routledge.

McDonald, Keiko (2006) *Reading a Japanese Film: Cinema in Context*. Honolulu: University of Hawai'i Press.

McGowan, Todd (2007) 'Affirmation of the Lost Object: *Peppermint Candy* and the End of Progress', *Symplokē*, 14, 1–2, 170–89.

McGrey, Douglas (2002) 'Japan's Gross National Cool', *Foreign Policy Magazine*, http://www.chass.utoronto.ca/~ikalmar/illustex/japfpmcgray.htm (accessed 11 June 2007).

McHugh, Kathleen, and Nancy Abelmann (2005) *South Korean Golden Age Melodrama: Gender, Genre, and National Cinema*. Detroit: Wayne State University Press.

McRay, Jay (2005) *Japanese Horror Cinema*. Edinburgh: Edinburgh University Press.

Mes, Tom (2003) *Agitator: The Cinema of Takashi Miiki*. Goldalming: FAB Press.

Mes, Tom and Jasper Sharp (2005) *The Midnight Eye Guide to New Japanese Film*. Berkeley, CA: Stone Bridge Press.

Miike, Takashi (2001) 'Interview' http://www.midnighteye.com/interviews/takashi_miike.shtml (accessed 31 July 2003).

Minh-ha, Trin Ti (1991) *When the Moon Waxes Red: Representation, Gender and Cultural Politics*. New York and London: Routledge.

Modleski, Tania (2005) *The Women Who Knew Too Much*. London and New York: Routledge.

Molony, Barbara and Kathleen S. Uno (2005) *Gendering Modern Japanese History*. Cambridge, MA: Harvard University Asia Centre.

Moon, Seungsook (1998) 'Begetting the Nation: the Androcentric Discourse of National History and Traditions in South Korea' Chungmoo Choi and Elaine Kim (eds.) *Dangerous Women: Gender and Korean Nationalism*, London: Routledge.

___ (2005) *Militarized Modernity and Gendered Citizenship in South Korea*. Durham, NC: Duke University Press.

Morley, David and Kevin Robins (1995) *Spaces of Identity: Global Media, Electronic Landscapes and Cultural Boundaries*. London: Routledge.

Morris, Meghan, Siu Leung Li and Stephen Chan (2006) *Hong Kong Connections: Transnational Imagination in Action Cinema*, Durham, NC: Duke University Press.

Noh, J. (2006) 'Korean Filmmakers Protest as new quota becomes a reality', *Screendaily.com*, 3rd July, www.screendaily.com/story.asp?storyid=26865 (Accessed 19th August 2007)

Nowell-Smith, Geoffrey (1997) *The Oxford History of World Cinema*. Oxford: Oxford University Press.

Nygren, Scott (2007) *Time Frames: Japanese Cinema and the Unfolding of History*. Minneapolis: University of Minnesota Press.

Okubō Kiyoaki (2007) 'Kimiko in New York', *Rouge*, 10. http://www.rouge.com.au/10/

kimiko.html (accessed 6 July 2008).

Paquet, Darcy (2002) 'Netizen Funds' http://www.koreanfilm.org/netizen.html (Accessed 1st July 2008)

___ (2003) 'Korean Filmmakers Rage Against the Quota Threat', Screendaily.com, 13 June, www.screendaily.com/story.asp?storyid=12847 (accessed 1 July 2008).

___ (2005) 'The Korean Film Industry: 1992 to the Present', in Chi-Yun Shin and Julian Stringer (eds) *New Korean Cinema*. Edinburgh: Edinburgh University Press, 32–50.

___ (2009) *New Korean Cinema: Breaking the Waves*. London and New York: Wallflower Press.

Park, Sung-hyun (2007) 'Korean Cinema after Liberation: Production, Industry, and Regulatory Trends', in Francis Gatewood (ed.) *Seoul Searching: Culture and Identity in Contemporary Korean Cinema*. New York: State University of New York Press, 15–36.

Phillips, Alastair and Julian Stringer (2007) *Japanese Cinema: Texts and Contexts*. London: Routledge.

Polan, Dana (2001) *Jane Campion*. London: British Film Institute.

Pyle, Kenneth. B. (1973) 'The Technology of Japanese Nationalism', *Journal of Asian Studies*, 33, 51–65.

Rayns, Tom (1997) 'Hana-Bi', *Sight and Sound*, 26–9.

___ (2000) 'This Gun for Hire', *Sight and Sound*, 19–21.

Rich, Adrianne (1979) *On Lies, Secrets, and Silence: Selected Prose, 1966–1978*. London: W. W. Norton.

Richie, Donald and Paul Schrader (2005) *A Hundred Years of Japanese Films: A Concise History, with a Selective Guide to DVDs and Videos*. Rev. Ed. New York: Kodansha.

Russell, Catherine (1995) 'Overcoming Modernity: Gender and the Pathos of History in Japanese Melodrama', *Camera Obscura*, 35, 130–57.

___ (2003) 'Three Japanese Actresses of the 1950s: Modernity, Femininity and the Performance of Everyday life', *Cineaction*, 60, 34–44.

___ (2008) *The Cinema of Naruse Mikio: Women and Japanese Modernity*. Durham, NC: Duke University Press.

Russell, M. (2005) 'Sector Report Korea' http://www.hollywoodreporter.com/hr/search/article_display.jsp?vnu_content_id=1000930566 (accessed 24 July 2008).

Ryang, Sonia (2002) *Koreans in Japan: Critical Voices from the Margin*. London: Routledge.

Ryan, Chris and Michael Hall (2001) *Sex Tourism: Marginal People and Liminalities*. London: Routledge.

Saïd, Edward (1978) *Orientalism*. London: Vintage Books.

Sato, Kumiko (2004) 'How Information Technology Has (Not) Changed Feminism and Japanism: Cyberpunk in the Japanese Context', *Comparative Literature Studies*, 41, 335-355.

Scofield, David. (2004) 'Sex and denial in South Korea' Asia Times 26th May. http://www.atimes.com/atimes/Korea/FE26Dg03.html (Accessed 1st Sep, 2008)

Shin, Chi-Yun and Julian Stringer (2005) *New Korean Cinema*. Edinburgh: Edinburgh

University Press.

Shin, Gi-wook and Michael Robinson (2001) *Colonial Modernity in Korea*. Cambridge, MA: Harvard University Press.

Shohat, Elaine and Robert Stam (1994) *Unthinking Eurocentrism: Multiculturalism and the Media*. London and New York: Routledge.

Sievers, Sharon (1983) *Flowers in Salt: The Beginnings of Feminist Consciousness in Modern Japan*. Palo Alto: Stanford University Press.

Smedley, Tim (2000) 'A Divine Comedy: The Films of Takeshi Kitano'. Available http://Kitanotakeshi.com (accessed 11 June 2008).

Standish, Isolde (1994) 'Korean Cinema and the New Realism', in Wimal Dissanayake (ed.) *Colonialism and Nationalism in Asian Cinemas*. Bloomington, IN: Indiana University Press, 65–89.

____ (2000) *Myth and Masculinity in the Japanese Cinema: Towards a Political Reading of the Tragic Hero*. London: Curzon.

____ (2005) *A New History of Japanese Cinema: A Century of Narrative Film*. New York: Continuum.

So Chong-yun (1990) 'Standing Alone' *Koreana*. Seoul: International Cultural Society of Korea.

Takahashi, Tetsuya (2005) 'Japanese Neo-Nationalism: A Critique of Katō Norihiro's "After the Defeat" Discourse', in Richard F. Calichman (ed.) *Contemporary Japanese Thought*. New York: Columbia University Press.

Taylor, Kate. E. (2013) 'East Asian Co-Production and the New Eastern Film Wave', in Saer Maty Ba and Will Higbee (eds) *De-Westernizing Film Studies*. London and New York: Routledge.

Taylor, Matthew (2006) 'Strategies of Disassociation: A Mimetic Dimension to Social Problems in Japan', *Anthropetics: A Journal of Generative Anthropology*, 12, 1.

Thompson, Kirstin and David Bordwell (1994) *Film History: An Introduction*. New York: McGraw-Hill.

Thornham, Sue (1999) *Feminist Film Theory: A Reader*. Edinburgh: Edinburgh University Press.

Thornton, S. A. (2007) *The Japanese Period Film: A Critical Analysis*. Jefferson, NC: McFarland.

Thorsten-Morimoto, Marie (1996) 'The nail that came out all the way: Hayashi Takeshi's case against the regulation of the Japanese student body', in Wimal Dissanayake (ed.) *Narratives of Agency: Self-making in China, India and Japan*. Minneapolis: University of Minnesota Press.

Tipton, Elise K. (2002) *Modern Japan: A Social and Political History*. London and New York: Routledge.

Trbic, Boris (2004) 'Park Chan-wook's world of personal introspection: The subtext of cinematic space in *Oldboy*, Available http://koreanfilm.org/trbic-oldboy.html (accessed 6 February 2009).

Truffaut, François (1976) 'A Certain Tendency of French Cinema', in Bill Nichols (ed.) *Movies and Methods: Volume I*. Berkley, CA: California University Press, 224–36.

Turim, Maureen (1998) *The Films of Oshima Nagisa: Images of a Japanese Iconoclast*. Berkeley, CA: University of California Press.

Uno, Kathleen S. (1999) *Passages to Modernity: Motherhood, Childhood, and Social Reform in Early Twentieth Century Japan*. Honolulu: University of Hawai'i Press.

Wada-Marciana, Mitsuyo (1998) 'The Production of Modernity in Japanese National Cinema: Shoichiku Kamata Style in the 1920s and 1930s', *Asian Cinemas*, 9, 2 69–93.

____ (2005) 'Imagining Modern Girls in the Japanese Women's Film', *Camera Obscura*, 60, 15–55.

Warner, Marina (1996) *Monuments And Maidens: The Allegory of the Female Form*. London: Vintage Press.

Werly, Richard (2001) 'Persécutés dès le préau au Japon', http://perso.fraise.net/liberation-japan-ijime.html (accessed 31 August 2008).

Wei, S. Louisa (2012) 'Women's Trajectories in Chinese and Japanese Cinemas: A Chronological Overview', in Kate. E. Taylor (ed.) *Dekalog 4: On East Asian Filmmakers*. London and New York: Wallflower Press, 13–44.

Yamahta, Yōsuke (1959) 'Genbaku satsuei memo' in Muneto Kiatajima (ed.) *Kiroku shasin: genbaku no Ngasaki*. Tokyo: Gakufû Shoin.

Yang, Hyunah (1998) 'Re-membering the Korean Military Comfort Women: Nationalism, Sexuality and Silencing', in Chungmoo Choi and Elaine Kim (eds) *Dangerous Women: Gender and Korean Nationalism*. London: Routledge.

Yates, Ronald E. (1990) 'Foreigners in Japan say openness all talk', http://www.davidapple-yard.com/japan/jp42.htm (accessed 13 September 1999).

Yau, K. S. (2009) *Japanese and Hong Kong Film Industries: Understanding the Origins of East Asian Film Networks*. London and New York: Routledge.

Yoneyama, Shoko (1999) *Japanese High School: Silence and Resistance*. London: Routledge.

Yoshimoto, Mitsuhiro (2000) *Kurosawa: Film Studies and Japanese Cinema*, Durham, NC: Duke University Press.

Yuval-Davis, Nira (1997) *Gender and Nation*. London: Sage.

Žižek, Slavoj (1993) *Tarrying with the Negative: Kant, Hegel, and the Critique of Ideology*. Durham, NC: Duke University Press.

Filmography and Further Viewing Suggestions

NB: where films have more than one English-language title, both have been given.

IM KWON-TAEK

Due to the amount of films that Im Kwon-taek has directed I have only included the films that have been referenced in this work.

1962 Farewell to the Tuman River/Dumanganga jal itgeola
1973 The Deserted Widow/Weeds/Jabcho
The Testimony/Jeungeon
1975 Parade of Wives/Anaedeului haengjin
1976 Commando on the Nakdong River/Nakdongkaneun heureuneunga
1979 The Genealogy/The Family Pedigree/Jokbo
No Glory/he Hidden Hero/Gitbaleobtneun gisu
The Divine Bow/Shingung
1980 Pursuit of Death/Jagko
1981 Mandala
1982 Daughter of Flames/Bului dal
1985 Gilsoddeum
1986 Ticket
The Surrogate Woman/Sibaji
1987 Adada
1989 Come Come Come Upward/Aje aje bara aje

1990 General's Son/Janggunui adeul
1991 The General's Son II/Janggunui adeul II
         Fly High Run Far/Gaebyeok
1992 The General's Son III/Janggunui adeul III
1993 Sopyeonje/Seopyeonje
1994 The Taebaek Mountains/Taebaek sanmaek
1996 Festival/Chukje
1997 Chang
2000 Chunhyang
2002 Drunk on Women and Poetry/Pained Fire/Painted Fire/Chihwaseon
2004 Low Life/Haryu insaeng
2007 Beyond the Years/A Crane of 1000 Years/Cheonnyeonhak
2011 Hanji

FUKASAKU KINJI

Due to the amount of films that Fukasku Kinji has directed, I have only included the films that have been referenced in this work.

1961 Vigilante With a Funky Hat/Fankii hatto no kaidanji
1964 Wolves, Pigs and Men/Okami to buta to ningen
1968 Black Lizard/Kurotokage
         Blackmail Is My life/Kyokatsu koso waga jinsei
         The Green Slime/Gamma daisan go: Uchu dai sakusen
1969 Black Rose Mansion/Kurobara no yakata
         Japan's Organized Crime Boss/boryokudan: Kumicho
1970 Tora! Tora! Tora! (co-director)
1971 Sympathy for the Underdog/Bakuto gaijin butai
1972 Under the Flag of the Rising Sun/Gunki hatameku moto ni
         Street Mobster/Gendai yakuza: Hitokiri yota
1973 Battles Without Honor and Humanity/aka The Yakuza Papers I/Jinginaki tatakai
         Battles Without Honor and Humanity: Hiroshima Deathmatch/aka The Yakuza Papers: Hiroshima Deathmatch II/Jinginaki tatakai: Hiroshima shito hen
         Battles Without Honor and Humanity: Proxy War/aka The Yakuza Papers: Proxy War III/Jinginaki tatakai: Dairi senso
1974 Battles Without Honor and Humanity: Police Tacticsaka The Yakuza Papers: Police Tactics IV Jinginaki tatakai: Chojo sakusen
         Battles Without Honor and Humanity: Final Episode aka The Yakuza Papers: Final Episode V/Jinginaki tatakai: Kanketsu hen
         New Battles Without Honor and Humanity/Shin jinginaki tatakai

1975 Graveyard of Honor/Jingi no hakaba

Cops vs. Thugs/Kenkei tai soshiki boryoku

New Battles Without Honor and Humanity: The Boss's Head/Shin Jinginaki tatakai: Kumicho no kubi

1976 New Battles Without Honor and Humanity: The Boss's Last Days/Shin Jinginaki tatakai: Kumicho saigo no hi

Yakuza Graveyard/Yakuza no hakaba: Kuchinashi no

1978 Message from Space/Uchu kara no messeiji

1980 Virus/Fukkatsu no hi

1992 The Triple Cross/Itsuka giragira suru hi

1994 Crest of Betrayal aka Loyal 47 Ronin: Yotsuya Ghost Story/Chushingura Gaiden: Yotsuya kaidan

1999 The Geisha House/Omocha

2000 Battle Royale/Batoru Rowaiaru

2003 Battle Royale II: Requiem/Batoru Rowaiaru: "Rekuiemu"

LEE CHANG-DONG

1997 Green Fish/Chorok mulkogi

1999 Peppermint Candy/Bakha satang

2002 Oasis

2007 Secret Sunshine/Milyang

2010 Poetry/Si

KITANO TAKESHI

1989 Violent Cop/Sono otoko, kyobo ni tsuki

1990 Boiling Point/3-4X jugatsu

1991 A Scene at the Sea/Ano natsu, ichiban shizukana umi

1993 Sonatine

1995 Getting Any?/Minna-yatteruka!

1996 Kids Return/Kidzu ritān

1997 Hana-bi

1999 Kikujiro

2000 Brother

2002 Dolls/Dōruzu

2003 Zatōichi

2005 Takeshis'

2007 Glory to the Filmmaker!/Kantoku Banzai

2008 Achilles and the Tortoise/Akiresu to Kame

2010 Outrage

2011 Outrage II

PARK CHAN-WOOK

1992 The Moon is the suns dream/Dal-eun...haega kkuneun kkum

1997 Trio/Saminjo

2000 Joint Security Area/JSA/Gongdong Gyeongbi Guyeok JSA

2002 Sympathy for Mr. Vengeance/Boksuneun Naui Geot

2003 Oldboy/Oldeuboi

2004 Three Extremes 'cut'

2005 Sympathy for Lady Vengeance/Chinjeolhan Geumja-ssi

2006 I'm a Cyborg, but that's OK/Ssaibogeujiman Gwaenchanha

2009 New York I love You

Thirst/Bakjwi

2012 Stoker

KAWASE NAOMI

1988 I focus on things that interest me/Watashi ga Tsuyoku Kyomi o Motta Mono o Okiku Fix de kiritoru

The concretization of these things flying around me/Watashi ga Iki-Iki to Kakawatte Iko to Suru Jibutsu no Gutaika

1992 Embracing/Ni tsutsumarete

1994 Katatsumori

1995 Memory of the Wind/Kaze no Kioku

See the Heavens/Ten/Mitake

1997 The God Suzaku/Moe no Suzaku

1998 The Weald/Somaudo monogatari

Wandering at Home: the Third Fall Since Starting to Live Alone, Tayutafu ni Kokyo – Hitorigurashi o Hajimete, Sannenme no Aki ni

2000 Firefly/Hotaru

2001 Sky, Wind, Fire, Water, Earth/Kya Ka Ra ba A

2003 Letter from a Yellow Cherry Blossom/Tsuioku no dansu

Shara/Sharasojyu

2006 Naissance et maternité/Tarachime

2007 The Mourning Forest/Mogari no mori

2008 Nanayomachi

2009   Visitors (Koma segment)

2011   Hanezu no tsuki

KIM KI-DUK

1996   Crocodile/Ag-o

Wild Animals/Yasaeng dongmul bohoguyeog

1998   Birdcage Inn/Paran daemun

2000   Real Fiction/Shilje sanghwang

The Isle/Seom

2001   Address Unknown/Suchwiin bulmyeong

Bad Guy/Nabbeun namja

2002   The Coast Guard/Haeanseon

2003   Spring, Summer, Fall, Winter... and Spring/Bom yeoreum gaeul gyeoul geurigo bom

2004   Samaritan Girl/Samaria

3-Iron/Bin-jip

2005   The Bow/Hwal

2006   Time/Shi gan

2007   Breath/Soom

2008   Dream/Bimong

2010   Arirang

Amen

MIIKE TAKASHI

Due to the amount of films that Miike Takashi has directed, I have only included his most notable ones.

1993   Body Guard Kiba/cBodigado Kiba

1995   Shinjuku Triad Society/Shinjuku Kuroshanki

1996   Jingi Naki yabō

Fudoh: The New Generation/Gokudō Sengokushi Fudō

1997   Rainy Dog/Gokudō Kuroshankai

Full Metal Yazkuza/Furu metaruGokudō

1998   The Bird People in China/Chūgoku no Chōjin

Andromedia

Blues Harp/Burūsu Hapu

1999   Ley Lines/Nihon Kuroshanai

Dead or Alive/DOA Deddo Oa Araibu – Hanzaisha

2000 Audition/Ôdishon
        The Guys from Paradise/Tengoku kara kita otoko-tachi
        MD Psycho (TV series)
        The City of Lost Souls/Horōryūgai
2001 Visitor Q/Bijita Q
        Family/Famiri
        Ichi the Killer/Koroshiya 1
2002 The Happiness of the Katakuris/Katakurike no Kofuku
        Agitator/Araburu Tamashii Tachi
        Sabu (TV)
        Graveyard of Honour/Shin Jingi no Hakaba
        Go! Go! Fushimi Jet (Music Video)
2003 Gozu
2004 One Missed Call/Chahushun Ari
2007 Sukiyaki Western Django
2008 God's Puzzle/Kamisama no pazuru
2009 Yattâman
2010 Thirteen Assassins/Jûsan-nin no shikaku

SELECTED FURTHER VIEWING: JAPANESE CINEMA

AOYAMA SHINJI

1996 Two Punks/Chinpira

1999 Shady Grove/Sheidî gurôvu

2000 Eureka/Yurîka

2004 Lakeside Murder Case/Reikusaido mada kesu

2006 Crickets/Kôrogi

2007 Sad Vacation

2011 Tokyo kōen

GOSHO HEINOSUKE

1931 The Neighbours Wife and Mine/Madamu to Nyobo

HARADA MASATO

1997 Bounce KoGals/Baunsu ko gaurusu

1999 Jubaku: Spellbound/Kin'yû fushoku rettô: Jubaku

2007 The Suicide Song/Densen uta

2008 The Mōryō's Box/Mōryō no Hako

ICHIKAWA KON

1956 The Burmese Harp/Biruma No Tatekoto

1958 The Temple of the Gloden Pavilion/enjo
         Fires on the Plain/Nobi

1963 An Actors Revenge/Yukinoke Henge

1975 I am a cat/Wagahai wa neko de Aru

IMMAMURA SHOEI

1963 The Insect Woman/Nippon Konchuki

1966 The Pornographers/Jinruigaki Nyumon:Erogotshi Yori

1979 Vengeance is Mine/Fukusu Saruwa Wareniari

1983 Ballad of Narayama/Narayama Bushiko

1997 The Eel/Unagi

ITAMI JŪZŌ

1985 Tampopo/Dandelion

ISHII SŌGO

1978 Panic in High School/Koko dai

1980 Crazy Thunder Road/Kuruizaki sanda rodo

1984 The Crazy Family/Gyakufunsha kazoku
2000 Gojoe
2005 The mirrored Mind/Kyoshin

KINUGASA TEINOSUKE
1926 The Page of Madness/Kurutta Ippeji
1953 Gate of Hell/Jingokumon

KOBAYASHI MASAKI
1951 The Human Condition Part I/Ningen No Joken I
1961 The Human Condition Part II/Ningen No Joken II
1964 Kwaidan

KORE-EDA HIROKAZU
1998 After Life/Wandâfuru raifu
2004 Nobody Knows/Dare mo shiranai
2006 Even If you Walk and Walk/Aruitemo aruitemo
2009 Kūki Ningyō/Air Doll
2011 I Wish/Kiseki

KUROSAWA AKIRA
1950 Rashamon
1952 Ikiru
1954 Seven Samurai/Shichinin No Samurai
1957 Throne of Blood/Kumonosu Jo
1961 Yojimbo
1962 Sanjuro
1980 Kagemusha the Shadow Warrior
1985 Ran

KUROSAWA KIYOSHI
1989 Sweet Home/Sûîto Homu
1997 Cure/Kyua
2001 Pulse/Kairo
2003 Doppelgänger/Dopperugengâ
2005 Retribution/Sakebi
        Loft
2008 Tōkyō Sonata

MIYAZAKI HAYAO
1986 Castle in the Sky/Tenkû no shiro Rapyuta

1988   My Neighbour Totoro/Tonari no Totoro

1989   Kiki's delivery Service/Majo no takkyûbin

2001   Spirited Away/Sen to Chihiro no kamikakushi

2004   Howls Moving Castle/Hauru no ugoku shiro

2008   Ponyo/Gake no Ue no Ponyo

MIZOGUCHI KENJI

1936   Osaka Elegy/Naniwa Ereji

1952   Life of Oharu/Saikaku Ichicai Onna

1953   Tales of Ugetsu/Ugetsu Monogatari

1954   Sansho the Baliff/Sansho Dayu

NAKATA HIDEO

1998   The Ring/Ringu

1999   The Ring II/Ringu II

2002   Dark Water/Honogurai Mizu No Soko Kara

2009   The Incite Mill/Inshite Miru: 7-kakan no desu gemu]

2010   Chatroom

NAKASHIMA TETSUYA

1995   Kamikazi Girls/Kamikaze takushî

2006   Memoires of Matsuko/Kiraware Matsuko no Isshō

2010   Confessions/Kokuhaku

NINAGAWA MIKA

2006   Sakuran

2012   Helter Skelter

ÔTOMO KATSUHIRO

1988   Akira

1995   Memories

2004   Steamboy/Suchīmubōi

2006   Mushishi

OSHIMA NAGISA

1968   Death By Hanging/Koshikei

1969   Boy/Shonen

1976   In the Realm of the Senses/Ai No Korida

1999   Taboo/Gohatto

OSHII MAMORU

1995   Ghost in the Shell/Kôkaku kidôtai

2004   Ghost in the Shell 2: innocent/Kôkaku kidôtai

2008   Ghost in the Shell 2.0/Gōsuto In Za Sheru/Kôkaku Kidōtai 2.0

The Sky Crawlers/Sukai Kurora

OZU YASUJIRO

1932   I was born but.../Otona No Miru Ehon-Umarete wa Mita Keredo

1949   Late Spring/Banshan

1951   Early Summer/Bakushu

1953   Tokyo Story/Tokyo Monogatari

SAI YOICHI

1993   All Under the Moon/Tsuki wa dotchi ni dete iru

2002   Doing Time/Keimusho no naka

2004   Blood and Bones/Chi to Hone

2009   Kamui

SATOSI KON

1998   Perfect blue

2003   Tokyo Godfathers

2004   Paranoid Agent/Mōsō Dairinin

2006   Paprika

SATOSHI MIKI

2005   Turtles are Surprisingly Fast Swimmers/Kame wa Igai to Hayaku Oyogu

2007   Adrift in Tokyo/Ten-ten

2009   Instant Swamp/Insutanto numa

SEZUKI SEIJUN

1964   Gate of Flesh/Nikutai no mon

1966   Tokyo Drifter/Tôkyô nagaremono

Elegy of Violence/Kenka erejii

1967   Branded to Kill/Koroshi no rakuin

2005   Princess Racoon/Operetta tanuki goten

SHINDO KANETO

1964   Onibaba

TANAKA HIROYUKI AKA SABU

1996   Dangan Runner

2000 Monday
2002 The Blessing Bell/Kôfuku no kane
2005 Dead Run/Shissô
2011 Usagi Drop/Usagi Doropp

TAKAHATA ISAO
1988 Grave of the Fireflies/Hotaru no haka
1994 Pom Poko/Heisei tanuki gassen pompoko

TESHIGAHARA HIROSHI
1964 Women of the Dunes/Suna no Omna

TSUKAMOTO SHINYA
1989 Tetsuo: The Iron Man
1995 Tokyo Fist/Tokyo ken
2002 Snake in June/Rokugatsu no hebi
2009 Tetsuo: The Bullet Man

SELECTED FURTHER VIEWING: KOREAN CINEMA

BAE YONG-GYUN

1989   Why did Bodhi-Dharma leave for the East/Dharmaga Tongjoguro Kan Kkadalgun

1995   The people in White/Geomeunga dange huina Baekseong

BONG JONG-HO

2003   Memories of Murder/Saliniu Chueok

2006   The Host/Hweomul

2009   Mother/Madeo

2012   Snow Piercer

CHANG YOON-HYUN

1997   The Contract/Cheob-sok

1999   Tell me something/Telmisseomding

2007   Hwang Jin-yi

2012   Gabi

HONG SANG-SOO

1996   The Day a Pig fell in the Well/Daijiga Umule Pajinnal

2000   A Bride Stripped Bare by her Bachelors/Oh! Soo-Jung

2002   On the Occasion of Remembering the Turning Gate/Saenghwalui Balgyeon

2006   Woman on the Beach/Haebyeoneui Yeoin

2008   Like you know it all/Jal aljido mothamyeonseo

2010   Oki's Movie/Okhuiui yeonghwa

2012   In Another Country/Dareun naraeseo

HUR JIN-HO

1998   Christmas in August/Palwolui Christmas

2001   One Fine Spring Day/Bomnaleun ganda

2007   Happiness/Hængbok

2012   Dangerous Liasons

JANG SO-YEONG

1968   Love me Once Again/Miwodo Dashi Hanbeon

JANG SUN-WOO

1986   Soeul Jesus/Seoul Hwangje

1991   The Road to the Race Track/Gyeongmajang Ganeum Kil

1993   Passage to Buddah/Hwaeomgyeong

1996 A Petel/kkotnip

1999 Lies/Gojitmal

JEONG JI-YOUNG

1992 White Badge/Hayan Jeonjaeng

1994 Life and Death of the Hollywood Kid/Hollywood kie Eu Saeng-ae

JO JIN-GYE

2001 My Wife is a Gangster/Jopog Manura

KANG JE-GYU

1996 The Ginko Bed

1999 Shiri/Swiri

2004 Brotherhood/Taegukgi Hwinalrimyeo

2011 My Way/Mai Wei

KANG WOO-SUK

1989 Hapiness has nothing to do with student records/Haengbpken Seongjeogsunoi Anjiyanchayo

1993 Two Cops/tukabseu

1996 Two Cops II/Tukabseu II

2003 Silmido

2006 Hanbando

KIM JI-WOON

1998 The Quiet Family/Choyonghan Kajok

2000 Foul King/Panch ilkwang

2003 A Tale of Two Sisters/Changhwa wa Horgryon

KIM KI–YOUNG

1955 Box of Dath/Ju-geon-eui Sang-ja

1960 The Housmaid/Ha-nyeo

1963 Garyeojang

1964 Asphalt

1968 Woman/Yeo

1971 Woman of Fire/Hwa-nyeo

1972 The Insect Woman/Chung-nyeo

1978 Earth/Heulk

KIM SANG-JIN

1999 Attack the Gas Station/Juyuso seubgyuksageun

2001 Kick the Moon/Shinlaui dalbam

2002 Jail Breakers/Gwangbokjeol teuksa

2004 The Ghost House/Gwishini sanda

KIM SUNG-SU

1998 City of the rising Sun/Taeyengeun Eodba

2001 Musa the Warrior

2003 Please Teach Me English

KWAK KYUNG-TAEK

2001 Friends/Chingu

2005 Typhoon/Tae-poong

2008 An eye for an eye/Noon-e-neun noon ie-neun ei

2011 Pained/Tong Jeung

LEE CHANG-HO

1974 Home of Stars/Byeoldeului Gohyang

1984 Widow's Dance/Gwabu Chum

1987 The Man with Three Coffins/Nageuneneun Kileseodo Swiji Anneunda

LEE JAO-YONG

1998 An Affaire/Jung sa

2000 Asako in Ruby Shoes/Sunaebo

2003 Untold Scandal/Scandal - Joseon namnyeo sangyeoljisa

2009 Actresses

LEE JOON-IK

2005 The King and the Clown/Wnag-ui Namja

2008 Sunny/Nim-eun-meon-go-sae

2009 The Happy Life/Jeulgeoun insaeng

2010 Blades of Blood

2011 Battlefield Heros/Pyeongyangseung

LEE KWANG-MO

1998 Springtime in my Hometown/areumdawoon Sheejul

NA WOON-GYU

1926 Arirang

PARK KWANG-SU

1988 Chilsu and Mansu/Chilsu wa Mansu

1990 Black Republic/Keduldo urichurum

1991 Berlin Report

1993 To the Starry Isle/Geu seome gago shibda

1996 A Single Spark/Jeon tae-il

1999 Uprising/Lee Jae-sueui nan

RYU SEUUG-WAN

2002 Die Bad/Jukgeona hokeun nabbeugeona

2002 No Blood No Tears/Pido nunmuldo eobshi

2005 Crying Fist/Jumeogi unda

2006 The City of violence/Jjakpae

2010 The Unjust/Budanggeorae

2012 The Berlin File

Key Electronic Resources for Japanese and Korean Film

Midnight Eye

An excellent overview of and guide to Japanese cinema.

www.midnighteye.com

KitanoTakeshi.com

This site offers articles and information about Kitano and his work.

www.kitanotakeshi.com

Korean cinema.org

Darcy Paquet's guide to South Korean film.

www.koreanfilm.org

Kawasenaomi.com

The official site of Kawase Naomi. In Japanese with some English.

www.kawasenaomi.com

Korean Film Council

KORIC offers a large amount of information and statistics concerning South Korean Cinema. In English.

www.koreanfilm.or.kr

Asian Film Connections

Online education resource that offers information of the cinema of Japan and Korea.

www.usc.edu/libraries/archives/asianfilm

Sense of Cinema

This online journal has several articles and reviews on both Japanese and Korean cinema

www.senseofcinema.com

Index